SACRED ART
OF THE EARTH

SACRED ART
OF THE EARTH

ANCIENT AND
CONTEMPORARY
EARTHWORKS

Maureen Korp

CONTINUUM · NEW YORK

1997
The Continuum Publishing Company
370 Lexington Avenue
New York, NY 10017

Printed in the United States of America

Library of Congress Cataloging-in-Publication Data
Korp, Maureen.
Sacred art of the earth : ancient and contemporary earthworks /
Maureen Korp.
p. cm.
Includes bibliographical references and index.
ISBN 0-8264-0883-4 (pbk. : alk. paper)
1. Earthworks (Art) I. Title.
N6494.E27K67 1996
709'.04'076—dc20   95-46735
CIP

Sources of Photographs
Figures 1a, 1b, and 2: Kathy Gillis; Figure 3e: Dawn Dale;
Figures 5, 6, 7, and 9: Jennifer Dickson, R.A.; Figure 8:
Esto Photographics; Figure 10: Edward Ranney; Figures 11a
and 11b: Margaret Dyment; Figures 13 and 15: John Weber
Gallery; Figure 14: Dia Center for the Arts; Figure 16:
Charles Ross. All other photographs are the author's.

In Memory of Avrum Malus
1939–1993

genius loci

A sacred art is not necessarily made of images, even in the broadest sense of the term; it may be no more than the quiet, silent exteriorization, as it were, of a contemplative state, and in this case—or in this respect—it reflects no ideas, but transforms the surroundings qualitatively, by having them share in an equilibrium whose center of gravity is unseen.

Titus Burckhardt

Contents

List of Illustrations

Acknowledgments

The voices of many people weave through this study. I want to acknowledge particularly the scholarly interest and encouragement of Mary Gerhart, Belden Lane, Charles Long, Daniel Noel, and Richard Pilgrim (who is the source of the coined word "religio-aesthetic"). Fred Popper and Margaret Dyment generously answered my requests for help. My far-ranging field trips would not have been possible without the assistance of my daughter, Meghan Dunn, and the help of friends. Many lent a hand: Bill Clausen, Paula Drewek, Roberta Huebener, Kathy Gillis, Jan Glyde, Jean Jarrett, Anne Jeanjean, Tim McCoy, Jenná Nehammer, Sheila Redmond, Patricia Robinson, Betty Steckman, and Meryl Tara-dash. Finally, and with particular importance, I remain ever in the debt of artists Jennifer Dickson and Charles Ross. Without doubt, their stories are the raison d'être of my work and their work the reason I could see the way home. Thank you.

My research was supported by a postdoctoral fellowship from the Social Sciences and Humanities Research Council of Canada (1991–93) and aided by the Canadian Museum of Civilization's program for associate scholars.

1

Introduction

In the summer of 1993, there was an interesting twin exhibition at the Galerie Montcalm—a public municipal gallery in Hull, Québec. The exhibitions were entitled "The Romance of Reality" by Cindy Deachman and "Labyrinth" by Kathy Gillis and Carolyn Davis.

Cindy Deachman hung large, delicately composed assemblages of bits and pieces of stuff—mostly brown—on the walls of the gallery. Her work reminded me of the detritus of ancient sites in old sepia photographs of nineteenth-century digs. That was part of what the artist intended the viewer to know. In her catalogue statement, Deachman explained the romance she saw in reality: "The shards that haven't been discovered may reveal themselves in time, but even then, we won't ever stand on sure ground."

Siting a Labyrinth

Deachman's work provided a counterpoint to that of Kathy Gillis and Carolyn Davis: they stand self-assuredly on the ground, as they know it. About the gallery, the two artists had hung fifty-four ceramic studies of labyrinth formations found in different parts of the world and from various time periods. Fourteen of the studies were from the New World, the others were from the Old World, the Pacific, or were of unknown origin to the artists (see figures 1a, 1b). In addition, out of builder's gray paper and dry wall, the two artists had constructed on the floor of the gallery a classical seven-circuit labyrinth, about 30 feet in diameter (see figure 2). It was a low thing, not much more than the height of my knee. At first glance the Gillis and Davis labyrinth series appeared to be the same sort of thing as Deachman's wall hangings. Color, material, forms—all were not dissimilar. The intentionality, however, of their labyrinth series was a good bit different.

The night of the opening, I and several others followed Kathy Gillis into the labyrinth. There was, as the artist promised, only one way in and one way out. After all had exited the construction, Gillis asked me quietly, had I noticed anything interesting about the center? I thought about this and answered, "Well, the floor seemed a bit mushy under my feet once I got there, but then it's hot, and I've had two glasses of wine. . . ." "Two glasses of wine?" the artist interjected; "Mushy, did you say?" "Yes," I answered, now looking at her warily, "come on, tell me: what do you know that I do not know?" Kathy Gillis explained: she had dowsed for the center of the labyrinth. She had used a divining rod. She and Carolyn Davis then built the structure outward from that divined center.

I was startled. There was no mention of their siting protocol in the artists' catalogue statement. Gillis explained that was a deliberate omission: the two artists had not wanted to seem "flippy."[1] Instead, for the catalogue they had written rather prosaic statements about the traditional meaning of the labyrinth as a life symbol—a symbol of passage from birth to death—and they had noted the use of the labyrinth worldwide as a teaching device. I asked Gillis what would she have done had she not found a centering point? The artist replied, "It never occurred to me that it would not be there. I just knew it would be there."[2]

The same week, my mail brought a flyer announcing a joint exhibition of area artists at six outdoor sites tucked into out-of-the-way places in Ottawa and Hull, sites located mostly near the banks of the Ottawa River and the old nineteenth-century factories of the region's early logging industry. The exhibition was entitled "Outside/Ex-site," and was organized by two nonprofit, artist-run galleries—one in Hull, the other in Ottawa.[3]

At one of the installation sites—"Snake Path Outaouais"—artist Dawn Dale constructed an effigy figure of a snake well hidden in a clump of city "trash plants," the sort that grow along the edges of parking lots, in between buildings and in other abandoned urban sites where nothing else grows easily. Here, the foliage bordered the old paper mill's parking lot (see figures 3a–3e). The visitor's eye first spotted an elegant serpentine drawing in crushed red brick at the edge of the parking lot. The drawing's curve became a spine leading to a low, grassy mound hidden deep in the undergrowth and trees, and then to the edge of a gorge, also hidden in the thick growth. The gorge was narrow, dark, and noisy with rushing water pouring along a broken and abandoned log flume. One would never have known the log flume was there had not the artist's discerning eye seized the analogical connections between time and place, red brick and grassy hillock *that were already present at the site.*

The year before in my university mailbox, someone dropped off a small catalogue that drew my attention to a nearby temporary outdoor exhibition called "Art Terre 92—a site-specific land art exposition" (see figures 4a–4b).[4] Spotted in among woodlands, a stream, a meadow, sites all on private land outside the rural community of Buckingham, Québec, were nine installations created by a group of artists who had been invited by the land's owners (themselves artists) to create site-specific work. All of the work created was temporary, intended to last but a few weeks, but all of it built to interact with sun, wind, weather, and night stars. The installations were of varying expertise. The exhibition lasted two months and included in its opening program circle dances performed at each of the nine sites. The dances were intended to be a sacred expression of the connection of the arts and the earth. One of the artists choreographed them.

I mention these events not because they are intended to document that I live in a major art center (I do not) or that the Ottawa–Hull arts community is uniquely placed to do great things (I do not know), but because my research indicates such work and the artists' concerns are *typical* of work artists are producing in number everywhere in North America. Theirs is a sacred art. The work is concerned with the earth and with demarcations of sacred places and events upon the earth. The earth itself is often viewed as an altar, although the artists disdain church patronage or the sponsorship of organized religion.

Certainly, theirs is an art about place. Moreover, their work valorizes the earth and human experience of the earth. The work is intensely and specifically site-oriented—whether found in or outside a gallery's walls.

Our public galleries are filled with work that was once site-specific—to some other place. What happens when a site-specific work of art is warehoused somewhere else? In some cases, we know one outcome may be the preservation of what might have been lost. One has only to think of the Elgin marbles—those fragments of Phidian frieze ripped from the metopes and pediments of the Parthenon in Athens, and now displayed at the British Museum in London—to know Phidias's sculpture would not have survived in situ. Nevertheless, the results are not always beneficient when site-specific work is removed from its site. The removal of such work is always, I think, problematic.

When site-specific work is removed from site, our understanding of the work changes. We may lose all sight of the artist's intentions. For example, there is in the National Gallery of Canada a pleasant work of neoclassical garden statuary installed so prominently many visitors are convinced Canova's *Dancer* is one of the treasures of Western civilization. It is not. The flirtatious minx is one of many the sculptor turned out for his patrons' gardens. In the gallery, however, the sculpture is placed on a tall plinth, and the visitor initially sees it at a long remove through an arched doorway. So placed, the sculpture looms over the visitor. No wonder the work seems important, and no wonder Canova's *Dancer* is a popular topic for my students' essays. The statue's placement makes it difficult for one to take note of anything else nearby.

More often than not, galleries display art as things in and of themselves, self-referential objects without specific places to be—thereby always removable or replaceable with another object from the collection. Even more troubling, the public has come to think of art in just those terms—as though exhibitions were comprised of disparate objects, each one a wholly self-contained *thing*, the whole a display of status acquisitions within privileged walls.

Although I saw the sculptures of Kathy Gillis and Carolyn Davis in a gallery setting, their work did not consist of precious gallery objects—things upon walls, or things placed upon floors. The value of the artists' work lay elsewhere: their labyrinth models were mementos of landscapes, of particular time and place connections with the earth. In their work, the artists charted an understanding of the earth as a site with its own dimensions, its own powers. If the Gillis and Davis labyrinth were moved elsewhere, the work's intrinsic power of place would be lost. Their large floor labyrinth drew the viewer to a reckoning point, to a place where the artists knew the earth pulsed—to a hidden waterspring. If the Gillis and Davis labyrinth were moved elsewhere, the work's intrinsic power of place would have been lost.

Earthwork—Marking the Landscape

Within the last fifty years numerous North American artists have written of their especial concern—if not reverence—for the earth, and of their desire to change our perception of the earth as something out there to be used, to be exploited. In blunt words or poetic words, artists have been challenging the public to rethink the notion that we enjoy any particular god-given dominion over the earth. Time and again, with something like apocalyptic fervor, many contemporary artists have insisted we change our perception of the earth, and thereby change our perception of life and of ourselves. Nevertheless, for all the words written by artists in the catalogue statements accompanying their exhibitions and the statements attributed to them in interviews, we have—scholars, critics, and public alike—tended to slide right past what the artist says the work means, or what the artist says prompted the work. Our experience of gallery exhibitions prompts us to think of art as discrete items, as part of temporary or permanent exhibitions curated by experts, but not necessarily part of our lives. That is the problem.

One result of our inattention is that some artists, who once talked freely about their work, no longer will speak of the how and why of its making. Kathy Gillis and Carolyn Davis, for example, chose not to mention their use of a dowsing rod to site their labyrinth construction. Another result has been the appearance within the last thirty years—primarily in North America, although there are examples extant in Great Britain and Europe—of a body of work created *outside* the gallery art exhibition and distribution system, a body of work difficult to ignore. This body of work is a visual text writ sometimes large, quite large, on the earth itself—the earthwork. It marks the landscape, shapes our perception of the earth as a landscape. It creates a geography.

Earthworks are architectonic constructions sited out of doors. Constructed on the site itself, the earthwork is often made of humble if not ephemeral materials—dirt and wood, found boulders, grasses, and trees—rather than of bronze or marble. If earthworks employ sophisticated technology and mathematical knowledge in their construction, they do not display it. It is hidden. Very often natural phenomena are part of the work's conception—running water, starlight and sunlight, wind, lightning, natural erosion, tidal flows, change of season, that sort of thing. Sometimes, too, the earthwork is located in hard-to-reach areas, private lands, remote regions. Usually the earthwork cannot be bought and sold.

The earthwork is most often known to the public through published photographic documentation. There are, however, some artists who do not document their work and omit the ones they have constructed from their professional résumés. These earthworks are most private. If there is no record of it, the work does not enhance either the artist's reputation or income.

In Western art history, the earthwork appears to be without precedent, or is it?

The Renaissance Italian garden and the eighteenth-century English garden folly certainly made use of sculptural forms in outdoor settings; so, too, the centuries' older practice of erecting commemorative arches and statues of the hero returned in public markets and thoroughfares. The contemporary earthwork is not a public sculpture in the grand heroic tradition—even those few built with funds raised by public subscription. The contemporary earthwork does not commemorate heroes or human victories. It creates, instead, a changed perception of the earth for those who walk its site.

In a special way, earthworks are related to the set-apart, cultivated, harmonized resting places we call gardens: both demarcate landscapes and create geographies. Although this relationship is not one that has been brought out in the art-critical literature, the connection to the garden gives the earthwork an ancient history. Worldwide, when people began to live in fertile river valleys, relying upon agriculture for their primary food source and city-states for their sense of social status, people also began to cultivate gardens. Ancient cities in the Americas, Europe, and Asia all had gardens.[5] The earliest known garden plan is that of an Egyptian court official in Thebes, c. 1400 B.C.E., and scholars assume that cultivated gardens are at least fifteen hundred years older.[6]

Like the garden, the earthwork is about landscape: a landscape of a particular place conceived as an architectonic space. Earthworks and gardens are both site-specific structures. They mark landscapes in suprasculptural ways to create landscapes of three dimensions, plus a fourth, natural time.

For viewers, earthworks often have an educative function because they reform perception. By placing the viewer within the site's ambit, the earthwork prompts the eye to see the shape of the site in relationship to a wider environment. As such, contemporary earthworks have also been labeled "ecology art," "environmental art," and "land art"—particularly in material written about them in the 1970s.[7] Such labels, however, are limiting. They suggest the earthwork is a mislabeled science-fair display project. They do not suggest it is a sacred art, one marking the landscape.

So-Called "Primitivism"

A few art historians and critics have called contemporary earthworks "primitive" constructions. Sometimes the art-critical reference is intended to draw attention to the materials used by both contemporary and "primitive" artists. Indeed, the material of contemporary earthworks is often roughshod, "primitive" stuff, material so seemingly unworked as to prompt the question, "Is that art?" Sometimes, however, the reference to "primitivism" in the art-critical discussion suggests something else—something akin to what anthropologists call "sacred space" or "sacred place." A sacred space or sacred place (both terms are used interchangeably in anthropology) is an area ritually demarcated. It is a site made holy because the gods are here or may be persuaded to appear here. It is a site pulsing with power.

The influence of so-called primitivism upon the art of the twentieth-century avant garde has been long acknowledged. The influence is usually dated to the fabled days of Picasso's tramp through the Parisian junk shops in search of African masks. The continuing fascination of contemporary artists with tribal art is usually viewed as part and parcel of an o'erweening eclecticism typical of the avant garde—one day Bakota masks, the next day soup cans, and tomorrow dirigibles and lasers. The art market is one hungry for novelty, and disparaged for its hunger. Some artists and art historians alike argue that Western art is only about art, building only upon its own history, fueled by a driven, sensationalized search for the novel, the exotic, the unknown. It is important to note here that earthworks are not bought and sold in the commercial gallery system, although other examples of twentieth-century primitivism can be and are. Earthworks do not accrue in value. You cannot buy one for investment purposes. Few are the important collectors of contemporary art who have underwritten their construction.

If it is art history—and only art history—that impels an artist to make art, then what would be so appealing about projects with so little commercial potential? The answer does not lie within the discipline of art history, but rather within the history of religions.

A Sacred Art of the Earth

The contemporary earthwork's archaic antecedents are suggested by their similarity in structure and form to ancient sacred sites, but the more important clue comes from the artists themselves when they talk about their work. The artists use a religious vocabulary, one devolved from archaic and traditional religion. Sometimes even art critics viewing such work can find no other words but religious ones to describe their own responses to these site-specific works. In these constructions, the wellspring of artistic inspiration is found authentically in the land; the artist is self-described as a transformer, a conduit of earth-centered visions. *Site-specificity counts for everything in the work itself.*

In a most important way, there is nothing new about the content and context of these artists' visions. Throughout the world, everywhere and in every human epoch, peoples have marked the earth, scraped clear a reckoning place, considered a rock, a star, the sunrise, cleared a bit of underbrush in order to sit and look and think purposeful thoughts. In these places, people have chosen to be receptive to change, to transformation, to trance, reverie, and ecstasy. They have chosen to mark the passages of theirs and others' lives. In these places some have claimed the gods have spoken. All of these places are crossing places of time and place, "patterns of power."[8] Many are ancient landscapes, first honored by lost and forgotten archaic peoples. Such landscapes seem particularly remarkable when they are found close at hand in North America because our intellectual, cultural construct for our continent is one of "new world." How old could anything be here? The artists, however, know there is nothing newer about this part of the earth than any other. It is all of one whole.

No archaic sacred sites exist by happenstance, we just do not know today what they meant then—why one rock and not another, one meadow and not another. They are all site-specific constructions. So, too, the constructions of contemporary artists who build earthworks, many purposively located in or near archaic sacred places, many built in a similar manner and, frequently, with stated referent by the artist to archaic and traditional cultures. Let us then suppose a respectful and respectable link between archaic and contemporary earth forms. What questions have we to answer?

First off, are the archaic earth forms art? The question may be irrelevant. Often in the languages of traditional peoples, one will find no word for either art or religion. Although anthropological literature has paid much attention to the discernment of religious practice in traditional peoples, little analytical attention has been given to describing material culture in art historical terms. Instead, the "use" of such items as soul catchers, masks, or drums is described, not the choices that went into their making. And almost no attention has been given to the construction of sacred places, yet these are many and known, even if we do not know today precisely why they are important.

Are the contemporary earth forms art? Yes. They have been made by artists. Visual artists make art, real things that can be seen, real things they call "art." We need not attempt to define it any more than that. Fascinating as the question "What is art?" may be, it is a question particular to Western culture and usually one more concerned with matters of taste and quality in the appreciation of art by the viewer than with the legitimacy of the artist's effort. Artists have no difficulty telling you whether the end product of their day's work is a painted wall or . . . a work of art, a painting. Whether the observer thinks the effort is worthwhile, and "deserves" to be called art because it is "good work" is entirely another question, and not part of this study.

May we then discuss the artistic qualities of the archaic and contemporary earth forms? Of course, but the discussion will be limited, even pinched. For example, having discussed the use of materials, placement of the forms, compositional qualities, prototypes and variations on formal themes, what then? A thoughtful person would still want to say what it all *means* (or meant). The archaic artist cannot tell us. The contemporary artist sometimes does.

In order to compare the contemporary earth form to the archaic form in more than just formal, structural terms, we will have to do it on terms set by the contemporary artist. What are those terms? Religious terms, sacred terms. Contemporary artists insist theirs is a religiously motivated endeavor. We assume the same of the archaic earthworks. Because we assume archaic earth forms are religiously motivated, we have the possibility of a valid comparison with contemporary earthworks. Having moved the discussion over to one of religious categories, our problem now becomes one of ascertaining if the contemporary forms are maps, markers of sacred events in a manner similar to archaic forms.

Pathways in and out

In this study, I have chosen to look at the work of several contemporary artists whose architectonic constructions are most often called "earthworks." In their work, the artists appear to be marking sacral aspects of the site. The artist's work is always as much a physical fact as the site itself. This book then is about the specificity of sacred places as *physical places*. It is not meant to be about theological interpretations of those places. Instead, it is about the marking of sacred places, the documentation of sacred sites, the components of sacred landscapes and geographies. It is about earthworks.

My argument, like the labyrinth, has two analogical pathways: there is a way in and a way out. The way into the labyrinth starts with a discussion of artist Jennifer Dickson's work. Since 1980, Dickson has been photographing elegant Old World gardens from England, France, and Italy. For her the gardens are sacred places, and she calls them that with good reason. Her experiences there have been revelatory, transcendental jumps across time. In her paintings and etchings based on these photographs and in her public lectures about gardens, Dickson imparts aspects of her revelatory experiences to the viewer. Many find her garden images not just beautiful, but also talismanic, inspirational. For some the garden images are pilgrimage destinations.

Jennifer Dickson photographs gardens built by wealthy people whose money came in some fashion from Europe's developing mercantilism of the postfeudal period, roughly the sixteenth to the eighteenth centuries. In a curious way, the gardens are linked historically to the colonialization of the seemingly "primitive" and "savage" New World. The gardens are also linked in Dickson's vision of them. The corporate imagery of her garden series comprises a work of collective memento mori.

The pathway into the labyrinth continues with a chapter providing an overview of Amerindian traditions concerning the earth and sacred place. We sometimes forget that the migratory trails of peoples who crisscrossed the continent for millennia are the routes of superhighways today. Ancient trails continue to define our landscapes, our cultures. Throughout North America, ancient earthen forms may still be fairly easily discerned. If we know something of the contextual reasons for ancient burial mounds, effigy figures, medicine wheels, and such—and we do—we still sometimes overlook the most important fact: the ancient forms mark the earth then and now. The earth beneath the asphalt is still fertile, still alive. It will outlast us. This chapter establishes a typology of built archaic forms that can be used to discuss contemporary built forms.

The experience of *place* as something sacred is not an uncommon experience. More than one scholar has attempted to describe these experiences in terms of the site itself. Mircea Eliade's work has been the most influential across academic boundaries extending from religious studies to art history, anthropology, geography, and architectural history. His theories, however, are limited to describing the experiences of site at places *known* to be sacred by a community of believers. What if one is not of that community? What if one does not know the site is sacred? Are sacred place experiences then unavailable to the uninformed, ignorant, or uninitiated? I think not, and in chapter 4 I propose a grammar of spatial organization that can be used to analyze and assess more anonymous site experiences for their sacral elements.

At this point, if the reader will indulge me my extended metaphor of labyrinth, we are at the labyrinth's center. It is time to find the pathway out by addressing the question: Is the contemporary earthwork a marker of sacred place?

Art critics and art historians find the earthwork a difficult form of art to assess critically because it appears to have no iconographical content. However, it does. Its subject matter is the earth itself. It serves to mark sacred sites and map religio-aesthetic visions.

Three of the most well-known of the contemporary earthworks are discussed in chapter 5 (because all three have been written about extensively by art critics and historians)—Robert Smithson's "Spiral Jetty," 1970, now under water in the Great Salt Lake of Utah, and two naked eye observatories currently under construction in New Mexico and Arizona—"Star Axis" by Charles Ross and the "Roden Crater" by James Turrell. Of these three, I have visited only one site—"Roden Crater" in Arizona, just before Turrell at that time stopped permitting visitors to the site. Charles Ross, however, spent many hours talking to me about his work, "Star Axis" in New Mexico, and was most willing for me to see the site. Robert Smithson's "Spiral Jetty" is a work whose mythic proportions are due in part to its loss in the rising waters of the Great Salt Lake and in part to Smithson's own death in an airplane crash shortly after its completion.

Three other earthworks are also discussed in this chapter; and all six are analyzed in terms of site specificity and sacred place morphological criteria. Several of the six contemporary earthworks do fit the typology for traditional sacred place; for others not enough information is known to complete the assessment.

What is the purpose of the contemporary artist's religio-aesthetic concern with the earth? The last chapter suggests an answer and a further outcome.

The artists appear to be pointing the way out of a labyrinth, an old puzzle—part ecological, certainly religious. How are we to live upon this earth? In their work, they sacralize the world we live in just as their visions sacralize the lives they lead as artists. Their work is that of a sacred geographer, a mapmaker of visions, a creator of sacred landscapes. Moreover, theirs are not the only contemporary visionary statements regarding the landscape of North America.

In New Jersey, the most densely populated of the American states, two Rutgers University scholars, Frank and Deborah Popper, have proposed the creation of a very large land restoration project in the American West. They want to return the land to its frontier, grasslands state. If the Poppers' proposal for a "Buffalo Commons" succeeds, the potential acreage could cover as much as a fourth of the contiguous United States. It will certainly affect federal and provincial land use discussions in neighboring Canada.

For almost a generation contemporary artists have been building earthworks in the American West. It is fortuitous the Buffalo Commons proposal should appear at this time. We may be ready to see it. If so, it is because artists have helped reform our visual perception of the earth.

There have been moments before in Western cultural history when artistic thought seemed to presage shifts in public policy, if not foretell stunning changes in a society's worldview. Artists know art has the power to change perception, to change our understanding of the world. The seemingly predictive powers of art lie in its ability to form new ways of thinking.

When I interviewed Yurok artist Rick Bartow for this study, he reminded me of the Biblical references to trees talking and rocks talking and said that what those references really mean is:

> Somebody has a *feeling* for that particular place. . . . People miss miracles all the time because they're not Spielbergian effects. Our experience of the spiritual is manipulated for us by what we think we *ought* to see rather than what we *do* see.[9]

No doubt Bartow is right. By thinking religious vision to be something still "other," it is we who sever art from religion, who indeed miss the forest for the trees—not the artist, whose vision is clear, whose vision may prompt changes of perception in others. At such moments of perceptual shift, garden may become earthwork, earthwork prompts another look at garden, and somehow . . . the buffalo strays into view, just at the periphery of possibility.

2

Jennifer Dickson's Gardens

The artist Jennifer Dickson's lasting legacy is likely to be the body of work she has been producing since 1980, work depicting gardens as set-aside places, as sacred places. For almost two decades Dickson has been photographing a small group of European gardens. She uses those photographs in complex ways to compose multiple series of lush pictorial images that critics find as worthy and breathtaking as do her collectors. Dickson works her study photographs of aristocratic gardens into evocatively titled sets of photo-etchings, serigraphs, paintings, black-and-white and Cibachrome photographs, and sometimes video and multiscreen slide presentations. The artist considers her work to be religious and says of religious art generally that it is both "truth revealing *and* cathartic."[1]

Of some of her experiences of garden sites, Jennifer Dickson speaks openly and in detail, of others she is more reticent. Nevertheless, the artist's ability to impart the framework of her vision to others through her imagery is consummate. Her photographs depict liminal landscapes of time, place, experience. She photographs gardens built in their own time as places set apart in a "wider landscape of fear," to use Yi-Fu Tuan's memorable phrase.[2]

Jennifer Dickson has not always been so concerned with garden imagery; in fact, the artist has no recollection of ever setting foot in an English garden before 1979 during all the years she lived and worked in England. Yet today when she speaks of the gardens she photographs, Dickson says, "The gardens are the only thing I live for. They are what keep me alive."[3] Her commitment to the garden is profound. She prays daily in her studio and explains this personal ritual by saying: "I do not know if I am going to be able to do it, to do my work well enough."[4]

Prefigured Images of Death

In 1980 at the age of forty-three, artist Jennifer Dickson was handed her own death sentence. Her lungs had become damaged after many years of exposure to the toxic chemicals with which she worked as a printmaker. There was not much that could be done. She had been working to the point of collapse. The preceding year, while a visiting artist and professor at Queen's University, Ontario, Dickson had produced a large portfolio of prints, "Three Mirrors to Narcissus." There were twenty-seven images in the portfolio and it was the largest and most complex sequence the artist had ever attempted.

In 1980 Jennifer Dickson's artistic reputation was solid, first-rate: she exhibited internationally, was represented in many of the world's leading public collections, and had earned the distinction three years earlier of being elected to the Royal Academy of Art, the only Canadian artist so honored in its 200-year history. Her other awards included the Prix de Jeunes Artistes pour Gravure from the 1963 Biennale de Paris and a special purchase award from the 1974 World Print Competition at the San Francisco Museum of Art. The artist was quite young when she demonstrated her talent in printmaking. She was only twenty-four when she went to Paris to study with S. W. Hayter—renowned among printmakers—and from 1960–65 she was an associate of Hayter's studio, the Atelier 17 in Paris.

Her work in the 1960s and 1970s was based on body imagery—problematic, curious images, sometimes erotic and, some said, sometimes offensive. Lelde Muehlenbachs of the *Edmonton Journal* wrote in her review of "The Secret Garden" (a traveling exhibition organized by the Still Photography Division of the National Film Board of Canada in 1975 and curated by Lorraine Monk), that Dickson not only showed male and female bodies in an "equally explicit" manner, but had also included "one totally unconscionable photograph which smacks of child pornography and shouldn't be allowed to skulk complacently behind the protective veil of fine art."[5]

Lelde Muehlenbachs' criticism is puzzling because Jennifer Dickson has never been so self-aggrandizing as to seek the publicity of deliberate confrontation and controversy via her art. She is not exploitive of public sentiment in that sense. In fact, the artist willingly chose *not to exhibit* several of the images from "The Secret Garden" portfolio. In Dickson's statement accompanying the exhibition on its travels, she noted the omissions and wrote gracefully:

> I am grateful to have the opportunity of showing this work, and hopeful, that at sometime in the future, the work can be shown in its entirety . . . in a less emotionally charged atmosphere.

Despite the series' title, "The Secret Garden" was *not* about gardens; nor, for that matter, did gardens figure in "Three Mirrors to Narcissus." Jennifer Dickson's work throughout the 1960s and 1970s favored the use of the nude as the primary motif in her explorations of mortality and sexuality. One critic wrote of her male imagery:

> In spite of their beauty, there is a fragility about the young men she portrays. Like butterflies, they have a short life span.[6]

Of the 1978 Narcissus series, Leo Rosshandler, then curator of the Montreal Museum of Fine Arts, wrote that Jennifer Dickson had "taken the subject of the nude and turned it inward, away from nature," and by retelling the story of Narcissus, the beautiful young man who falls in love with his water-reflected image, the artist was using a myth to "take the burden of cosmic fear from our shoulders."

What Jennifer Dickson strove to confront again and again in her work of those two decades was the anger she recognized in her own fear of death. In 1967 she said of her work, "I accept the definition of art as being an act of transformation. I want to kick time and mortality in the teeth."[7] A few years later in 1970, she expressed that fear again when she said to an interviewer, "I feel the terrible waste of death putting an end to all there is to do."[8]

Not long after that interview, however, the artist seemed to have quieted the soul-searing anguish she felt over the commingling of life with death. Interviewed in the *Montreal Star* in 1972, Jennifer Dickson said of her new series of twenty-six etchings, "Sweet Death and Other Pleasures," that she had gone into the work "very frightened" but had come out of it "feeling that I had lived several lives and had come to terms with mortality. I feel that one has other lives and has had other lives."[9] Her sense of peace was short-lived: whatever terms the artist had struck with mortality, the terms were shaky.

African Images

Jennifer Dickson had good reason to be concerned with her own mortality: as a young girl in South Africa she had been stricken with polio. She credits her ability to walk normally to her mother who, daily for hours on end, had massaged her daughter's legs, working a miracle by will alone.[10] Unlike so many other people who survived the polio epidemics of this century, Dickson walks today without a limp.

In the memories of her childhood, South Africa itself was a place of lived violence. As the artist explains, "The rains when they came were floods; when there was drought, the sand dunes blew round; when there were blooms, they were brighter. The parameters were set at extremes."[11] Dickson was mindful of those extremes.

Jennifer Dickson was born on the edge of Swaziland, in the town of Piet Retief, but grew up mostly on the desert plateau of the interior. Her father, Captain John Liston-Dickson, was a government veterinary officer, a position that required the family to relocate several times. The artist remembers being younger than six and bathing with crocodiles (and her father) in a river named aptly the Crocodile River. Dickson also recalls vividly her fear during the Durban riots of 1947 and speaks of seeing "brains and blood all over the street"[12] in the rioting that broke out between the Zulu and East Indian communities, and the nightmares that followed for months. Yet when the artist recollects another childhood experience of extremes—a conversation with a Basuto man whose job was killing sheep—she tells a story that is talismanic for her:

> When I was about eight years old, I went to spend a school holiday with some friends who had a house in the Eastern Orange Free State. I wandered for hours across the *kopjes*, across the hills. I felt extremely attuned to this bleak, rocky landscape. There was a man who came once a week to kill the sheep which provided meat to be sold in the farm shop. One day I asked the old man who he was.... He said to me: *"Ek is die Moerdenaar van die Skape."* I am the murderer of the sheep and at night their eyes surround me and glow in the dark, thousands and thousands

of sheep eyes. I watched him kill a sheep that week. . . . I felt he was partaking in a ritual."[13]

Jennifer Dickson's African childhood provided her with, she believes, a respect for "water, sky, earth, cloud, rain,"[14] a respect fostered by the influence of the African women she knew as a child—the women who were nannies and household servants. Until quite recently Dickson had always denied any influence of Africa upon her or her work: now she sees its having been there all along in her feeling for ritual, in her apprehension of liminality, in her experience of numinous events. When she speaks of her memories of the desert plateau of her childhood, the artist speaks of a beautiful night sky, "a darkness uninterrupted by light . . . a landscape in which you have no place to hide, but I think its very openness gave me peace."[15]

The First Garden

When Jennifer Dickson collapsed in 1980, she was in England. Upon her return to Canada, she was seen by occupational health specialists at St. Michael's Hospital in Toronto. For several years, she had experienced warning signs of lung damage—but these were all variously attributed by Dickson's doctors to asthma, exhaustion, stress. The damage was misdiagnosed even though there were frightening periods when the artist had to curtail her time in the studio. Dickson had first become ill in 1971 when she was intensively working with and teaching metal-plate etching. Artists, like coal miners, work in hazardous and toxic environments; but that fact was not generally known before the late 1970s by either artists or their doctors. Dickson had worked in unsafe conditions for almost two decades as a printmaker, *and* she had taught printmaking classes and workshops as a visiting artist in fifteen different colleges and universities in Canada, the United States, Jamaica, and England during that time period, thereby increasing—and dramatically so—her exposure to toxic chemicals and fumes.

In 1980 Jennifer Dickson was sick and weary of being sick. In her effort to understand her condition she found herself yearning to spend time in a garden in England, yearning to take with her a camera . . . and, in the artist's words:

I thought I would borrow Ronald's camera.[16] I thought maybe I might do a few watercolors. I really did not know I had found my life's work. I went to England that summer with Ronald's camera. The first garden I went to was Haddon Hall. In the whole of my life, nothing had given me such an intense pleasure as that garden. It gave me an intense peace of mind, intense pleasure. It was the most extraordinary thing.[17]

What the gardens showed her was another sense of time, another image of death—an image of death as timelessness. Dickson believes that without a spiritual base one cannot accept death.[18] The gardens provide her with that spiritual base, which is why she credits them with saving her life. Of the work that preceded the gardens, the artist says,

I was dealing with sexuality and love. What happened in the gardens was that people turned into statues. It wasn't that people disappeared. What had been nude young men now became statues of Bacchus. . . . What is important for me about the gardens is the sense of timelessness . . . that moment in which the clock stops. It is neither the present time, nor the past, nor the future.[19]

"Il Paradiso Terrestre"

Jennifer Dickson returned from England with rolls of film shot in the gardens of Haddon Hall, Chatsworth, and Castle Howard.[20] She was thinking about making some paintings, so she took her slides to one of the first color xerography machines available in Ottawa in order to make some inexpensive color study prints. Because she was not thinking of herself as a photographer, the quality of the color prints surprised her and so did the positive appraisal of others looking at her prints. One of her colleagues[21] suggested the artist keep working with those images, there was something there . . . and Dickson did. Then Martha Langford of the National Film Board of Canada's Still Photography Division became interested in Dickson's garden photographs. One thing led to another, and a few months later Langford included Dickson's work in an extraordinary cross-Canada traveling exhibition entitled "Paradise." The exhibition also included photographic work by Taki Bluesinger, Glen Lewis, Tim Porter, and Francis Sanagan.

In the exhibition, Martha Langford broadly explored the theme of "paradise." By no means did the curator interpret the concept in expected terms of afterlife or with references to the Old Testament story of the Garden of Paradise. As Langford selected images from the artists' divers portfolios, she found reason to select for the exhibition images of Ontario prisons, gardens, and the Taj Mahal—all included under the rubric "Paradise."

Jennifer Dickson's own contribution to Martha Langford's "Paradise" was explosive in number and theme. In a series of images Dickson termed *"Il Paradiso Terrestre,"* the "Earthly Paradise," the artist engaged the viewer in a monumental exploration of the garden. *"Il Paradiso Terrestre"* included twenty-one paintings documenting the environment of a mythical garden, plus preliminary drawings and watercolors; thirty-eight color xerography prints with a mythic (and properly ambiguous) story line; three serigraphs; *and* a seventeen-minute multiple 35mm color slide presentation accompanied by an original score written by Michael Baynger.[22]

The critics were stopped in their tracks. While commending Dickson's work as a bravura performance, many seemed to find it beautiful, *if* melodramatic; literal, *although* symbolic; complicated, confusing, *but* exquisite; abstrusely intelligent, *yet* highly romantic; idealistic, *but* realistic.[23] Granted, many were confused by Dickson's work; however, their written, critical descriptions must have seemed even more confusing to their readers.

What the critics were encountering, and certainly being discomfited by, was the multivalent nature of religious vision. Religious vision is extreme, it breaches boundaries. Religious vision is often contradictory, insistent, dense, and layered in its reification. No wonder many flinched at the sight of Dickson's garden imagery. But not all. Rosalie Smith McCrea of the *Ottawa Citizen* saw in the Dickson imagery places of isolation where "muted words hover in the air."[24] When "Paradise" finished its cross-Canada tour, the exhibition went on to Paris under the further sponsorship of the Canadian government.

In recent years Jennifer Dickson has undertaken an additional task— one often neglected by contemporary critics and curators—that of public education. The artist has become a popular and proficient lecturer on the history and thematic symbolism of gardens. Her lectures are perceptive, ambient, witty, and well illustrated by her slide selection. She uses her photo resources intelligently, having documented more gardens than many university historians of landscape architecture. As a lecturer, Dickson imparts to scores of people an appreciation of the garden as the loci of her own sacred experiences, while suggesting the possibility of theirs.

Jennifer Dickson combines and recombines photographic images in

her lectures and in her garden series. She ponders her study photographs taken on site and ponders her memories of those sites, then she
works to convey those visions to others. Her study photographs are not
in and of themselves realized works of art. They are working documents,
notes, drafts of ideas. Nevertheless, even in the study photographs, we
can see how the artist's unerring sense of composition works to impart
to the viewer the sense of a sacred landscape—there, in those places.
Dickson seems to interweave a ribbon of liminal experiences with the
muted words of old stories from the gardens.

Chantmarle Manor, Somerset

In the late winter of 1988, Jennifer Dickson and her sister Jane traveled
to the county of Somerset because the artist wanted to photograph
gardens in the area. They stayed at an old pub called "The Quiet
Woman," a pub whose name had intrigued them with its promise of
serene surroundings. They learned, however, upon arrival that the
"quiet woman" was one beheaded. The pub sign showed a woman holding her own severed head—indeed, a quieted woman. The pub was not
crowded with guests and, during the course of their week there, they
became friendly with the pub's cook. She told them she cooked on Sundays at an old estate with gardens she thought Dickson should certainly
see before leaving the area. Quite unwittingly, the artist had obtained
an entrée to Chantmarle Manor.

Early the following Sunday, a dank and gray morning, Jennifer Dickson and her sister accompanied the cook to Chantmarle where she left
them on their own to stroll about the grounds of the estate. The two
women spent several hours there, Dickson with her camera photographing the gardens.

Chantmarle Manor is an old estate with a house that has been added
onto over the years in a random sort of way. Jennifer Dickson spoke of
entering Chantmarle Manor as an experience of "entering a waiting
place, empty but not abandoned."[25] About the house itself were tended
borders of perennials and striated lawns. There were individuated garden plantings—some of which had been worked upon, others yet waiting to be reclaimed. The artist sensed there a landscape "poised on the
edge of something."[26] Then, as she explored the grounds, Dickson located a water system—a series of channeled streams and ponds. Had
Chantmarle Manor originally been a monastery? Such systems were
sometimes built to feed water to fish tanks within the monastery's walls.

The stocked fish tanks would then provide the monks with a ready source of food permissible during those long periods of the year when meat was forbidden the holy. Dickson followed the gravity feed of the water to its source.

The watercourse began in the upper reaches of the garden—its source, an underground spring. There the stream was gentle water, meandering by clumps of flowers—primroses, daffodils, bog plants—and Jennifer Dickson thought of the stream as a lullaby flowing softly through a series of channels, bordered by flowers interwoven with hedges. At the terminus of the watercourse was a formal pool walled in stone, one part cut away in a stepped, concave curve. Here she saw the whispering, murmuring stream narrow and darken, then spill over a low wall and into the pool. The water was quieted. The pool itself, the artist noticed, was deep, silent as stone, its walls covered with moss and lichen.

Dickson's memory of that morning is one of tension as she observed the shift in mood the descent of the watercourse created. At the pool's edge the artist sensed feelings of melancholy in a foreboding atmosphere. That, indeed, is what she photographed in "Whispering Stream" (figure 5), the tangled, overgrown trees with their bare branches, the concave curve of the spillway into the pool, and the opposing curve of the stone arch behind it. The curves of both images shimmer into darkness nearest the viewer as the walls plunge deep into the pool.

As Jennifer Dickson walked about the grounds photographing the elements of the gardens, she was unaware that the estate today is used for training by one of the British army's antiterrorist squads. She learned of that later. Yet she was well aware that morning there were secrets here: the garden whispered them and she listened.

The experience of that walk, of the secrets murmured, stayed with the artist. Of the several images Jennifer Dickson photographed that day, one was particularly haunting—the one she called "Whispering Stream." The artist felt she had been drawn to that site. Certainly, she had photographed it, fixed it on a picture plane; but what deeper story did the site hold? More than half the picture plane of "Whispering Stream" is entangled with vegetal matter, fecund lichens. In the center, a moist channel leads to darker recesses. In the foreground the plane is dark and deep with curved and vertical lines pulling the viewer gently to the very center of the image and beyond. Everything in the scene is of the earth and charged with powers abiding within the earth—rotting leaves, sere branches, weathered stones. Here, with mordant longing, Demeter awaits Persephone's return from the Underworld.

The photograph "Whispering Stream" became the first image in a series of eight hand-tinted photo-etchings Jennifer Dickson entitled "Sonnet to Persephone." Persephone, as we recall in the old Greek story, is the beloved daughter of Demeter, most fertile of the goddesses. Persephone is kidnapped by Hades who carries her deep within the earth. Angered and grief-stricken, Demeter wanders the earth, refusing to eat, refusing to clean herself, refusing to care for the plants, for the animals. All falls into ruin, decay, and silent death. Zeus intervenes, proposing a solution: Persephone will return to her mother, but for only part of the year. The rest of the year Persephone remains the bride of Hades. Her people are the dead. Demeter accepts, reluctantly. The annual return of Persephone to the earth and the concomitant joy of her mother was the central myth of the Eleusinian mysteries, of which we know so little today.

In "Whispering Stream" Jennifer Dickson gives us an image of Demeter sullenly awaiting the appearance of Persephone; "Whispering Stream" is a birth canal. The landscape photographed here is most sacred, blood ritual sacred. One of the stories the landscape tells is of passage and renewal; another story is of mother love and the primal bond of mother and daughter, the life bearers; and yet another story is of the dead, the terror of the dying and of the living. In this context, it seems no accident to learn that one of the secrets of Chantmarle Manor today is its current use as a training place for a British army antiterrorist squad.

"Sonnet to Persephone" was previewed in Ottawa at a private exhibition before the series was shipped to London, England, for its official exhibition in 1990 at the Royal Academy of Arts. Chantmarle Manor is not open to the public and the artist has not been able to return to the site.

Studley Royal, North Yorkshire

Unlike Chantmarle Manor, the gardens of Studley Royal are well known, and are now public gardens. Jennifer Dickson believes the gardens may be more beautiful today than when first designed because Studley Royal's original garden statuary remains on site, the water system has been newly and completely restored, and all of the ponds have been relined with clay.[27] The gardens were begun by John Aislabie in 1716 and completed by his son, William, in the last half of the eighteenth century. Studley Royal is large, so large in scale and conception that the visitor usually does not experience crowding or congestion anywhere on the grounds, yet the site is one of the most visited of the National Trust properties. According to Dickson, John Aislabie's grounds crew once numbered 400 groundsmen, gardeners, and laborers who were employed on the structure and maintenance of the gardens.[28]

It is not possible to see the whole of the gardens in a single day; nor was it possible in the eighteenth century either, even before the full realization of the garden's design. In 1744, Philip Yorke, second Earl of Hardwicke, visited Studley Royal and noted in his journal:

> It is impossible from a single survey, however well conducted, to conceive oneself or give a stranger an adequate idea of Studley . . . and what seems almost peculiar to Studley is that the same object, taken at a different point of view, is surprisingly diversified and has all the grace of novelty.[29]

Dickson concurs with Philip Yorke's observation and notes that the same pleasing feature persists today: "There is no one way you are forced to look at it; the vistas seen depend upon the path you take."[30]

The entry into the garden typically begins at the Fountains Abbey, a ruined twelfth-century Cistercian abbey, where there is a choice to be made by the walker—the path to the right or the path to the left—and, comments Jennifer Dickson, "either right or left, the circuit is labyrinthine."[31] The artist views the design of the garden as a sequence of experiences that move one from the high "sacred ground" of the ruined abbey into the "profane ground" of the Valley of the Moon Ponds and its Temple of Piety (figure 6). The design is also metaphorically a transit from ruined Christian to pristine pagan space.

The garden's spatial transitions are water-modulated ones demarcated by the reengineering of the River Skell's meander into a set series of canals, ponds, channels, and streams. The Moon Ponds are part of this complex water design. They are a series of ponds, set about the Temple of Piety, and configured into the phases of the moon. The ponds are precisely inscribed on the temple's greensward—reflecting mirrors creating inversions of reality. The effect is ethereal: the moon is brought to earth; the moon is the earth; the waters are mirrors joining heaven and earth.

Water has always been a special feature at Studley Royal. When

Philip Yorke wrote in his journal what it was like to visit the gardens, he found the water system particularly enchanting:

> Imagine rocks covered with wood, sometimes perpendicularly steep and craggy, at others descending in slopes to beautiful lawns and parterres, water into 20 different shapes—a canal, a basin, a purling stream, now gliding gently through the plain, now foaming and tumbling in a cascade down 8 or 10 steps. In one place it is finely turned through the middle arch of a rough stone bridge.[32]

Jennifer Dickson is passionate about the role of water in a garden. She declares that a garden without water is "like someone who has lost her soul, she is damned;"[33] nor can there ever be, she feels, too many statues.[34] Dickson's opinions are not idiosyncratic. The sight of water and the sight of sculpture placed outdoors are among the events that usually prompt reflective thought in the viewer. Studley Royal is rich with outdoor sculpture, all of it placed well for viewing, and all of it of male figures.[35]

In Dickson's photograph of the Temple of Piety reflected in the central Moon Pond, a statue of Bacchus (also known as Dionysus to the Greeks) fills the right third of the picture plane. Bacchus holds aloft two of his attributes—the skin of a panther and a bunch of grapes. At his feet a panther beseeches Bacchus's attention and Bacchus bends his head towards it. The composition itself blends beautifully positive and negative spaces. Bacchus's raised elbow accentuates an upward line of tension on the left side, while his downturned head signals the start of a more relaxed line on the right side of the figure. Right and left together outline a mandorla, or almond shape, holding man and beast together in a unified and balanced composition. At the same time, the mandorla is nicely evocative of the feminine form, as is the supplicating panther and youthful Bacchus himself.

Seemingly, the photograph of temple, statue, and ponds is simply composed of verticals and horizontals. Vertical and horizontal lines on a picture plane usually create stable images. Not so here. The bottom third of the picture plane is reflective water and the top two-thirds (more or less) is dense vegetal growth. So dense are these vegetal forms, they pour from the heavens: there is only foreground and middle ground. Reversions proliferate. Dark masses tumble downward from the skies. If they are leaves growing on trees, they are unlike any ever seen before. If they are leaves, they are also heaven-sent murmurings of unrest, confusion. The photograph is eerie. We are looking at a crystalline moment on the verge of splintering; we see it just before the moment shatters.

By printing the photograph as a reverse negative, Jennifer Dickson created an image that collapses distances, reverses usual expectations, and opens the viewer's eyes to the dissolution of ordinary time and space. This is an experience the artist herself has known in gardens.[36]

Unlike "Whispering Stream," the Temple of Piety negative has not yet been used in any of Jennifer Dickson's finished work, although she has used other photographs of the temple, the statue, and the Moon Ponds—most recently in "The Haunted Heart," 1993, a suite of photo-etchings. In this composition, the artist is being explicitly faithful to what she has experienced at Studley Royal and implicitly faithful to key elements of the Dionysus myth that survive to this day.

The Dionysus myth is a complex one. Hera made the Greek god mad. In this condition, Dionysus wandered the earth. Where he was treated kindly, he gave the gifts of civilization—including the gift of wine—and where he was not worshiped, he left madness. Dionysus is usually depicted as a beautiful, naked young man at rest, a man whose body has a certain feminine delicacy. The god is sometimes shown draped with a deerskin or—as in the Studley Royal version—draped with the skin of a panther. In Greece, the followers of Dionysus were mostly women whose rituals in his honor were bloody and orgiastic. Rome outlawed the Dionysiac religion in 186 B.C.E., the only time the Roman Senate acted to ban any religion; and according to some scholars, several thousand people may have been subsequently executed before the faith was extinguished. The rituals were replaced by a far more tempered, and officially condoned, devotion to Bacchus, the god of wine.[37]

The viewer notes, however, the Studley Royal sculpture is not of Dionysus; it is of Bacchus, the god of wine. But as all know, wine is not only the bringer of truth, it is sometimes the bringer of madness. Dickson's composition invites the viewer to ask previously suppressed questions. For example, the temple in the photograph is called Piety, but what is piety? Devotion to a god. Which god? And what of the temple itself? We know it was used as an intimate, private dining pavilion. What transpired there? We do not know.

The photograph was taken in late winter. There was no one about in the gardens. Jennifer Dickson approached the site of the Bacchus sculpture by walking along the perimeter of the ponds, a path now forbidden because the turf is fragile. The artist said she sensed all the while "strongly erotic undertones in this landscape of languid privilege."[38] That is what she photographed. One need not know the story of Bacchus or the temple's name or its use. One need not even know that this is a photograph of a site at Studley Royal. The image itself is one of liminality, of the edge of revelation—a revelation of wild natural forces, forces so intense that even marble sculpture pulses and shimmers in an energy field of reverse light.

Villa Farnese, Caprarola, Latium

Unlike the carefully maintained and restored grounds of Studley Royal, the next photograph (figure 7) is of a small, richly ornamented stone and brick terrace fallen into decay. The terrace is located on the grounds of the Villa Farnese, Caprarola, a hunting retreat outside Rome designed by Giacomo Barozzi da Vignola for Cardinal Alessandro Farnese, the grandson of Pope Paul III. Vignola was probably responsible for all of the villa's features, including the gardens,[39] with the exception of a small summer casino, or pavilion, in the woods. The design of the summer casino is credited to Giacomo del Duca. It consists of a chapel and two terraces.[40] There is also a winter garden. The iconography of both gardens is based upon river symbolism, in this case, that of the Tiber and Arno rivers.[41]

The Villa Farnese (sometimes called the Palazzo Farnese), was completed in 1587.[42] Unfortunately, between the two World Wars, the villa has fallen into ruin. It is now being restored by the Italian state. Casual visits, therefore, are not possible. One must write to Rome for a special permit to see the grounds at appointed hours.[43] All visitors are accompanied by guards.

The Farnese were once a family of wealth, prestige, and discernment, producing numerous cardinals, a pope, and a queen (Isabella of Spain). When Alessandro Farnese became Pope Paul III, it was he who commissioned Michaelangelo to paint the *Last Judgment* in the Sistine Chapel, so when his namesake and grandson, Cardinal Alessandro set about rebuilding the old papal summer retreat, the choice of architect for the building and its gardens was no small matter.[44]

In this crowd, aesthetic choices counted. One wanted to be known as "discerning," drenched in *maniera*, as it were, a person uncommonly well educated, of creative and inventive intellect, and bloodless. *Ma-*

niera was a courtly grace not so much learned, but discerned, and *Manierismo* (Mannerism) was the style of a sophisticated elite. Emotion was mimed, never experienced. *Manierismo* governed everything from the letters written to painters to the architects hired. It has aptly been called the "stylish style."[45]

To the modern eye, as a visual arts style, Mannerism's elegance reads as a style of tension and irony, a composite quality architectural historian Nikolaus Pevsner calls its "magic suction effect."[46] It has a surreal quality. Like it or not, one cannot help but stare fixedly at a Mannerist composition. The Mannerist composition is frontal, if not confrontational, and the tension inherent in its often bizarre symbolism (frequently sexist by today's standards) is exacerbated by the rigid boundaries of the forms themselves. There is only one point of view, even if it stands things on end.

Vignola, Alessandro's choice for the villa's architect, was one of the leading practitioners of Mannerist architecture. His design for the Villa Farnese's facade illustrates the surreal quality of Mannerist thought (see figure 8). The visitor's first sight of the villa is of a rectangular building at the top of a hill fronted by a double staircase. A closer look, however, indicates the staircase is big, bigger than any staircase need be.

Vignola's grand entry staircase is composed of a double oval with a sweep to its curve that seems to pull the visitor onward and on high or, alternately, seems to render the villa itself a loathsome, predatory, great horned beetle of a structure crawling over the back of the hill. In all, the villa and its elevation might be a proto-Fellini movie set. Off to the side and in back is the place where one finds the little terrace Jennifer Dickson photographed one September day in 1989.

Jennifer Dickson located the little terrace after a lengthy walk up the grand double staircase, a thorough exploration of the villa, the water garden, the casino. Finally, the artist came upon the little terrace, the Cardinal's alfresco dining room where he and a few intimates dined so elegantly in the dark evergreen wood of ancient Roman cedar.

In her photograph of the terrace (see figure 7), Dickson did not photograph the site as a Mannerist composition. She shunned that point of view. Her experience of the site was more complicated, yet there are facets of the composition that are mannered. For example, the artist chose to emphasize—with a delicate attention to detail—the ground level view rather than the more ordinary one of eye level. She also constructed the view as a composition based on the intersection of diagonal lines *outside the picture plane*.

The left third of the photographic image is crushed with the vertical placement on an angled wall of a large, carved, stone urn on a plinth, placed between two stone volutes pushing against the plinth like steadfast giant snails. The eye then travels from the near foreground to the middle ground of the photograph. Centered there, one finds a delicate arrangement of four intricate, free-standing, stone niches (there are actually five, but one is hidden)—each one looking like a blind doorway. They are, however, half basins for small fountains. When the Cardinal and his select guests dined here, their conversation was masked by the splash of water sprays in the nearby fountains. In Jennifer Dickson's photograph, they are sentinels standing guard against the woods. Behind these stone sentinels, there are ancient trees that extend a great distance beyond and outside the picture plane. The eye completes its inspection of the photograph by swinging around to the foreground of the picture plane. The last object seen is a stone globe delicately balanced on the brick wall against a fragile field of wildflowers—poppies, daisies, dandelions.

But wait, another look at the stone sentinel cluster appeals to the eye. In a second, much closer look, one can see two, or three, are surmounted by elaborate stone urns. Two more sentinels are crowned by sculpture of women riding goatlike creatures. All appear to be festooned with the bearded heads of the river god, a feature of garden statuary that dates back to the ancient Roman gardens.[47] Strange, but not inexplicable.

The trees seem to be particularly massive and dense in the photograph. Wild boar inhabit those woods. How odd then to think of Cardinal Alessandro and his guests, attended by pages, eating their evening's repast while bristly, tusked boar root about in the woods beyond. Did those men at the table see in the dark the eyes of the boar they had slain that day? Did they speak of themselves as the "murderers of the boar?"

Or did they perhaps talk of the Protestant rebellion, the peasant uprisings, the parlous and terrible state of the European fiefdoms, the new popularity of witch burnings and public maimings? Certainly, their conversation must have been of travelers' concerns. When the Cardinal's guests traveled to his hunting retreat, they did so at risk of attack by highwaymen. If they talked of civic affairs in Rome, perhaps they spoke of the numbers of heads of bandits impaled on the Ponte Sant Angelo. The display was intended to be a deterrent. It failed.[48] Surely, we can imagine the Cardinal and his guests speaking of the theological issues that fueled so much of Europe's civic strife. Whatever, all the while they talked and dined, the boar with glowing eyes surrounded them.

Jennifer Dickson notes there was nothing to stop her from leaving the garden and walking into the woods that day, but she sensed a "menacing border" and stayed put. She did not venture off the terrace. The artist felt "held within the space, held by the sense there was an avenging angel nearby."[49] The terrace haunted her dreams for months.[50]

Dickson suspects her sense of the terrace's absurd barrier and boundary may have been even more explicit in the sixteenth century. She thinks the stone sentinels were once linked together with evergreens, creating a gateway leading from the terrace to the wild woods, a ceremonious transit from the civility of the Cardinal's table to the "lived violence" of a blood sport. In the artist's composition all these possibilities exist. One can even imagine the reverse: boar stampeding through the gate onto the terrace, routing all the Cardinal's guests.

Unlike the Mannerist devotees of the sixteenth century, artist Jennifer Dickson is engagé with the world at large, then and now, by virtue of her vision's clarity. The Mannerists knew only a walled-in garden, one built by their own intellectual constructs.[51] Her photograph honestly witnesses the site's history: where blood is shed, the ground is sacred.

Some of the photographs Jennifer Dickson took that day of the Summer Casino and its terrace were eventually used in her 1992 suite of photo-etchings, "The Spirit of the Garden."

Villa San Remigio, Pallanza

Usually, Jennifer Dickson is able to return to a garden. Sometimes the artist returns often. She likens her longing to see a garden again to that of the lover's longing for the beloved:

> One seldom enters a garden in an innocent or empty mode. Always there is a feeling of tremendous anticipation. It is very close to embarking upon a love affair. You have to be very patient. Once I find a garden that moves me, it is rather like building a friendship. You keep going back. The layers of meaning and subtleties of that understanding of the garden are not always obvious. . . . It is a form of meditation, of purification. This relationship is a solitary activity.[52]

Each visit heightens the "reverberations—*rimeditata*—of thinking about the garden over the winter."[53] In time, the reverberations of those visits produce a suspension, literally, a suspension in time: the artist creates an image, a work of art. With that, the artist's work is done. It is a further cause for celebration, a celebration to be shared with the beloved. The artist returns to the garden.[54] Her love of the garden is as direct, necessary, and intimate as that of Radha calling out for her Krishna, as that of the bride seeking her bridegroom in the Song of Songs.[55]

The work of art created may be etching, watercolour, photograph. In whatever medium the image is revealed, the image is art and artifice, revelation and pure invention. Its integrity is what holds it together and that integrity is solely the artist's responsibility. Further, because it is a work of art, the gaze of the viewer matters.

Dickson believes many of her images are comforting to viewers because they remind some of "a space linked with childhood memory or places they know or have gotten to know."[56] This effect, however, is not one she "consciously" intends in her pictures.[57] As the artist notes, she does not usually know who buys the work.[58] Nevertheless, often enough the artist receives a letter from someone who owns an etching, a photograph. Often enough, someone unknown approaches the artist at an exhibition. What do the letters say? Or the exhibition visitor? Usually, simply "thank you" for a sorely needed and wanted beauty found in the artist's work.[59]

Jennifer Dickson observes of her photo-etchings: "There is little that is photographic about the etchings."[60] What is kept in the etchings is the structure of the photograph, the composition. As working documents, the study photographs have their own integrity. The transformation of any one of them into a work of art is not a paint-by-number exercise. Let us consider the intrinsic qualities of Jennifer Dickson's study photograph of the garden she has renamed the "Betrothal Amphitheater" (see figure 9), although its designer, Sophie della Valle di Casanova, may have called it the "Garden of Sighs."

The amphitheater is part of the grounds of the Villa San Remigio on the shores of Lake Maggiore in the north of Italy. The villa was built at the end of the nineteenth century by a devoted couple—Sophie and Silvio della Valle di Casanova. The design—according to Jennifer Dickson—is based on visions, on Sophie's dreams. The garden was intended to be a testament to the love these two held for one another. The garden's sundial inscription appears to attest to that: it reads "to measure only happy hours."

The garden is framed within a semicircular amphitheater containing, as part of the mosaic work, the portraits of Sophie and Silvio, in addition to several installations of classical statuary (replicas all). In another part of the garden is the mausoleum where the two lovers are buried.

In Jennifer Dickson's photograph, we do not see either portraits, statuary, or mausoleum. Her composition is a subtle and difficult balance of formal symmetry and enveloping curve. The picture plane is divided almost evenly along horizontal and vertical axes through the center, yet the curve of the pond belies this four-square symmetry. The impression the eye first receives is one of curves, a set of multiplying, graceful curves drawing the eye to the center portal, and beyond it to a faraway white light.

The light beyond that opening is dull. Nevertheless, it pours through the portal and illumes the water of the silent fountain, the petals on the surface, the drift of algae, and the blossoms of the plantings. The portal itself is framed by Corinthian columns, tall and slender, the most graceful of the three classic orders. Even the lintel connecting the columns is curved. On the right, the mosaic wall is festooned with a design of slender diadems and swags, an attenuated eternal flame. On the left, massed topiary are intermingled with climbing plants and low flower bushes. The garden is pure artifice. Nothing here is possible within nature—either by luck or happenstance alone—except for the algae on the still water. In this sweet *paradiso,* the choices were many, carefully considered, designed and dreamed.

The lesson presented the visitor is as delightful as it is difficult. And of course, there is a lesson to be learned, for we are looking at a paradisial scene: Sophie's garden of love came to be not by chance. It was conceived in her dream and maintained by her careful hand, the hand of an avid horticulturalist. The lovers, however, died. Gracefully the world of their perpetual betrothal slips away. The masonry is destabilizing, ivy climbs the walls of evergreen, the roses grow wild.

Jennifer Dickson describes the garden as a site of "tumbled profusion at the brink of anarchy, and that's what makes it interesting."[61] In her photograph, the artist provides the viewer with a dreamworld of light spring scent and possibility—the possibility of love everlasting, of promises remembered and honored. The curve of the pond invites the viewer forward, invites the viewer to step carefully along the edge towards the portal. Here, time is magic—all art, artifice, the desire for beauty and love everlasting.

Border Crossings

Jennifer Dickson said that when she came upon the Villa San Remigio's garden, she began to weep,

> feeling if I died right there, it wouldn't matter because everything had fallen into place in the world in that moment in the garden.[62]

The feeling the artist describes is one historians of religion called revelatory, religious, numinous—the transcendent moment of understanding. It is why Jennifer Dickson knows in an inviolate way that the garden is a sacred site because such has been her own incontrovertible experience of these set-aside places. She has herself walked there.

All four of the photographs discussed here are of liminal sites where there are choices to be made, longings expressed, promises enjoined, and borders crossed. At Chantmarle, the turbulent stream plunged into a deep pool, whispering the promise: Persephone will return, winter will not last, the daughter will return to her mother. At Studley Royal, Bacchus promises the freedom of madness and pulls the moon down to earth, capturing it in its own reflection. In the wood surrounding the Cardinal's summer casino, the boar survive. The hunters did not kill them all. Their survival ensures that we can never eliminate every animal, every beast, or every risk. The deaths of the hunted enjoin us to remember civilization is a temporary construct of the wild and improbable. So, too, Sophie's betrothal promises. They could not last: the lovers would die. The promises, however, can become something else, another sort of memory. Time throws down the gauntlet and the artist picks it up: promises can be transformed into works of art and, in that way, live in memory.[63]

In her work Jennifer Dickson accepts that challenge: her work maps the borders of mortality—life and death. She works in liminal places.

Old World and New World

When Jennifer Dickson considers as a whole the gardens she has been photographing, she notes the ones she favors most cannot be built today.

Not unimportantly, the chief reason is the obvious one: the gardens are old; when built they were new. The sites are poignant to the artist because they are storied places, she hears whispers there, the accretion of memory over time.

Jennifer Dickson has photographed new gardens in North America and Europe, gardens no older than fifty or sixty years, but she photographs them differently. Her photographs do not suggest the sites are loci of any especial sacrality—no borders, no tensions, no inversions, no passions. They read more as records of horticultural displays, records of landscape architecture, even records of landscape as sculpture. What they are not are images of sacred sites. In fact, in her public lectures, the artist's commentary about new or modern gardens tends towards the subject of material, texture and color, what flowers grow in the gardens. The viewer senses that Dickson is searching for an older, more substantive story. It is clear in her lectures[64] that she is delighted, for example, by the imported limestone columns of the Dr. Sun Yat Sen Garden in Vancouver and the bamboo grove of the Jardins Albert Kahn in Paris.

Jennifer Dickson's interest in the ancient and the old—survivors from other times and places transported into modern settings—is one that the designers of the Old World gardens of the sixteenth to nineteenth centuries also shared. Their gardens were constructed with borrowed plantings. By the eighteenth century, there were nurseries in England that specialized in providing gardeners with plants from the New World.[65] Seemingly, the makings of whole forests were transplanted to the Old World from the New—oaks, pines, firs, spruces, sycamores, walnuts, chestnuts, laurels.[66] Consequently, the deforestation of New England was not due entirely to the burgeoning shipbuilding industry. The young trees of the American forests were also wanted for landscaping the grounds of European estates.

The history of the Old World garden is a complex one. It is a history interweaving the exotica of the explorers' contact with distant places with the ecological despoliation of Europe and Europe's subsequent colonialization of much of the rest of the world. The glories of the Old World garden derive in part from the success of European mercantile policies and the subsequent accumulation of wealth by the merchant classes. The shifting of wealth and the accumulation of wealth prompted a redefinition of state and commerce. In the early 1700s,

enormous estates in England were defined by forcing landless people
to move elsewhere—often into the growing cities, sometimes overseas
to the colonies. Unfortunately, an economic and political history of the
garden is one beyond the scope of this study, so a few connecting points
must suffice instead.

According to historian Kirkpatrick Sale,[67] by the sixteenth century,
there were almost no primeval forests left anywhere in Europe. The
Mediterranean had been depleted of many of its food stocks, and once
common animals like the bear and the wolf could be found only in
remote corners. Others, like the marten and the fox became species
protected for the hunt of the noble and wealthy. Life had been and
remained stressful, dangerous. There were many sources of fear—nature was one, and religion provided yet another. Many believed the Day
of Judgment was soon upon them. One date cited was 1650 (earlier
millennial dates had been the years 1000 and 1500). If time was running
out, and there always seemed to be some Christian thinkers who were
sure it was, the exhaustion of the land and the exhaustion of the resources of nature were only to be expected.

Generally, up to and including much of the Renaissance, Europeans
viewed nature as a fickle source of provender. Nature was not viewed
as a source of beauty or revelatory knowledge.[68] The European attitude
is one that can be traced to a number of sources, Genesis and Pliny
among them. We are, however, the heirs of a later Romanticism. We
can hardly imagine what it must have meant to encounter an entirely
new world, one having seemingly unending resources of land, forest,
water, animal.

One of the European responses to this extraordinary expansion of the
known natural world was wonderfully imaginative. It was the garden.
People began to build gardens—places where they could sit (safely)
and look upon nature, places where they could entertain (safely) their
friends. The first garden designs were rooms outdoors—designs whose
concept was not unlike the Cardinal's dining terrace at the Summer
Casino of the Villa Farnese. In short order, however, the concept of the
garden changed from that of a room outdoors to that of a site-specific
journey—one taking you to places where you might gaze upon and be
part of poetical views. In this world, nature could be explored on a
larger and larger scenic scale, yet still remain a garden, a place set
apart. Studley Royal reflects this sort of expansive, optimistic thinking.

Nevertheless, whether built large or small, grand or intimate, the
gardens built in the developing age of European mercantilism and ex-

ploration were conceived to be places where one might find a way to understand a world of fear, change, collision, and contact. The making of a garden was not a frivolous activity—even in the New World's colonies. In fact, in the seventeenth century Governor John Winthrop of the Massachusetts Bay Colony urged the making of gardens upon the Puritans as their Christian duty.[69] For Governor Winthrop such activity ensured that an "appropriate" relationship to the land would be maintained by the Puritans. The story the land spoke to Governor Winthrop was couched in the terms of Genesis.

The indigenous stories of the New World were not easily heard by the first explorers, missionaries, and traders from Europe, and many of the stories of North America were lost. The devastation of the First Nations in those early days of contact meant there was no one to tell the stories and no one to hear. Ever since—native and nonnative alike— we have all been inventing idyllic versions of those stories that were lost.

The known Amerindian traditions concerning the earth are complex and by no means idyllic. The earth is holy, but the beliefs are various and not well understood. For example, the Cahuilla people of southern California describe a landscape in which death is twinned to ecological pollution. They have a story[70] that recounts their righteous anger when Muhat the Creator introduced—by trickery and with the innocent help of Menil the Moon—death into their perfect world. The people poisoned Muhat. They forced the creator to die, and they poisoned forever all of creation—the world. Death remained, but so did life and regeneration because Menil stayed too. The Cahuilla story is an unusual one. Its complexity is reminiscent of qualities I also see in Jennifer Dickson's work.

When Jennifer Dickson maps her garden experiences, she makes it possible for the viewer to experience something of the same truth the artist has known at that site. Her compositions are intended to map and reveal something of the artist's experience of the garden as a liminal site, as a sacred place. The truth the artist finds in her garden experiences is the fundamental one of mortality, the borders of life and death, the borders of time.

Each of the gardens the artist selects to photograph is a set-aside place, a place where the world is sensible, beautiful, sensual. None of the gardens she selects are wild, unnamed places. At each site there have been events of passion and intellect; the sites have history and they have names. The gardens are complexly storied. Part of Jennifer

Dickson's work has been to find the stories in the landscape, to find them with her artist's eye and sensitivity, and then to tell us sacred stories of the gardens.

In the New World, too, there are sacred stories and they are also extant in the landscape.

3

To Speak of the Earth— Ancient Landscape Markers

Perhaps 65,000 years ago, perhaps even longer ago than that,[1] the first peoples of the New World were wandering along the riverbanks and running brooks, lake, and ocean shores, foraging here and there, following game herds through the meadows and vast plains of North America. We know these long-ago peoples looked for food, looked for shelter. But what did they talk about? I believe we have to assume the first New World wanderers were people who saw the world in terms of personal and sacred significance because we know of no instance at any time and any place when people have not made some mark upon the earth to mark it as a place known, to assign it significance, perhaps even to be themselves remembered in that place by whatever forces they apprehend there. What were the landscape markers that mattered to these long-ago peoples, markers they noted as particular to place, or to time, to season, markers that may matter to us still? What do the markers look like? How shall we know them? What do they mean?

We may be able to get some hint of what the answers to these questions could be by examining the attitudes towards land, or towards the landscape, known to be held by the first peoples of North America since contact (1492, the date of Christopher Columbus's "discovery" of the New World), and presumed to be held precontact. By so doing, I do not mean to suggest the indigenous peoples of North America are "Stone Age survivals." Quite to the contrary, I am only following a useful precept established by Edward Sapir: "the more frequent and stereotypical such a reference, the more reason, generally speaking, we have to assign the cultural element great age."[2]

There is little we can be certain of underlying the known Amerindian reverence for land and its uses because the forms that reverence takes are various and not at all well understood. Of one thing we can be certain, however; the traditional cultures of the first peoples of North America are not "primitive"—if by that we mean "simple." The cultures are old and long-lasting. They are also different.[3] All cultures—be they "primitive" or supposedly "civilized" ones—are equivalently complex with regard to fundamental human relationships and religious experiences. These are the things that carry us through from birth to death and provide us with our sense of place in the world.

Historically, scholars have been reluctant to credit fully the complete range of human diversity found among the native traditions of North America. We have either struggled against or, sadly in some measure, accepted a stereotypical Indian as our model. We have never been able to approach any ethnological description with virgin eyes. There may be a generic "Hollywood Indian," but there is certainly no historic generic Indian in any wise. More than one scholar—native and nonnative alike—has skidded down a slippery slope of imposed, second-order interpretation when attempting to write a clear, first-order description of native beliefs. For example, scholars who know one tradition well, sometimes present other traditions as though they were but variants of that one.[4] Other scholars sometimes make hopscotched equivalences between the cultures of divers indigenous peoples all over the world today and those of long-ago Paleolithic Europe as though today's indigenous peoples have somehow been frozen in time for over 30,000 years everywhere.[5] Not true. Not true of any group anywhere at any time.

Marks upon the Land

The importance of land in traditional Amerindian beliefs is rooted in its inherent potential to inscribe an earth-centered hierophany that is itself part of a unitary cosmos. Although there are many themes in traditional Amerindian myth, one attitude appears pervasive: any part of the world may unfold the whole—upperworld, lowerworld, and the ground we stand upon. Any part of the world may unfold the whole more or less according to the strength of individual vision and the cogency of the tribal metaphorical tradition for interpreting that vision. Thus, vision is personal, but not private. All dreams must be discussed at some point with another.[6] All dreams are validated in time by events that do happen. The realization of vision is community-based and therefore ethical or moral. Similarly, native land-use patterns, including architectonic spaces—the marks people make upon the land—are both fluid and fixed. As built forms, they are forms built to weather, to change, to be impermanent. But, they are also forms built in places to which one can return. Thus, they are forms well suited to a sacred geography in which the cosmos is perceived to be structured, ordered, yet fluid, ever-changing in its degree of animation, power, energy.

Sacred and secular uses of land are thereby so commingled throughout North America that our usual scholarly constructs of sacred and profane (i.e., that which is not sacred) are inadequate explanatory categories for an earth-centered reverence so personal, yet so traditional.

Marks upon the land are real marks, visions made tangible in form, even if they be no more than a clearing of brush or a respectful distance obtained. Built things persist for a while—sometimes for a great while. When a burial mound is plowed back, we can still see in aerial photography where the ground was cleared, compacted, formed. We can still find postholes where wood has rotted and discolored the earth. We know when trees are first or second growths, and we know when rocks are moved, burnt, or chipped. It is important to collect this information of times past because we will not know where we are now if we do not know how we came to this place; and, paradoxically, as Christian Norberg-Schulz notes: "Soon, if we do not know where we are going, we no longer know where we are."[7] That is why so much archaeological study rests upon the painstaking classification of such mundane items as projectile points and potsherds. These remnants trace where we have been and where we wandered off to. Marks upon the land are similarly persistent.

Throughout all of human history and prehistory, people have been wanderers as much as they have been settlers. Whenever a group moves, the group must recenter, re-create themselves in the world. They must also re-create the world to do so. That means they must find a fixed center and build a harmonious structure to affirm their own balancing point in the world along with everything else in and of the world. The harmony desired is a synoptic one. It is an affirmation that, indeed, "all's right with the world."

To be of the earth is an affirmation that one is standing under the sky and above all that below. To be of the earth is to know where you are. In his great cosmological vision of 1870 Black Elk stood upon Harney Peak in the Black Hills of South Dakota. At that moment the center of the world in his vision was there. Nevertheless, many years later, he told John Neihardt, "But anywhere is the center of the world"[8] because what is important is what you make of that place, how you come to know it.

The demarcated landscape, the sacred place is a built thing. It is not nature primeval. The sacred place is paced off as a separate place. It is set apart. There is *always* some human modification of that natural space. Even on the walls of a natural form as daunting and magnificent as the Grand Canyon there are petroglyphs and built shelters still visible. The modification of any place that demarcates it as a sacred place can be as simple as a pathway up a hill, or a thank offering of red cloth tied to a branch. The modification can also be as elaborated as the building of a cathedral church with plaza. No sacred place persists only in memory; it exists also in fact.

Because sacred place is a built space, a space architectonically conceived and inscribed, it involves the notion of territory. The New World notion of territory has never been one of simple possession. For the original peoples of the New World, territory is to this day a mythic concept with much potency. Territory is not just where people live and where their bodies are buried. Territory includes the notion of origin— where the people have come from—and, therefore, territory is the continuity of life itself. In this sense, territory is multivalent in its meaning and in its expression.

Territory is both a metaphorical image and a concretized one. Each tribal group particularizes their own notion of territory, often a specific geographical place told in myth, a place that has always been theirs and to which they are to return, a place that is always someplace in the New World. That is why many tribal groups organize their cosmologies into layered orders—mininally three, but often five, seven, even nine—in order to illustrate the relationship of underworld powers, the powers of this world, and the powers of the dome of heaven, the upperworld. All actions thus are in mind of a cosmological layering or structure placing a people upon the earth, one enabling them to continue to be of the earth.

Typically, tribal traditions and beliefs have placed little or no importance upon living life *in order* to get to some better eternal place beyond the earth at the time of death or to avoid a hellmouth horror somewhere vaguely below or out there. For example, the Dineh or Navajo[9] place of emergence is bounded by four sacred mountains—the names and characteristics of which are well known, but not their precise identification and location in the physical landscape of northern Arizona and

New Mexico.[10] All four "are said to be located just beyond the Navajo Earth (since the Earth is to rest on them)."[11] Territory, thus, for the Dineh, an Athapaskan people, is as specific as a grouping of mountains and as mythic as the one farther off in the misty mists of time. Nevertheless, that place, too, is real, and all of it together comprise *this place. This* is where the people have come from. As Sam Gill notes, the literal translation of the word "Blessingway"[12] in Dineh is: "the way to secure an environment of perfect beauty."[13] The four mountains are part of that multilayered, multivalent environment. There is no perfect beauty in death; the dead are fearful powers feared by the living who do not willingly speak of them.

The Ojibway, on the other hand, have constructed an elaborate healing and rites of passage ceremony specifically for the dead. It is a contrariwise midéwiwin, a ghost midéwiwin, in which all ritual gestures are the opposite of the midéwiwin performed for healing the living. The reason is obvious. The dead are not alive; therefore everything must be different.[14] Among other Algonkian tribal groups, the Cree for example, beliefs in reincarnation are expressed in a number of variant ways as the continuance of life on this earth and life elsewhere. In some expressions of reincarnation belief, for example among the Haida, this is possible because people are believed to have several souls—one to remain, one to go elsewhere. Thus, a child born soon after the death of an elder may signal the continuance of the dead person's personality and particular wisdom in the new life of the child.[15]

It is interesting to note that the Algonkian, and before them the Mound Builders of the eastern woodlands, align the bodies of the dead along an east-west axis in relationship to the rising sun—an astral body commonly thought to transit all layers of the cosmology in its daily circuit through day and night, recycling and regenerating its powers daily. The orientation of dead body to rising sun is an orientation found worldwide[16] just as there are examples found worldwide of beliefs more like those of the Dineh—they do their best to avoid all contact with the dead.

Territory is also physical sustenance, the usage of land to obtain food and shelter—be it by hunting, gathering, farming, fishing, or some combination thereof—and that involves kinship relationships (tribal groups) and the relationships among smaller and larger groups of people, and everyone's (or every group's) travel and migration patterns. These patterns are often told in myths recounting epic journeys of the people, myths explaining how they came to be here. Among all Amerindian tribal groups, it was ordinary to move from summer to winter quarters, or from summer to fall to winter quarters. Even farmers in supposedly settled agricultural villages would move to dwellings appropriate to the season and the work to be done.[17] As people shifted about, they intermingled. The shifts were not always peaceful ones even before the disruptive European incursions, and are not so today between neighboring groups of native peoples. For example, the Hopi and the Dineh have long disputed each other's land claims or geographic entitlements.[18] The reserve boundaries that place Hopiland flat in the middle of surrounding Navajoland graphically illustrate their ongoing argument.

To some extent, territory can also be the shared usage of land by neighboring groups of native peoples.[19] As groups of people shifted—in search of game or fertile ground or because there were no more young trees to cut down for fuel or building material or because living conditions had become unsanitary—tribal areas also shifted, and population groups changed. Nevertheless, it seems unlikely that years and years ago the first marks upon the land were ever fixed borderlines to be defended against all comers. It was always possible to negotiate a border or a trading route—until the Europeans arrived.[20]

A Structured Cosmology

All efforts to place a mark upon the land, to define space, are efforts to order the world,[21] to make it possible to *see* what is *felt* or *apprehended* about the world. As a number of Gestalt psychological studies have made abundantly clear, we have difficulty seeing those things of which we know nothing.[22] For example, just as nongolfers have difficulty spotting a ball on the fairway, the first sight of the high chaparral is baffling to the gaze of city dwellers, who cannot see bird, snake, or antelope, but the Jicarilla Apache hunter can. Bird, snake, and antelope are not distinctive parts of the landscape unless their presence is already supposed possible. We, who are city dwellers, only see myriad forms of cacti and scrub brush, and presume the land desolate.

Marks upon the land bespeak the use we make of land, what meaning we take from it, what we see there. There is a uniformity of use about traditional sacred space in the New World. It is commonly limited to burial grounds; places of revelation, vision; and the performance of traditional ritual (healing, rites of passage, thanksgiving, invocation, gathering). Its meaning derives in part from its exemplary usage.

People who are hunters and gatherers build ceremonial structures and dwellings replicating the order of their universe, structures that re-create their own creation and renew the cosmos. Farmers and traders, city dwellers, too, also build villages and cities replicating the order of their universe, often a more structured and ranked—if not autocratic—cosmology. For example, the highest point in all of Cahokia, the premier center of the Mississippian culture near present-day St. Louis (Collinsville, Illinois) was an earthen mound in the form of a truncated pyramid. This mound, called today "Monks Mound," is ten stories tall and covers an area of about 14 acres. It was built mostly between C.E. 900 and C.E. 1200 and is the largest earthen mound ever built anywhere in the world. Upon its summit the priest/god dwellers could look out over the palisade surrounding the ceremonial complex to four woodhenges—measuring nearly 263 feet to 476 feet in diameter on a cleared plain almost 3,280 feet to the west—which delineated important astronomical alignments.

Over the years scholars have noted the frequency of astral orientations and configurations in ancient sites, very often to the direction of the rising sun. In North America, the sunwise direction—east to south, to west, and return again to east, the rising sun—is sacred everywhere. Only one ancient site in North America is known to have been oriented to the moon's circuit about the sky—Casa Grande, a Hohokam structure built of clay about C.E. 1350 in the Sonoran Desert of southern Arizona.[23] That does not mean, however, that an orientation to the sun or, exceptionally so far as we know now, to the moon would be the only primary astral orientations possible. It simply means, to date, that is all we know.

Other possibilities do exist. For example, in the high Andes of Peru where the sky view is severely limited by craggy mountain ranges, spatial organization is significantly different. The mountains rim the sky in a stepped configuration of many levels. Some scholars see this stepped configuration of natural forms mimicked in the built forms of the ancient terraced architecture of the farmlands, the ancient stone carvings, and as a motif still persisting in today's woven tapestries.[24] The stepped motif first appears on ancient Moche pottery dated to 900–200 B.C.E.[25] There may be a deliberate mimicry of natural form in the built forms of the high Andes. Certainly, the analogy is an evocative one that helps us, as outsiders, to comprehend the images.

Let us consider another example from the high Andes. In the night sky of the Andes, the Milky Way appears to be part of a vast circle—a remarkable sight for those of us who are used to seeing the Milky Way as a wide river across the sky. The circle configuration is remarkable because it is so different from what we expect to see. But does that make it significant to native Peruvians? In ancient Andean work, a circular motif is commonly used. Shall we call it a Milky Way motif or a sun depiction? Both or neither? Could it be another mountainous enclosure? One of the highest heavens? We would be more certain of the strength of any of these associations had we studies from these areas that assessed Peruvian sacred myth for mountain or star images and stories. I do not know of any.

For all peoples everywhere the built space is a way of creating a concretized personal and group identity. By building ceremonial structures (all native domestic architecture is ceremonially based), all peoples—hunter or farmer, herder or trader—place themselves and their world into a known and fixed locus of meaning, sometimes behind walls, sometimes not.[26] Each tribal group devises its own form, and these forms are responsive to social needs of the time and of the particular place. In fact, Yi-Fu Tuan argues that the only reason this tribal self-sufficiency ever collapses among tribal groups is when villagers come to realize:

> their lives are governed not so much by the motion of the sun and moon overhead as by events (reflecting the laws of supply and demand or government policy) in other parts of the country.[27]

There are no architects among tribal groups of people; the forms of the built structures are told in myth; everyone knows the story, so everyone knows who it will be to wrap, notch, tie the forms together. As Peter Nabokov writes, it is in the myths that we find the "zoning codes, blueprints, and labor unions."[28] Nevertheless, we are often flummoxed in our use of myth to read backwards into native traditions. Myths change, too, according to personal vision and understanding. They are also highly sensitive to and dependent upon the language in which they are told. Sadly, as we well know, we have lost many native languages since contact.

Unfortunately, when an oral tradition is lost, we may be at a loss to know why some groups dramatically revised their inventory of building forms. The built form, the architectonic space—in other words, architecture—has the potential to respond quickly to any early need for change or modification in a people's *Weltanschauung.*[29] Language, myth, and social structure also change, but they change more slowly. That is why we must be doubly careful about the interpretive statements we make for any built form. For example, in the Shenandoah Valley of Virginia, in one area continuously occupied for more than ten thousand years with seemingly little change in architectural structure, suddenly in the midsixteenth century stockaded villages were built.[30] We do not know the precise reason or combination of reasons for this—perhaps warfare, perhaps disease, perhaps competition for hunting territories from groups belonging to larger confederations, perhaps something else completely different—the whim of a charismatic leader, for example.[31]

Presumably, the Shenandoah Valley people belonged to or were allied to the Powhatan confederacy.[32] Nevertheless, only some of the Algonkian peoples of that confederacy built stockades; others in the confederacy did not.[33] Moreover, there are some Algonkian groups, as far as we know, who have never built stockaded walls about themselves— the Algonkian peoples of the subarctic lands, for example. We cannot, therefore, even ascribe certain building customs to various groups within a language family. All we can observe is that there are always variations, always multiplicities, of forms possible within any group's building inventory.

Very generally speaking, of the precontact New World groups, it is those who fenced themselves in who did not survive and were forced into dramatic changes, including relocation. These changes may have occurred in part because their populations came to exceed what the land could support.[34] For example, the stockaded walls of Cahokia were constructed four times. The surrounding forests were depleted and the wildlife habitat of the surrounding area destroyed.[35]

Community settlement carried with it another grave danger. At the time of contact, because of their population concentrations, settled groups were particularly vulnerable to the terrors of European-introduced diseases.[36] Smallpox, plague, measles were among the diseases introduced into the New World by the first European explorers, diseases that spread rapidly throughout North America in advance of the actual arrival of colonists.

Did similar mythic concepts of territory as place of origin and built structure as the renewal and re-creation of the cosmos once pertain among the Old World tribes too? The Gauls, and the Celts, the Picts, and all the others? Perhaps. There are certainly hints of something from the same ballpark when we consider the prevalence of the Graeco-

Roman custom of marking the end points of territory with terms or herms, little squared pillars in honor of the Roman god Terminus or the Greek god Hermes. Unfortunately, that sort of comparative inquiry is beyond the focus of this study.

Whether the ancient Amerindian communities lived within walls or without walls, all native communities demarcated gathering places, be they council grounds, feasting grounds, or grounds of sacrifice and ceremonial competition. These grounds were ritually set aside, with circumscribed approaches and uses. The first European travelers knew these places were significant and recognized them as special places, set-aside places of particular import. Their accounts—essays for other European readers describing the strange, peculiar, interesting customs of the so-called savages of the New World—are often illustrated with drawings and paintings of tribal village layouts showing cleared ritual grounds.[37]

A Typology of Set-Apart Space

In a most general way, the built sites of ancient America share a number of commonalities. They are remarkably alike in formal terms, that is, in terms of what they look like and of what are they made.[38] For example, it is obvious that the shell rings of the southeast coast and the medicine wheels of the northern plains are essentially flat circular shapes. It is just as obvious that the ceremonial ball courts and plazas of the southwest and southeast are flat rectilinear shapes. The sun dance lodge and the tepee of the plains are conical shapes, just as are the burial mounds of the Ohio and Mississippi river valleys. The plank house of the Northwest Coast and the midéwiwin lodge of the Great Lakes region are rectangular, enclosed, roofed forms. The prairie wickiup is dome-shaped. In other words, the constructions are all simple shapes in edge and volume: isolated, separated circles or polygons, each one two-or three-dimensional in volume.

Most structures are free-standing, but there are a few notable architectural exceptions: The pit houses of the west coast and the plateau were dug into the earth; some of the granaries and storage rooms of the ancient pueblo people were tucked high up in mesa walls and rock overhangs and layered into horizontal multilevels—stories and plazas. Nevertheless, even these so-called cliff dwellers spent most of their days and many of their nights sheltered by simple frame ramadas on the ground below the cliffs.

The ancient North American sites were built from the materials at hand. This means dirt, fiber, tree bough, stick, grass, skin, bone, clay, stone, even snow. Materials were seldom transported long distances to the construction site although in at least one notable case they were. More than 600 juniper, fir, and balsam tree trunks were carried by Hohokam laborers almost 50 miles[39] in the middle of the fourteenth century to provide the framework for the clay structure of Casa Grande, previously mentioned.

All of the Amerindian building materials used were chosen purposively—not just because they were usually near to hand and practical, but also because they fit the story, they had their own intrinsic meaning, their own potentiating powers.[40] Care was taken in gathering the materials and in using them correctly, but that did not mean people thought of their structures as lasting ones to be built for forever.[41] Quite the contrary. Because the structures are themselves powerful, animated, they cannot be expected to remain fixed. They change, just as does everything else upon the earth.

The raw materials used are those of the earth—its stones and river-bed clays, the animal skins and sinews, trees and grasses. Sometimes the materials are combined and sometimes not. The structural types are just as straightforward: bent frame, post and lintel, compression. Some of the built forms are volumetric: they have walls and roofs. Others are not: they are drawings upon the earth. In all cases there is an appropriateness of form and material that is appealing to those of us schooled in the Bauhaus dicta of modern classicism. The right material has been used for the right purpose. It is honest work.

It is important, too, to remember that all of the tribal groups used a number of different shapes and forms. Further, no tribal group stayed exclusively within one form. Thus, it is an error to say the circle is a configuration most important to the Plains groups if by that the importance of the elevated burial platform to some of the Plains groups is thereby overlooked. Each group must be studied individually because each is a separate people with their own mythology and traditions, although there are, of necessity, wider groupings that can be made, with circumspection, on the basis of culture areas, climate, the building materials at hand, and local economic needs.

Indigenous architectonic forms may also be summarized in another way. They could be categorized as spaces that are primarily Euclidean shapes (e.g., the circles and squares of forms such as medicine wheels, ball courts), or spaces that are primarily topological volumes (e.g., the domes and cones and shallows of forms such as tepees, wickiups, pit houses). They could also be described as projective spaces—spaces that are measured in relationship to some feature of the terrain or ourselves (e.g., big, little; near, far). Regardless of whether one chooses to emphasize shape, volume, or measure in the description and categorization of an architectonic form, all spaces are combinations of spatial relationships. They all have shape, volume, and measure.[42]

Some ancient New World earth forms are zoomorphic shapes; that is, they are architectonic forms sculpted or drawn upon the earth in the shape of animals or parts of animals. One of the most renowned zoomorphic forms is the ancient serpent mound, over 1310 feet in length, near Cincinnati, Ohio. It may have been built between 800 B.C.E. and C.E. 400 by the Adena people.[43] A somewhat similar, but less well known serpent mound, is found at Rice Lake, Ontario. It is approximately 197 feet in length and was built about C.E. 130.[44]

Other earth forms are hybrids, part human perhaps, part animal, fantastic biomorphic figures. It is not known, for example, if the great mound at Poverty Point, Louisiana, built between 2000–700 B.C.E.[45] is bird or monster or . . . ?

Still others are geometric figures, meanders, spirals, enclosures. They can be as large and complicated as the famous Nazca lines of Peru, comprising more than 800 miles of straight lines, 300 geometrical figures, and perhaps thirty-five biomorphic drawings, all built between C.E. 200–1000.[46] They can also be as unremarkable and hard-to-find as the large intaglio drawings of Quartzite, California, near the Arizona border for which no date is known. They may be as miniaturized as a single, small petroglyph drawing pecked away on a rock outcropping. (Some petroglyph drawings can be sizable and complex compositions, particularly if the site was long known as a place of pilgrimage—the Peterborough, Ontario, petroglyphs, for example, where approximately 900 drawings are engraved into a single limestone outcropping of the Canadian Shield. Some of the Peterborough drawings may date back to 3500 B.C.E., others have been added since contact.)[47]

We do not know if many of the drawn or sculpted petroglyphs, intaglios, and zoomorphic earth forms are abstracted forms, ideograms, astral or terrestrial maps of some sort, or . . . ? Many of the earth forms and intaglio engravings have only been found in aerial survey, a most puzzling feature. Others, now known, slip away. For example, there are petroglyph sites in Nova Scotia that are now under water. In 1977 artist Anna Sofaer documented a previously unknown solstice configuration of sunlight and spiral petroglyph at Chaco Canyon, New Mexico, an ancient Anasazi site. In 1990, only thirteen years later, a brief update note in the June issue of *National Geographic Magazine* states that the "sun dagger" image is now lost due to a combination of erosion and inadvertent damage by visitors to the site.[48]

From a nonnative point of view, the loss of the Chaco Canyon configuration is troubling. One wonders if site access should not have been even more tightly restricted by the federal National Park Service (visitor access was limited to supervised groups). From a native perspective, however, the loss may not be at all troubling because it is one due to natural forces. It is something that happened in the usual way of such things.

All Amerindian structures are traditionally understood to be part of a life cycle of wind, rain, sun, and dark of which all things are part. It is as though one way of understanding the cosmos is as an ever-renewing pool of energy, ever-metamorphosing into one shape and another. Thus, you simply walk away from a sweat lodge, from a sun dance lodge; you do not burn it to the ground when the ceremonies are over. These lodges, like every other built tribal structure, are built in the image of the cosmos, and, in fact, are the cosmos in that place.[49] It is possible to desecrate a structure by using it for other than its intended purpose instead of letting it return simply to a state of grace, a state of nature. However, there is no way to desacralize the structure because there is really no way to sacralize it. By making it, one is only temporarily concentrating energy, connecting powers already inherent in the materials chosen.

One can add more rooms, whenever wanted, to the side or on top of adobe structures; or leave and start again somewhere else. Tepee poles can be dragged along from camp to camp, not just because poles may not be so readily found at the next campsite, but because the poles, too, are part of the migratory journey of the camp. Powers may be beseeched, they may be guided. They may not, however, be controlled in any way that attempts to subordinate them. There is no way to have dominion over the earth's powers. This is an attitude quite unlike the Judaeo-Christian notion of the world as one made for human benefit, a world in which we concomitantly grieve the loss of those things we made in the world. The Amerindian relationship to the world is an interaction with it of reciprocity, an acceptance of loss as appropriate change.

Among the ancient Pueblo cultures when pots are buried with the dead as grave offerings, they very often are marred with a "kill hole." A hole is punched into the pot to allow the power of both the maker of the pot and the power inherent in the clay itself to escape, to return—powers of reciprocity fused within the pot and now released back to the world. A modern Santa Clara Pueblo artist, Nora Naranjo-Morse speaks of this reciprocity exquisitely:

> The ground and the clay used to make this house are so absorbent, and the clay used to make the pottery is so absorbent that when you laugh, I can almost see it going into the walls. And when you are holding the clay in your hands, there is no way that your emotions can be separate. So that I always think it holds you in more ways than you can even imagine.[50]

In short, there are two points. First, all building shapes are simple. Even complex ones are only combinations of shapes. A shape is either big or little—in relationship to you. It rises, or it sinks—i.e., is concave or convex, vertical or horizontal—in relationship to the horizon line and in relationship to you. A shape may be spread out—pooling, puddling, a plane; or dense, compacted, fused. A shape may be broad or narrow, straight or curved, even meandering. Secondly, the position of any form is always determined in relationship to the horizon line and in relationship to you. Those are the two sublimely existential coordinates requisite to fix a place, to make it comprehensible. No one can see the same point on the horizon as you do. No one can stand in your shoes.

Architectonic shapes also exist in relationship to one another, and in that way they can be seen to be part of an ever more complicated webbing of coordinates with multiple nodes of intersection. Nevertheless, we *see* one thing at a time. We *scan* wider possibilities and imagined configurations. The essential coordinates remain but two: your personal angle of vision and the ineluctable horizon line, the rim of the earth where sky meets land or sea and where you can never be.

"The Earth Is My Mother"

Is there something further to be said about the meaning of traditional land use patterns and architectonic spaces in North America? Scholars and native elders alike are in agreement that the patterns and forms constitute ways of expressing and realizing a cosmological balance, harmony. Other statements have also been made—most notably that the cosmological patterns and forms are multivalent instances of a specific sort of hierophany, a theophany of mother-goddess. For these statements there is less agreement.

The Amerindian reverence for land, the earth, has been expressed many times metaphorically and religiously in such language as "the earth is my mother," a statement first attributed to the old Shawnee war chief Tecumseh and supposedly spoken in 1810 in a meeting with General William H. Harrison.[51]

Without doubt, land is a key concept of native beliefs and traditions. It is a sacred geography of origin. It is the source of well-being and personal identity, fundamental to most Amerindian faiths, emblematic of traditional Amerindian religiosity. This need not mean, however, that land, the earth, be necessarily female, a goddess in the sense of the Old World goddess traditions. The claim of a traditional earth-centered reverence is, I believe, a valid one, but the earth metaphor of mother may not necessarily be a traditional one. In fact, the metaphor is problematic for several reasons.

First of all, by referring to the earth as mother, the speaker often intends a reference to the beautiful and justly famed speech of Smohalla.[52] (Tecumseh's somewhat earlier statement has been eclipsed by the better known speech of Smohalla.) However, it is unlikely that any historic religious statement attributed to one or two nineteenth-century tribal leaders would be specifically true of the beliefs of any other North American tribal group then, now, or long ago. When we as scholars fail to recognize and appreciate the diversity of belief among the Amerindian peoples, part of our difficulty rests in today's creative and energetic pantribalism. It is subsuming the older individuations and older distinctions among the traditional sacred beliefs.

Secondly, none of the native languages we know of today are organized in terms of male and female gender—unlike the Indo-European languages. There is, therefore, no linguistic substratum supporting an ordering of the world into dualistic categories of male or female, and not-male or not-female. The importance of language in shaping worldview cannot be emphasized enough. In the Amerindian native languages, linguistic gender is derived from recognizing what is animate or inanimate, alienable or inalienable, about the noun.[53] It is not based on any sort of sexual differentiation. Sex is simply not an important attribute. Animate nouns take animate verbs. Much, very much, depends upon the speaker's perception and understanding of the object to be named, whether it is animate or inanimate.[54]

Third, although there are goddess formulations within several native cultures—for example, Changing Woman and Spider Woman of the Pueblo cultures and the Three Sisters of the Iroquois—most of them appear to be found within agricultural groups, not hunting groups. (Sedna of the Inuit would be one notable exception, and there are a few others.) Moreover, although it is by no means certain, a number of agricultural groups seem to have been at some point within the sphere of influence of the corn-growing Meso-American agricultural groups. Is it possible that many (or some) of the New World agricultural groups share some common point of origin—perhaps long ago in the Old World? That conjecture, although appealingly simple in its promise to provide us with an answer (if true) for the appearance of mother-goddess theophanies in the New World, is beyond the range of my inquiry. The evidence for an Old World link is particularly sketchy.

Nevertheless, mother goddess imagery has been traced by some scholars who subscribe to a diffusionist interpretation, Rachel Levy for example, as extending outward from an area of origin in southeastern Europe dated to the late Magdalenian period (c. 10,000 B.C.E.) thence to the south of Asia through western Asia.[55] Mircea Eliade, another subscriber to an Old World diffusionist theory, while agreeing that the earth is everywhere "mother," speculates that "before being represented as a Mother the Earth was felt as a pure cosmic creative power—asexual or, if one prefers it, supra-sexual."[56] He says this is a "fact." Unfortunately, there is no way to know that is so; however, I think Eliade is essentially correct when he observes that even when there are myths to explain how the first people came out of the earth itself "feminine attributes of this maternity may not always be in evidence"[57]—particularly, I hasten to add, when there is no language substratum to support an attribution of the earth as feminine. It is we who call the earth "mother" because that is what mothers do—give birth. As Eliade notes, birth giving can be a sort of a "mystical autochthony," something sprung from the land itself. Scholars are far from reaching consensus on any of these aspects; fortunately, the questions are open ones and being actively researched today.

Finally, as San Gill argues in *Mother Earth: An American Story* (1987), there is a case to be made for "Mother Earth" as a nineteenth-century white formulation of romantic, pious guilt that arose from white awareness of the deprivations wreaked upon the native peoples by dint of their conquest and removal from their hereditary lands by Euro-Americans (both United States and Canada), a formulation carried forward by other scholars such as Mircea Eliade and Åke Hultkrantz, according to Gill.[58]

There is yet another side to this argument. In her study *The Lay of the Land* (1975), Annette Kolodny notes that from her review of literary sources, it appears that the first European explorers *never* called the North American landscape "mother" or Mother Earth.[59] Instead, they *always* described it as a "virgin land," one of ravishing beauty.[60] Kolodny then argues provocatively that:

> our literary heritage of essentially adolescent, presexual pastoral heroes, suggests that we have yet to come up with a satisfying model for mature masculinity on this continent; while the images of abuse that have come to dominate the pastoral vocabulary suggest that we have been no more successful in our response to the feminine qualities of nature than we have to the human feminine.[61]

If Gill and Kolodny are right that the feminization of the North American landscape is a European construct, a foreign intellectual imposition, the contemporary Amerindian contribution to this discourse takes on even more poignancy—for it is traditional native speakers who insist that the earth is our mother, our grandmother. It is native speakers today who insist the earth is *not* a maiden to be ravished, but a woman worthy of respectful attention, a grandmother.

To call the earth "grandmother," as many native speakers do, is a respectful honorarium used in a number of tribal cultures. It is consistent with many native practices for yet another reason. In a tribal culture, it is often the grandmother who raises the children and teaches them all they must know to be fully human. For example, the saint most revered and to whom most Catholic churches on the Algonkian reserves are dedicated is Anne, the grandmother of Christ.[62] Grandmothers are not maidens (to be ravished), nor mothers (to bear children); they are women who have loved each of us unconditionally, no matter how many grandchildren there were.

The appellations "Mother Earth" or "Grandmother Earth" are richly evocative earth metaphors, ones that serve well as a pantribal religious formulation of ancient native reverence for land,[63] feminine metaphors enhanced by supporting concerns for land usage—both ecological and political—by natives and nonnatives alike. As English-language phrases, these earth metaphors are piquantly comprehensible to nonnatives. The metaphors work well to urge upon us a respectful, intense, individual interaction with the environment. Joseph Epes Brown says this interaction with the environment is so characteristic of native practice that he calls it a "metaphysic of nature."[64]

In any event, one of the few things non-Indians are sure to know about Indians and to believe sublimely characteristic of native traditions is a seemingly superior respect and reverence for the earth. That the earth is holy, the earth is sacred, the earth is life giver, wise elder earth is a prayer poignant and pregnant with hope for native and nonnative alike distressed by contemporary civilization's despoliation of the land. By directing our attention to the earth as we know it, the earth metaphors of mother, grandmother, prompt our reconsideration of the earth's geography as sacred. The womanly metaphors provide us with a sense of fitting place in the world, a place where we may indeed in the legendary words of Tecumseh "take our rest upon her bosom."

Impact of Language

One reason why earth-centered hierophanies are so readily comprehended within native cultures may lie in the structures of the native languages themselves. Unfortunately, summary statements concerning the native languages of North America are hard to come by. There are so many languages and not nearly enough linguists working with native speakers.

In Europe there are but three language stocks (Indo-European, Basque, and Finno-Ugric), and one is predominant, Indo-European. In the New World linguists commonly recognize six.[65] (Some anthropologists have argued that once long ago there was a protolanguage, a sort of "superstock" known by all of the peoples east of the Rocky Mountains.)[66] At the time of contact, there may have been more than 2,000 spoken languages; certainly, there were at least 1,000.[67] In Canada today there are eleven language families still existent, although only the Algonkian languages of Cree and Ojibway and the Eskimo-Aleut language of Inuktitut are likely to survive as modern languages.[68]

It is difficult to describe native languages in terms of Latin grammar (as we can the Indo-European languages with relative facility) because, as anthropologist Harold Driver notes, "Each Indian language has its own grammar which differs more or less from the grammars of other languages."[69] On the whole, nouns are more complexly inflected with more possible combinations of morphemes than nouns in European languages[70] (some argue that this characteristic enables Amerindian languages to be spoken with more exactness of meaning than European languages);[71] and, as noted before, in most native languages the gender of a noun is not one based on any form of male, female, or not male, not female sexuality.

There have been studies that have attempted to specify how a particular Amerindian language is keyed to a particular tribal culture. These studies are inherently fascinating and provocative. Every study that raises and answers one question for one group presents us with a question to be asked of another group. For example, in English we classify things into nouns and verbs, implying that nouns are more stable or lasting than verbs and, as Benjamin Whorf notes, "Our language thus gives us a bipolar division of nature; but nature herself is not thus polarized."[72] In Hopi, a Uto-Aztecan language, the major classification is not one of nouns and verbs, but rather one of duration—the long and short of it.[73] Nature is not split into two; it is rather more of a whole and events go on and on, always "storing up an invisible charge that holds over to later events."[74] This certainly tells us something about the Hopi landscape, but not about any other landscape.

In Wintu, a Penutian language, careful distinctions are made in the verb form chosen, which convey whether the action spoken of is one that the speaker is personally knowledgeable of or knows of only because someone else said it happened.[75] Thus, it is clear that Wintu places great stress on the speaker's veracity, ability to be accurate, and personal honesty. But is that also true in other Amerindian languages?

All languages are practical. If, as in Kaska, an Athapaskan language, there are no cardinal directions, it is not because that group of people lack any sense of direction, it is because their directional grid is one based on the flow of rivers—"a system that makes sense in a land where the sun almost disappears each winter."[76]

All languages have complex grammars. None are primitive; none more highly developed than another in terms of structure.[77] Moreover, "there is much evidence to suggest that language is more stable than the rest of culture."[78]

Let us look more closely at one exemplary study that considers the relationship of language to religious beliefs. Religious historian Werner Müller has studied carefully the grammar of the Dakota language compiled by anthropologists Franz Boas and Ella Deloria. Dakota is a Siouan language, one of several Siouan languages found among peoples of the plains and the eastern woodlands. Müller notes that what he terms "uniquely passive" verb forms in Dakota enable "attitudes of suffering, of enduring, and of passive acceptance [to] dominate the character of the entire language."[79] For example, things do not happen; they change states of being. Thus, I do not tremble; I am in a trembling condition. I do not turn about; literally, my inner power turns me around. Whenever possible, states Müller, the active first person statement is avoided, thereby retreating "to a view in which all actions and events are understood as happening to oneself (as a *Widerfahrnis*),[80] a sort of passive egocentricity.

Without questioning Müller's understanding of Boas's and Deloria's grammar, we might, however, query Müller's interpretations. Perhaps Müller's observations could be expressed in another way. Perhaps the speaker is not "enduring" or "suffering"; perhaps the speaker is waiting, watching, giving fully of a respectful attention to all forces, energies, possibilities in the landscape. Perhaps the waiting is one of self-confidence that *this* is the right place to be.

I suspect my restatement of the Dakota *Widerfahrnis* as a self-confident, respectful attention is one with which Müller himself would agree because he writes further that the passive nature of the Dakota language particularly permits a *Weltanshauung* in which the "Dakota accepts all phenomena with a kind of loving reverence."[81]

In Dakota, there is no past tense verb,[82] all time is now. Thus, all places are potentially animated. Instances of hierophany are everywhere possible, instances of power, instances of kratophany. It is easy to find oneself living in a mythic time in a sacred place when everywhere about you the world is vibrant, always talking to you, always changing the state of your being. Such a world is charged with potency; you would have to be there to know it. As Müller concludes, this seemingly (but not really) passive language "and the Indian world view, which is completely given to experience, fit together perfectly. It seems as though the one has created the other."[83]

What are we to do if we do not speak these native languages, do not know them as our mother tongues? We must then attend to the visual grammar of built forms—thus, my emphasis upon identifying the typology, the grammar, of built forms in the sacred landscape. Spatial organization is a grammar as potent as linguistic. Spatial organization specifically organizes the world and makes it formed, comprehensible.

A Reverence for the Earth

If one *knows* the earth is sacred, then one lives in a setting where all human endeavors may be instances of hierophany. Instances of hierophany are matters of perception, not of fixing something in its immutable place. All endeavors to survive are fixed in a cosmological understanding of the necessity of maintaining balance, harmony. That means at times there is loss as well as increase, qualities that are perhaps better expressed as change and transformation. The world is always renewable, and our own centering points in the world are always ongoing activities of personal vision realized in built forms and architectonic spaces.

In the Amerindian worldview, because the earth is sacred, no built forms are intended to be permanent ones. All built forms are concatenations and assemblages of power, of energy, assemblages that can be made again and again. The forms may be isolated ones, simple structures—bent frames, post and lintel, compression forms—visible in the landscape and made of materials at hand. The forms may be monumental ones, as indeed the Adena and Hopewell burial mounds are. There is no proscription to be found anywhere against building large things on or out of the earth. Big Horn Medicine Wheel in Montana is almost 80 feet in diameter; the Pinson burial mound in Tennessee is nearly 75 feet tall; and the mounds at the Cahokia site in Illinois, and the Troyville site in Louisiana are even taller. Many traditional architectonic forms continue to be built today—for example, totem poles and great houses in the northwest, adobe structures in the southwest, midéwiwin lodges in the upper Michigan peninsula, and sweat lodges everywhere. All are built to provide us with human centering points in an earth-centered cosmology.

If some call this earth-centered reverence "mother" or "grandmother," it is because that is one way to express in ways all can understand that the earth is holy—bone, flesh, sinew, blood, and hair; mountain, stone, tree, river, and grasslands. In the traditional cultures of the First Nations of the New World, earth-centered visions are moments of the sacred made visible. They are well and traditionally understood existentially through personal and powerful vision.

The Amerindian built form is itself a reified expression of those beliefs and traditions. It is not anything other or less than that.

4

The "Look" of a Sacred Site

For four years artist Charles Ross crisscrossed the American Southwest, driving thousands of miles through Utah, Arizona, Texas, New Mexico. He was looking for a particular place, a place to build "Star Axis"—a naked eye observatory (see figure 10). He was not looking for a building site, however. As Ross describes it, "I knew the site had to be the center of the universe, that I would have to feel that sense of centeredness in the site before I could build it."[1] Yet when Ross found the "Star Axis" site, he did not know where he was. That was all right, too. The name of the site could be found on a map later. The important thing was that he knew he was in the right place. As Ross explained further, "I've been guided in some ways to this place, I really have been."[2] What does this sort of statement mean? "Guided"? How could Charles Ross know he was where he should be if he did not know where he was, or how he had come to be there?

Seemingly inexplicable events, such as the one Ross relates, are typical descriptions of encounters with "sacred places." Sacred places are powerful visions realized and reified in architectonic space. They are loci for earth-centered kratophanies. Sacred places can be described—not just in terms of their affect (Ross's sense of having been led, guided, of being centered there), but also in terms of their physical setting (what the place looks like) because they are *also* architectonic sites. All of these events take place somewhere. The question arises: do "sacred places" have physical features in common? If so, what are they?

Any sacred place is an organized space. As an organized space, the viewer, or site visitor, responds to it in particular autonomic ways. That affect is one of the recognition of power, sacred power (kratophany), a power particular to place, which may or may not be intermingled with the recognition of that power as a sacred being (theophany). People from different cultures—even from cultures removed in time and geography—do experience religious responses (hierophanies) at sites sacred to other people. These are more likely to be experiences of kratophany rather than theophanies. Nevertheless, they *are* religious responses. Thus, if we can begin to see sacred sites in terms of their common physical features, we should be able to trust and understand better site-specific religious responses.

Astral Alignments

Religious historians have focused much of their study of sacred place on known sacred sites that are astrally aligned. This is consistent with the scholarly emphasis in religious studies on the importance of sky gods, gods of the heavens, even if they be the god who went away, a *deus otiosus*.[3] Moreover, it is true that astral configurations are important in a number of Old World religions. In fact, Christian Norberg-Schulz credits the development of the three major monotheistic religions—Judaism, Christianity, and Islam—to their having arisen in a part of the world where the sky is ordinarily visible as a vast expanse above and on high. As a result, says Norberg-Schulz, in this region, the landscape can be described as a "cosmic landscape" whose most important feature is the sky because the earth is desert, a barren ground, but the sky is an "immense embracing vault."[4]

Astral alignments can be determined for almost any site almost anywhere. All that is needed is a sky above and a horizon line upon which to fix a point. In the simplest methods we need only a place of fixed reckoning and the time to observe what happens over a year. Most sacred sites will appear to be aligned astrally to something significant in the sky because the sites are clearings of some sort. But, in order to be sure it is appropriate to look for an astral alignment for that site, it is important to know that sky gods mattered to the people of this place and/or to identify some sort of a built structure in the place as being astrally oriented, e.g., placed in a sunwise direction. If we do not have a few independent facts at hand of this order, any astral orientations we determine for the site from its natural configurations will all be imposed interpretations. Thus, we need to be wary of assuming that any naturally configured astral alignment demonstrates the site is sacred.

Two of the best archaeoastronomical studies of ancient Old World sites were done almost a century ago by Sir Norman Lockyer and W. R. Lethaby.[5] Lockyer's work is particularly remarkable because he convincingly explains how simple it is to calculate accurate solstice and equinox alignments and a number of other seemingly mysterious astral configurations. Following their lead, Vincent Scully argued in his still controversial study of Greek temple sites—*The Earth, the Temple, and the Gods* (1969)[6]—the necessary alignments of Greek temple sites with sacred topographical features. In fact, Scully uses his alignments to recapture lost archaic sacred sites in the landscape. Unfortunately, few archaeoastronomical studies[7] have been completed of New World sites. There are even fewer New World site studies that attempt to discern linkage or interpenetration of religious beliefs, landscape, and architectonic formulations. Again, one of these very few is also by Scully, *Pueblo* (1975).[8]

Boundaries and Enclosures

As important as astral alignments can be in recognizing a sacred place, or in saying something about why the place is sacred, there are other features of the site that must be noted in its physical description. Some sacred places are sites that appear to be enclosed spaces, rather than open or elevated spaces. Sometimes our attention is directed down, not up, or inward, not outward, when we enter the site. Sometimes there is something centered in the site, some recurrent or aberrant phenomenon to command our attention—for example, a geyser, a blowhole, a volcano—something that bespeaks powerful chthonic energies.

Similar sorts of places appear to attract our attention worldwide. Often they are very ancient sites. Sometimes they are sites sacred to cultures now lost or of which we know little. The sites are usually beautiful in proportion and often monumental in built or architectonic scale—for example, Machu Picchu in Peru, Big Horn Medicine Wheel in Montana, or Chaco Canyon in New Mexico. Why do these sites prompt pilgrimages even today?

Historian Kees W. Bolle calls the significance of place "presence," a "topographical religiosity," the "symbolism of being there." He argues[9] that our ability to recognize that ancient sites are religious places does not tell us anything at all about what forms religious expression took in those places. The important thing, as Bolle warns us, is that we avoid falling back upon old, exhausted theories of evolution in the history of religion, theories which equate "earth-centeredness" with animistic superstition, magic, and the lack of "true gods."

Bolle argues that what is quintessentially important about a sacred place is that it is an enclosed space. In Bolle's line of reasoning, the importance of a sacred place is not the figure of any deity within, for there may be nothing at all within.[10] The god could be away; the god may be waiting to be called to return to that place. What is more important is that there be a physically built enclosure to set the place apart. Because the god has come before, and may again, that possibility is what makes the place sacred. In other words, it is the process of enclosure that makes a place significant because it is there that the locus of presence is known. Enclosure means separation. Because the space is enclosed, it is centered upon something and is thereby more intensely animated than spaces that are not enclosed.

Although Bolle emphasizes the importance of physically building an enclosure, his line of thinking also suggests that what might be built would not need to be "built" per se. The "built" aspect of the space could be the pathway to it. For example, the enclosure could be wholly a natural form—mountain or valley, river or lake, the ocean, perhaps even a recognized astral configuration. In order to get there, the viewer leaves another place to enter the set-apart place. The viewer follows a path to a point of entry. What makes boundaries enclosing is that they have openings, as Christian Norberg-Schulz notes.[11]

To some degree also, the meanings ascribed to a place—what we call it, what we do there, in short, its metaphorical aspects—are also its "built" aspects. Metaphorical aspects are constructed meanings and emphases of importance. For example, among the Saami of Norway, one study[12] delineates eight different types of sacrificial sites (of reindeer, fish). All of the sites are located upon sacred mountains or within high meadowlands. For the most part, the sites are natural configurations of terrain, for example, rock formations, boulders, springs, lakes, and cracks in the ground or in rocks. Only one of the eight different types (the stone circle type) is a "built" site in the sense that it must be physically constructed of stones set in a circle with a diameter of nearly twenty to thirty feet, yet all of the eight types are set-apart spaces. All of the places are bounded, even as natural forms. They are all places that have a directed approach, a proper point of entry within. They are *known* by the Saami as sacred sites.

Tadehiko Higuchi, in his study[13] of the ancient sacred sites of Japan, noted that the viewer's angle of vision upon entering the sacred site is also determined by the type of enclosure and/or the point of entry to the site. For example, upon entering the site, does the viewer look up or down? How far up or down? Can the viewer see the site in its entirety or only in part? The answers to these questions identify the viewer's angle of vision and, thus, are also part of the site's constructed meaning.

Higuchi conducted a comprehensive physical survey of the best-known archaic sacred sites of Japan. His survey enabled him to identify seven sacred landscape types based upon their spatial configurations and their necessary angles of vision for viewing by pilgrims.[14] Each type is composed of four elements: center (the focus of our attention, or the goal of our approach), the approach itself (the directionality of our attention, how we get there), the boundary of the site (that space in its defined particularity), and the site's "domain" (its affect).[15] In this schematic, Higuchi is much influenced, as he acknowledges, by the typology of space established by Christian Norberg-Schulz.

Higuchi's writing in translation is dry and somewhat technical. Norberg-Schulz's writing is sheer poetry, precise in a very different way. His analyses of Old World sites, both ancient and modern,[16] attempt to determine what the space means, what makes a space a "place"—how its "genius loci," or "spirit of place," is realized. According to Norberg-Schulz, the particular genius of architecture is its ability to ground us both psychologically and physically. In other words, by means of a spatial form, an architectonic form, architecture provides us with a foothold in space and time. As Norberg-Schulz writes in *Genius Loci* (1979):

> Things always tell several stories; they tell about their own making, they tell about the historical circumstances under which they were made, and if they are real things, they also reveal truth.[17]

In Norberg-Schulz's analysis of what constitutes an architectonic space, we speak of things "taking place" because we cannot imagine any activity without place. All activities exist in vertical and horizontal dimensions equivalent and proportional to the dimensions of the earth, the sky, and ourselves as we perceive these ratios of measurement. All activities also exhibit aspects of centralization, direction, and rhythm—the concrete properties of space, as well as of time.[18] Thus, Norberg-Schulz is concerned not just with architecture, or with space conceived architectonically; he is also concerned with existential space.[19]

According to Christian Norberg-Schulz (and here we see most clearly

Tadehiko Higuchi's debt), the spatial aspects of architecture are three: place, path, and domain. All of these aspects are interrelated and dependent upon each other.[20] (Higuchi added center, the goal, and angle of vision to the analysis.) All place is bounded, or has a boundary whose enclosure is recognized because there is some sort of an opening into this seemingly closed-off or set-aside place.[21] Thus, built space boundaries (floor, wall, ceiling) are no different from the boundaries of nature (ground, horizon, sky). Path is the way we take to approach the opening. Path involves the notion of time.[22] We must transit from here to there; we must get there one way or another; thus, our activity takes place in time. The domain of a place is its metaphorical meaning, what we make of it, its "genius loci." When we perceive a space as "place," we are perceiving the space as being animated and formed in a particular way. There is a spirit or an energy to that place, one that we call "genius loci."

The approaches of Bolle, Higuchi, and Norberg-Schulz in combination not only enhance one another, they clarify our understanding of what makes a sacred place so attractive and attracting to us. Thus, one reason we are attentive to such places is that we see the area as an animated one. The place is enclosed, set apart. We may choose to enter or not. We may stand outside, at the rim. The site has presence; we hesitate; we know there is a reason for us to pay attention to it, even if there be no "thing" there. Our body tenses with concentration; we look up or down or into the set-apart place. We look closely at it. We have left some other place behind and journeyed in actual time from somewhere else to get there. And in all these ways we know that this site matters because we perceive it as being animated. It is an organized, defined space; it is a place.

We can very often get from here to there almost unaware of what we are doing. This may seem paradoxical but it is not. We are quite capable of doing one thing, while thinking of another. It is possible to journey without knowing one is following a sacred way—for a while. Once there, however, we must look. Our attention is fixed, concentrated, however briefly by the boundary of the site, by its set-apartness and concomitant animation. As the site is placed, so, too, are we placed. If we perceive the site intensely, if it is a sacred place, we cannot help but apprehend it as an organized space and as a point of orientation for ourselves in this world—at least the world as we know it. Sacred sites are earth-centering places, and our experience of them is to be ourselves earth-centered, to be most exquisitely, particularly centered here and now—for forever, in this moment.

Two Sites—Sacred or Non-Sacred?

Kees W. Bolle, Tadehiko Higuchi, and Christian Norberg-Schulz all worked their analyses from known sacred sites. Will their recognition formulae work on other sites? Yes. To the extent a site can be accurately described in terms of its features of enclosure, center, path, angle of vision, goal, domain, so, too, can its sacred aspects be identified if there are any. It is also helpful to know if the site or structure can be described as site-adapted or site-imposed. In other words, is the site or structure one built from materials at hand and built in response to the land's terrain? Or, is the site one that could be described as "improved," "developed," a site built upon with little regard for the original features of that particular terrain?

In 1989, within the space of a week, two lead articles appeared in the *New York Times Magazine* and the *New York Times Book Review* on the same homely subject—domestic land use. But that is something of a misstatement. Both articles, in fact, were about the ability of land to center people and to prompt personal moral decisions. They were religiously oriented articles, however unwitting their authors may have been about that aspect of the experiences they chose to describe in their essays.

One article, "Why Mow? The case against lawns,"[23] was about lawn mowing, a peculiarly American activity its author Michael Pollan insisted. He described the unfenced American front lawn, a greensward stretching from coast-to-coast, as "an egalitarian conceit, implying that there is no reason to hide behind fence or hedge since we all occupy the same middle class."[24] While pushing his lawn-mower back and forth on his own front lawn, ruminating and mumbling, all the while keeping the forest that abuts his property at bay, Pollan considers the lawn and concludes that lawns are "a symptom of, and metaphor for, our skewed relationship to the land. . . . They [lawns] bend nature to our will."[25] He decides he will have no lawn. In its place, he plants a garden—to keep the forest away, and because gardens "instruct us in the particularities of place."[26] Pollan soon recognizes his decision may be an imperfect compromise. Perhaps there is a place in his life for a lawn after all. If there is, Pollan wants his lawn to be a clearing *inside* his garden, a "distinct and private place."[27] At the end of the essay we learn that Pollan has not yet cleared a space in his garden for a lawn. He decides (wisely, I think) to wait a bit to see if he should. In the meantime, he erects a fence and plants a hedgerow.

In the second article, "A Shelter for Dreams," E. V. Walter[28] reviews a book by Witold Rybczynski, *The Most Beautiful House in the World* (1989). Rybczynski, a Canadian professor of architecture at McGill University, wanted to build a boat, a rather large boat. He decided it would be more comfortable to build his boat if he could do it in a shed. Because the boat would be big, the shed would have to be big. Thus, to build the boat, he needed to build a shed; to build the shed, he needed to buy some land. One day out looking for land, he and his wife found just the right spot: "Shirley and I looked at each other and knew we had found the place."[29] It was easy to decide to build a boat on that land. The chosen place was "a particularly comfortable spot,"[30] an old orchard south of Montreal, a gentle clearing in the landscape. Time passed. The Rybczynskis never built their big boat. Seemingly in an unintended, intuitive, graceful, natural way, the two began to build a house, their home, *there*, in *that* place—all the while thinking they were building themselves a boat shed: "My home had begun with the dream of a boat. The dream had run aground—I was now rooted in place."[31] The wanderers were now settlers. Walter comments, "a house shelters day-dreaming. . . . And dreams contain houses."[32]

What are the "sacred" aspects of these two seemingly nonsacred experiences? There are several. The Rybczynskis recognized the inherent "presence" of their land when they saw it. The little orchard provided a natural framework—path, enclosure, center—for house building, for centering. As they built upon their land, built their house by hand, the Rybczynskis came to know their land intimately. They came to know its domain and were led in some necessary way to build something that amplified the inherent structure of that clearing.[33] The contentment of the Rybcynskis with their "most beautiful house in the world" suggests that theirs is a site-specific, site-sensitive piece of architecture.

Not so Michael Pollan's garden. Pollan wants to keep back the forest. He does not want to let his garden revert to meadow or forest because, he writes, "I don't go in for that sort of self-effacement."[34] Instead, Pollan builds himself a fence and plants a hedge in order to secede from being part of the "national lawn."[35] It is possible Pollan will never find a natural place of presence, a clearing, in his garden. Pollan appears to be busy defining and defending the garden's perimeter against all comers, including those who spend their Sundays cutting the grass. Pollan's garden, thus, seems to be a site-imposed effort, not one of site-adaptation for learning the "particularities of place."

Monumentality

What I thought significant in my chance juxtaposition of reading those two essays in the course of a week was that both essays, for seemingly similar reasons, lacked illustrations of what they purportedly were about—a garden and a shed. The articles were illustrated in other ways.[36] The articles told the reader about personal responses to particular land sites—ordinary, unremarkable land sites, except that each site was a *place* that the authors had come to know as a place, and in that way their lives had been changed in an intimate way.

Had an art historian been asked to assess the relative site-adapted or site-imposed merits of Michael Pollan's garden or the Rybczynskis' boat shed from the written description provided in the two articles, the scholar would be at a dead loss. Art historians are trained to work their analyses from photographs. Often, what the art historian is really analyzing is the photograph itself, not what has been photographed. At times the analysis is skewed. Art historians are not usually trained to consider what the land looked like and felt like as an original naive construct.

In John W. Dixon's essay "Towards an Aesthetic of Early Earth Art," published in a special earthworks issue of *Art Journal* (Fall 1982), Dixon attempted to establish a "way of looking at and thinking about early earth art."[37] Dixon opens with a cogent statement that there are three classes of earth forms: cave and mountain (things upon the earth, things within the earth); the menhir (any isolated object); and, "patterns" (avenue, spiral, labyrinth, and mandala). The first two classes are self-explanatory, Dixon writes. The third class requires explication. For Dixon, it is pattern making that is "the first act in generating a distinctively human mentality [because a pattern requires a center and that] . . . inexorably carries with it the establishment of pathway, level, direction, and ultimately shape."[38]

According to Dixon, true innovation in form occurred only once—between 30000 B.C.E. and 7000 B.C.E., from the Old World palaeolithic to neolithic periods, inclusively. From 7000 B.C.E. onward, Dixon believes that all that has been done since has been only a matter of adapting, emendating, and varying a handful of basic intellectual patterns—because that is all that we can possibly think about anyway.

There are problems with Dixon's analysis. His analysis makes it possible to write nice, neat histories of form—the dome throughout history, the menhir throughout history, etc. Unfortunately, it suggests that people never solve problems, but only adapt known solutions. What if someone does not know there is a solution already at hand for a problem? No matter how many times the wheel is invented, each time it *is* a new invention—to the inventor.

What makes a statement innovative is not that it is the first time it has ever been stated, but rather that it is a new statement for the time in which it is made. There are many lines of primogeniture in human thought.

Secondly, Dixon is not current on the archaeological information he uses in his essay to substantiate his argument. For example, he mentions mound building briefly (the essay is a short one) and notes that many are burial mounds. He writes, however, that no "truly early example of an artificial (i.e., symbolic) mountain survives."[39] Not so. In 1979 a superb example dated to 14000—17000 B.C.E. was located in a small cave in northern Spain.[40] The El Juyo cave mound is a small burial mound, about three feet high, containing layered, charred bones and shell. The mound was carefully built of colored clays in seven-part rosettes. No doubt there are other similar burial mounds just as ancient that we may yet find.[41]

Dixon believes the shape of a burial mound is of no particular significance.[42] Most unlikely. Although we do not know what that little mound in Spain meant so long ago, it would be incorrect to say it lacks significance. The mound means something. Sacred mountain? Pregnant belly? Or maybe something else. Stars? Flowers? Further, if there is any human activity that is paradigmatically religious, quintessentially ethical, I would argue that the ritual care of the dead qualifies. The forms constructed to mark the places of the dead are meaningful, deliberate and deliberated.

Underlying all of Dixon's account is a suspect art-historical notion that real art is "monumental," i.e., made of stone or other lasting materials. Useful as his three classes (cave or mountain; menhir; flat pattern) could be in describing sacred sites, they remain bird's-eye views. What was the view that the viewer was intended to see at the site? The three classes delineated by Dixon omit the viewer's point of view, and they tell us nothing about the effect upon the viewer of the site itself.

Nevertheless, John W. Dixon brings out a salient point for our understanding of earthworks when he turns his attention in the essay to the work of contemporary earthwork artists. He believes they are "helping to rediscover the energies of a past human act . . . [by interacting with] the energies of the earth."[43] In other words, one way to know the meaning of something is to do it yourself. In that way you can "rediscover the energies" of someone else's effort from long ago. I do not know what Dixon means by "the energies of the earth," presumably something like "forces of nature," or perhaps those astounding events ironically described by insurance companies as "acts of God" for which no one is responsible, and for which there can be no indemnity. He may mean those instances of kratophany that bespeak the power of place.

Mircea Eliade's Theories

In his essay on earthworks, John W. Dixon acknowledges the influence of Mircea Eliade's work, especially *Patterns in Comparative Religion* (1958).[44] Eliade (1907–86) was one of the most prolific historians of religion. His morphological studies of non-Western and Western religions are significant; the vocabulary lists he established have been critically important in facilitating the development of religious history as a cross-cultural academic discipline. Over the many years of Eliade's scholarship, he refined and emendated his thoughts in a number of key areas. One of these concerns sacred place.

Patterns in Comparative Religion is an early work, written mostly in the mid-1940s, although it was not available in English until the late 1950s. In it Eliade writes that a space becomes sacred because "every kratophany and hierophany whatsoever transforms the place where it occurs: hitherto profane (i.e., not sacred) it is thenceforward a sacred area."[45] (Earlier in his text Eliade establishes a definition for kratophany that makes it an accompanying "notion of force or effectiveness connected with hierophanies,"[46] a force not necessarily proven to be sacred. Kratophany is not further discussed in relationship to sacred place.) Eliade explains further: "*There*, in *that* place, the hierophany repeats itself."[47] This may occur in one of three ways: by virtue of a "dazzling hierophany" (evidently something unique and, one presumes, involving kratophany); by the use of an orientation ritual, a form of geomancy (e.g., the charting of ley lines; the ritual calculations of *feng shui*); or by the appearance of some sort of sign (i.e., various known omens).[48]

In Eliade's schematic, the sacred place is an enclosed space with a particular approach by which its center may be obtained.[49] The center is what has the most import because it is there "where hierophanies and theophanies can occur, and where there exists the possibility of breaking through from the level of earth to the level of heaven." In this explication hierophany is equivalent to the experience of theophany. A bit further on Eliade speaks of the center as the center of the world, the omphalos, the sacred mountain and as a "point of junction between heaven, earth, and hell,"[50] a trilevel irruption.

Because Eliade believes hierophany to be a godly experience that always comes from outside, "from without,"[51] the hierophany itself is always a permanent manifestation[52] necessitating that there be an enclosure built for it that will last for all time.[53] Moreover, because hierophanies (or theophanies) are everywhere possible, there are many, many sacred places.[54] One wonders then if the enclosure must be built at all. Perhaps the enclosure could be a natural form recognized as enclosing the sacred place. If it must be a built place, need it last for all time? Eliade's description in *Patterns in Comparative Religion* does not happily apply to the architectonic places and structures of the New World. They are, as discussed in chapter 3, structures that are more assembled than built, structures left to weather, to return to nature, because that is the correct order of things.

There is a problem, too, with Eliade's insistence upon describing the sacred as something outside, a permanent something sometimes intrusive, something rather equivalent perhaps to a form of monotheism. Eliade's description appears to be a subjective statement of personal faith (that the sacred is outside and everlasting). It is not one of phenomenological description. The description of sacred place overlooks other objective and mitigating factors: for example, such common denominators as natural boundaries, means of approach, angle of vision—all factors that Tadehiko Higuchi, Christian Norberg-Schulz, and Kees W. Bolle consider in their studies of sacred place. Importantly, too, Eliade's description of sacred place also overlooks one important variable—the psychological receptivity of the individual to such experiences, a key factor in Jennifer Dickson's experience of the garden, as described in chapter 2.

Parts of *Patterns in Comparative Religion*, according to its foreword, are in large measure based on Eliade's lecture notes from the 1940s. In *The Sacred and the Profane: The Nature of Religion* (1957), Eliade again takes up the matter of what constitutes a sacred place.[55] His argument here is more tightly drawn. There is no mention of kratophany at all. Hierophany is now stated to be an experience of the sacred precisely equivalent to theophany. What makes a place sacred is "an irruption of the sacred that results in detaching a territory from the surrounding cosmic milieu and making it qualitatively different."[56] It becomes absolutely real.[57] (One might say better that it becomes suprareal, or hyperreal. The world is after all quite real.) As in his earlier work, Eliade also states that the sacred is something that comes from outside; hence the equivalence of its hierophany to theophany. He continues to omit the importance of personal receptivity to the experience.

The irruption of the sacred anywhere into any place signals that in that place a repeatable "break-through from plane to plane"[58]—heaven, earth, hell—is always possible. Thus the irruption *"founds the world* in the sense that it fixes the limits and establishes the order of the world."[59] The irruption centers the world, it makes it clear that only *this* place is real, all other places are chaotic, profane, without form. The irruption creates the world. Without irruption, without that necessary break in the planes, we cannot find a fixed point, an axis mundi, a sacred mountain, a temple, an orderly world with limits, a place of origin, an omphalos. We cannot re-create the world; we condemn ourselves to living in a world of linear time and profane space. If we are religious, and by definition Eliade says humans are *homo religiosus*, we must live in a world we know to be sacred. Only there can we have a *"real existence,"*[60] a religious one.

Eliade's emphasis in *The Sacred and the Profane* on the existential necessity of living in a sacred world, one in which we know the whereabouts of our origin, provides us with a formulation of sacred place much more in keeping with many Amerindian traditions than his earlier exegesis in *Patterns in Comparative Religion* emphasizing the importance of a permanently built sacred place. (The *Sacred and the Profane* version of Eliade's theory is also a formulation that extends and enhances Norberg-Schulz's thoughts about *genius loci*.) An existential sacred place can be carried about. It can be established by erecting a sacred pole in the center of a nomad's tent. It can be the entire countryside and beyond. It can be a country, even a continent. It can be as small as a built temple sanctuary. What is necessary is that it always be perceived as the midpoint, the center where, in a rupture of three cosmic planes, the world was created and can be created again and again.

It is not clear why in the *Sacred and the Profane* Eliade equates hierophany with theophany, and omits entirely the experience of kratophany. Eliade hardly discusses the role of god or gods in the irruption of hierophany into the profane world other than to say some cosmogonies are "tragic, blood-drenched."[61] (These are the ones requiring the repetition of similar godly sacrifices in the sacred place.)

A Sacred Place Morphology

The morphologies of sacred place proposed by Kees W. Bolle, Tadehiko Higuchi, Christian Norberg-Schulz, Mircea Eliade, and—to a more limited extent—John W. Dixon are compatible. Thus, a sacred place is enclosed, set-aside or set-apart space. It has a boundary. A correct point of entry obtains. The path to this place requires a separation of oneself from one kind of space to another, a space more animated, more intensified, more focused, centered. There is something we apprehend about that place that requires our attention. Symbolically, we may understand it as an irruption of power—a fluid energy from above and below. This power may or may not be concretized or contained in the form of pillar, mountain, mound. We may or may not recognize it by name as a god, an experience of the sacred personified in a theophany. We may only apprehend this power as a sort of energy from time before time, certainly from time before now. The place is not like other places, and in that way we experience it as a localized, site-specific kratophany.

A Walk in the Woods

Let us see if we can apply this simple morphology to three fairly typical experiences. First, to one recorded by Belden Lane, an American theologian whose work for several years has been to find out what it means "to experience the holy within the context of a spatially-fixed reality."[62]

Lane is indebted to Eliade's work on what constitutes a sacred place. Like Eliade, Lane assumes (but deemphasizes) the role of a god or gods in marking a place sacred or in making the world sacred. Lane's study *Landscapes of the Sacred* (1988) emphasizes the individual's capability to enter into and understand the import of a sacred place. Lane's paradigmatic journey is most personal. It is one undertaken, as he writes, in exhaustion to a nearby state park where:

> I finally escape in desperate loneliness to the river and woods, there (as I hope) to rediscover God in some grand mystic encounter. . . . But of course, it never quite works out as well as I had hoped. . . . I expect too much of the place. . . . Yet it is at this

precise moment, where I give up looking for the burning bush, that my retreat usually begins.[63]

The language is Christian and couched in theological terms, yet it is obvious that the "retreat" Lane describes is the age-old one of vision quest, and the end to be obtained—hierophany.

Lane is a devout Christian whose faith has been sustained and enhanced by his experiences of hierophany in the American landscape—nevertheless, as he explains, all the encounters have been "momentary, ambiguous . . . smaller than one dreams, yet larger than one expects."[64] Still, the encounters have certain formal elements in common that Lane calls "axioms," and presents as four "phenomenological categories describing how places are perceived in the process of mytho-genesis."[65] First, there is a sense of having been called to that place; secondly, the "sacred place is ordinary place, ritually made extraordinary;"[66] third, recognition of the sacred place is dependent upon the individual's particular state of consciousness at that moment; and fourth, the world is perceived as being itself entirely imbued with hierophany—because one has been profoundly centered in one localized place of significance.

The first characteristic—the sense of having been called to that place—is not one we can examine. It simply says that the event of being there is an extraordinary one, one that is not part of usual volition, an event that breaks through our daily sense of ordinary time and place. That, indeed, is just what a sacred place does. The remaining three characteristics are, however, familiar because they are restatement of the sacred place aspects previously discussed in this chapter. They include: passage; boundary or enclosure; center or domain; plus angle of vision.

Lane's paradigmatic encounter with hierophany took place in a clearing in the woods, a clearing in which he waited in silence. He first spotted the clearing from above where he stood on the bluffs overlooking the river, then he entered the clearing. In the clearing he saw a deer, a young doe. Lane claims he *knew* beforehand that he was "invited" to the clearing and that he would have to wait and be still when he entered the clearing to find out why. Lane insists the clearing was really an ordinary place, and credits its sublime appeal to his having entered it in silence.

Was it really such an ordinary place? I think not. First of all, he saw *that* place, not some other place, and decided—however whimsically—that he wanted to be *there*, not where he already was. Lane's desire is a wish to change two coordinates: where he was then, and what point on the horizon line he was using for orientation. Those two coordinates are the two irreducibly personal coordinates of our own persons. Further, because the clearing Lane wanted to enter was a clearing, he had to find his way in. *Autonomically*, Lane perceived the clearing as an enclosed, set-aside place. Moreover, when he first espied it as a clearing, he was looking down and into it. There was always the possibility, in his scramble down the hill, that Lane might not find it. He had to find a point of entry, a passage or an approach to get there—thus, perhaps, his existential feeling of having been "called there" because Lane risked not being able to find it. Perhaps he risked becoming disoriented, lost, as he scrabbled downhill. Lane entered the clearing in silence. That is important, too, because the combination of all these factors established the possibility of revelatory trance. The experience that resulted was significant *and* it was rooted in that place.

But what about the deer? Was not the sighting of the deer the point of Lane's pilgrimage? Yes and no. The deer itself was entirely circumstantial. Any animal seen there would have confirmed the rightness of Lane's experience because *all* encounters with wildlife matter to us in such places. It was the sighting of *something* that mattered. The sighting was what was privileged. In such places we are privileged to talk to the animals, or the trees, or the wind. Something always happens in places we approach with clearness of attitude. These are old experiences. For example, in the cave at El Juyo so very long ago there is a carved rock, rather large. It is a face—two profiles forming one frontal image. On one side a bearded man, on the other some sort of fanged cat.

Lane's understanding of hierophany is, as we have indicated, theistic. He writes from a Christian perspective. If his experiences of the landscape as sacred have been less than he hoped they would be, that is because his metaphorical construct still requires "burning bushes." If they have been more powerful than he thought they should be, again that is because he is not fully oriented to the possibility of landscape as sacred *in and of itself* since Christian beliefs are not earth-centered ones.

Lane might more easily find his "burning bushes" in the landscape were he to adopt a more pantheistic god (he appears to be headed in the direction of bio-or ecotheology), or if he were to eschew all expectation of theophany altogether. When hierophany is experienced as kratophany, there are no "oughts" or "shoulds" about it because experiences of kratophany are wholly original. Experiences of hierophany as theophany, however, are always reassessed and reinterpreted against a background of preexistent faith and theology. The experiences become as Lane admits, "ambiguous"—they are "smaller than one dreams, yet larger than one expects."[67]

The Medicine Wheel

In the summer of 1988, Canadian short story writer Margaret Dyment[68] began to write a story about a scholar's visit to a medicine wheel. Dyment herself had never seen a medicine wheel, but she did her research well and wrote a powerful story entitled "The Sacred Trust."[69] The medicine wheel in her story was Moose Mountain Medicine Wheel in central Saskatchewan (figures 11a, 11b). Having written the story from her imagination, Dyment very much wanted to see the site itself. In the fall of 1989, with the assistance of a travel grant from the Ontario Arts Council and the help of her sister, Kathleen Slavin, Dyment set out to find the Moose Mountain Medicine Wheel. She and her sister's family journeyed overnight from Saskatoon to Regina, then set out early the next morning to find the medicine wheel.

The Dyment party knew the medicine wheel was somewhere in the vicinity of Moose Mountain Provincial Park. They also knew it was on private land belonging to Cree Indians. Dyment's sister had once been there, but that was long ago and Dyment had not known of her sister's journey when she was writing her story. Stopping in the village of Kisby for directions to the site, they asked if they should get permission from the native people to see it before venturing onto the site. The answer was a laconic "You could." However, when they made their way to the farmhouse that seemed to be nearest the site (and reasonably the people from whom they should seek permission to visit the medicine wheel), they found no one at home. With some hesitation, the group decided, since they had come this far, they would try to locate the medicine wheel on their own. They had little difficulty in finding it, although the wheel was not visible from the road, and the hill upon which it lay was little different from any other rise of land surrounding. But there it was. They found the medicine wheel amidst rolling hills, on weathered range land, land sere and dry in the October winds.

Several things occurred at the medicine wheel that are significant to Dyment. The first was the appearance of the site itself. They found the medicine wheel at the top of a long hill that took almost a half-hour to walk to its crest. "The ascent," said Dyment, "was one you felt in your legs." From a distance the hill appeared to be no different than any other hill in that landscape of low rolling hills. But it was. Once there, it was obvious that the center cairn of the medicine wheel was the center point of a broad landscape circling about them. The little cairn on the rise focused and centered a vast open plain. The cairn was the highest point of the landscape, and the stones were radiating lines that drew the site together in a centripetal and centrifugal movement. As Dyment described the powerful appearance of those stone radii: "There was no way you'd be making this thing up. It was very clear this was what was intended."

The second thing that seemed remarkable to Dyment was the site's effect upon everyone. She had very much wanted to see the medicine wheel, but not in a crowd. She had come with a crowd because it was the only way to get there. No one asked anyone to be quiet, yet everyone was. There was a stillness that pervaded and persisted. When they arrived at the wheel, all talking stopped. Each person wandered off separately, one by one drawn outward along the stone directional pointers and back again to center, each person centering herself or himself there upon that landscape. The fourteen-year-old niece wandered out to the end of a stone pointer and began to sketch the site; the nine-year-old nephew wandered quietly down another stone pointer; their parents strolled out along the grassy prairie and found tepee rings by the score. No one asked, "Can we have lunch now?" (They had brought with them a picnic basket.) Each person seemed enthralled in the quietest sort of way as each came to realize that what appeared to be wild land was, indeed, land quite familiarly known by many other people, very ancient people. Dyment said of her own response to the Moose Mountain Medicine Wheel site:

> It moved me to think that human beings had created it and that all the human beings since hadn't destroyed it. What makes it special is how fragile it is.

Of the five people, only Dyment could be considered in any way expert on medicine wheels. That was not important. What was important was that each person took away from the site something that could not have been learned from a book. Each person experienced the site's domain. Each person paid attention to a presence of place, a *genius loci*.

The experience of Moose Mountain Medicine Wheel satisfies all of the sacred site typological requirements identified earlier in the chapter. Dyment and her family came from afar, leaving their own culture and the routes with which they were familiar. Trusting to the moment, they searched for and found without difficulty the site they wanted. The site was a centering place, bounded. The effect was sublime, quieting. Of the group, only Dyment had projected herself there beforehand in her imagination, but she said she had not known how centrally placed the medicine wheel really was until she trod upon the little rise of land to the central cairn of the wheel.

Oahu Lava Flow

Margaret Dyment and her family knew they were looking for a place known to be sacred to the native peoples of the prairie, but it is not always necessary to know that a place has ancient import. In the winter of 1989 I spent several weeks on the island of Oahu. There along the road I traveled almost daily was a small paved lookout point, one of several coastal viewing areas along the road. The lookout point to the south of it was a popular spot for watching the Pacific sunset, and the one just north was famed for its spectacular blowhole. There was nothing of particular note about this point—nothing unless you were there and had left the car, climbed over the highway barricade and worked your way down the slope of the ancient lava flow a ways. Then all perspectives changed.

The lava flow was a landscape of contoured, ribboned plains and canyons (see figures 12a, 12b.) Directly in front and far below at its bottom crashed the Pacific in great waves into frothy, murmuring tidal pools. In back of the barricade, behind the road now far above, loomed the exhausted volcanic mound that had created this site. The mound's slopes were ridged, fierce rivulets that clawed their way to the sea.

I never climbed the volcanic mound, nor did I ever work my way all the way down to the sea, although the descent would not have been difficult. Sometimes I did see fishermen down there in the tidal pools. I did not want to explore either of those edges—the end points of the vertical axis of mountain and ocean. Instead I usually worked my way over on the lava slope to a broad area, a ledge, where I could sit down comfortably. A rough visual measurement would place that broad ledge halfway down from the crest of the volcano or halfway up from sea level. Halfway was as far as I cared to go in either direction.

I returned there many times over the next several weeks. In that place I began to think clearly about the things troubling me so about the island, and I thought about things I had not even dared to think about previously. Oahu is a war machine. Beyond its thin coastline perimeter of hotels, shopping districts, and local attractions broods an immense armed fortress of worldwide reconnaissance and surveillance. Oahu has been the deployment point for American and allied action in four wars[70]—all fought in my own lifetime, all fought by men I have known. I had not thought about those things before. There on that ledge I could and did think about them. That was not the whole of my thought, however. I also thought about photographing the lava slope. In fact, my initial reason for clambering over the highway barricade onto the slope was to study the site, to know the lava flow well enough without my camera so I might be able to photograph some aspect of it accurately. I was not looking for a place to ponder the state of my soul or anyone else's, or to think any lofty thought at all. I just wanted to solve a photography problem.

The day before I left Oahu, I picked up an especially detailed map of the island. My lava flow (I had for some time been calling it "mine") was identified on the map as "site of ancient fishing temple." Somehow, I was not surprised. In my study of the lava flow, I had come to know it as my own place of petition, a place of blood sacrifice. Those were some of the things I had been thinking, so why should someone else not have thought those thoughts too once long ago in that place halfway between exhausted volcano and bone-breaking undertow.

Heirophanies

It is satisfying to read "site of ancient fishing temple" on a map. but that gives me no reason to claim I have some sort of mystic, particular sensitivity to place, and certainly no reason to claim a past life on Oahu. I have so often before found myself taking note of sacred sites of which I have no knowledge that I no longer think "ancient fishing temple" incidences especially curious or coincidental. These events seem to me to be an affirmation that my eyes see as well as others have seen and my brain works as well as another's once did. Locating any sacred site, known or unknown, is not particularly difficult when there are so many ancient sites about. Human beings have walked this earth for a very long time.

Thus, of the three sites, two—the lava flow and the medicine wheel—are known sacred sites. The wooded glade is not known to be an ancient sacred site; however, it is in Pere Marquette State Park, and that is not far from the ancient sacred city of Cahokia. The glade has not yet been explored by archaeologists. Perhaps there is something there.

All three sites can be accurately described as bounded areas; all three sites required that the travelers come from afar and find a path, a way in which was not at first obvious. Once the approach was located the passage from here to there was easy. All three sites were experienced as centered places having a centering effect upon the viewers who were themselves in a contemplative frame of mind. From the perspective of that place, the world obtained balance. Belden Lane described the experience of his wooded glade in terms of theophany; Margaret Dyment and I described our experiences of the medicine wheel and the lava flow in terms of kratophany. All three of us were aware that our experiences were visionary ones dependent upon the power of place. All of us carried away from those sites something of personal importance, something particular to the presence of that place. In short, our experiences were ones of hierophany.

For some the meaning of a sacred site, an ancient earthwork, is occult, hidden, a survival of a religiosity from times past—earth-centered and usually feminine in form, neglected but not forgotten, an old way. As John W. Dixon notes, many of today's "earth mystics" (his apt phrase) regard ancient earthworks as the "icons for a new religion," ones intended "to give access to the ultimate meaning of things, to unity with the fundamental energies of the earth."[71]

Typical of the "earth mystic" sort of approach are John Michell's several ley line studies. Michell argues that ancient earth forms evidence a unitary metareligiosity of earth magnetism and long-ago devotion to the "earth spirit"—a spirit that he describes as a universal deity, living, female, a spirit animated and made fertile by the sun.[72] Michell's studies and those of his followers hinge on the careful observation of astral configurations—usually the solstice and equinox, and usually those of Old World sites.[73] Stonehenge has drawn much attention.

Christopher Chippendale, reviewing the studies of Stonehenge as a naked-eye observatory, concludes that it probably does not matter to many of the people who visit Stonehenge today what scientists will eventually conclude was Stonehenge's original function for the people who built it, because Stonehenge is well on its way to becoming a religious monument for our time.[74] Stonehenge now draws so many pilgrim-visitors that access to the site has been restricted to peering through a chain-link fence—hardly an enclosure with opening.

(Modern-day Druids, however, are sometimes allowed into the circle for their summer solstice ceremonies.)[75]

From time to time other theories appear concerning ancient sacred places—chief among them those that posit "helpful visitors." One version argues that the worldwide similarity of structure among built sacred sites portends certain evidence of helpful visitors from outer space.[76]

Another version of the helpful visitors theory states that the similarity of archaic structures throughout the Old and New World is evidence of the New World's long-standing interaction with Old World mariners.[77] Unfortunately, the notion of helpful visitors lingers on, no matter how often debunked by scholars.

Art and Religion

There is yet another response possible. Why should I call my sense of awe when I encounter a so-called sacred site an experience of hierophany? Why not call my sense of awe an aesthetic response? Perhaps my experience of the lava flow, for example, was no more than my appreciation of a particular harmony of boundary, passage, center, angle of vision, and domain that I perceived there.

The question of aesthetic response vis-à-vis religious response (particularly that of kratophany, which we have already claimed to be religious) may be a red herring. As we have already seen, there is little difference in the formal aesthetic analysis John Dixon presented for ancient earthwork sites and the descriptive analysis presented by religious historian Mircea Eliade for sacred places. There is a significant overlap in the analyses of sacred place presented by theologian Belden Lane, religious historian Kees W. Bolle, and architectural historians Christian Norberg-Schulz and Tadahiko Higuchi. I am not sure aesthetic and religious distinctions matter when we speak of ancient sacred sites.

In our culture today, when we call something "aesthetic," we are usually labeling it "not religious." We have words for art and religion and we ascribe very different meanings to them. This is not true of all cultures today, and it most especially has not been true of past cultures. Few indeed are the cultures with separate words for "art" and "religion." Those few do not include the North American native cultures where there are no equivalent words for art or for religion.[78] Franz Boas, many years ago, noted "the mental processes of man are the same everywhere, regardless of race and culture."[79] When we call something "art," usually what we mean at a minimum is that it has achieved a certain excellence in its technical use of the materials at hand.[80] We may also mean something more besides, and we usually do.

In native cultures, very often that which is supposedly "aesthetic"—let us say, a beautiful pot or a well-honed projectile point—is also understood to be powerful.[81] We could say it has mana, if by that we mean to say it has animating power. More properly, within the particular tribal context, we should use the appropriate words—for example, *wakan, manitou, orenda*, perhaps even *inua*. If we do, then when we say the pot or projectile point is beautiful, we can also point to its power—it breathes, it is alive, animated, *and* it is beautiful. These words all refer to the same thing, the experience of working power in nonanthropomorphic terms, the experience of sacred power.

In English, some of this meaning of animating, nonanthropomorphic power survives—appropriately enough—in the slang contemporary North American artists use to voice approval: "that works"; "now we're cooking"; "now you've got it." Are the artists describing aesthetic effects or experiences of kratophany? Typically, an artist expresses dismay with a composition by saying, "It's dead, lifeless." The artists appear to be describing what is happening *in* the work as though it were alive. They are not describing the appearance of the work so much as they are describing its effect as a *work* of art.

The artists' jargon suggests a particular percolation of power, of life force, of creative energy *in* the work itself, something that can be alive or dead, and can be dependent upon point of view. In these instances, artists seem to be describing "soul"—not soul as a European religious term, but soul as in "soulful," soul as the word would be used today in a black American ghetto to describe something that is alive, potentiated, actualized, pulsing—in short, to describe a vibratory creative tension. Clearly, whatever the artists' aesthetic judgments may be, what they are describing are experiences of kratophany.

Further to this point, artist Andy Fabo suggests that the reason we prize so much more the work of dead artists rather than living artists is not an economic one (because the artists cannot make any more). Rather, Fabo believes, it is because the work of a dead artist is actually more animated than it was when the artist was living. Fabo is sure that when an artist dies, his or her life energy is drawn into the work that person produced over a lifetime.[82] Thus, individual life goes on, even when the person dies.

Fabo's belief is analogous to the Pueblo practice, described earlier, of punching kill holes into pottery in order to release and return the energy of the potter and the energy of the clay to the cosmos at the time of the potter's death.

Photographer Marilyn Bridges recently completed a series of aerial photographs of North American Mound Builder sites. She said of her experience photographing the Adena serpent mound in Ohio:

> The serpent's angular, twisting body in its forest locale was so realistic that in the evenings after shooting, it was a constant, even welcomed presence in my dreams.[83]

Bridges is describing a visionary experience of kratophany, a religious experience. Her experience, however is not one of theophany because the serpent (or what the serpent might represent) is no god to her. She keeps the image firmly rooted in its real place, the "forest locale," yet the serpent is so realistic (we might say "hyper-real"), she welcomes it into her dreams, her visions. Note, too, that the Adena serpent fully satisfies all the formal physical criteria of a sacred place—boundary, approach, angle of vision, center—in addition to the existential criteria of domain or hyper-realness.

Of the two formulations of hierophany—theophany and kratophany—kratophany, power specific to place, is the more appropriate one to use generally when discussing sacred place. This does not mean that a sacred site cannot be an instance of hierophany rendered as theophany. By no means. Of course it can be. I wish only to be clear that I believe the recognition of named gods in particular places to be a culturally bound metaphor. Devout Christians do not usually have their prayers answered with visions of Brahma and Amaterasu.

Kratophany, on the other hand, names no god. Having no god to be named, it is in a general way a true cross-cultural metaphor of power, energy, animation. For example, a thunder-booming night thick with lightning flashes is in and of itself an experience of kratophany. It is a marvel. Anyone in that place will know that. You might call the experience "Thor," but you would have to be taught to do so. You might tell the story of old Ben Franklin with his kite and how-he-discovered-electricity, but someone taught you that story, too. No one taught you to stand amazed at the ancient, crackling, wing-fingered pterodactyls of the sky. You simply are.

All experiences of hierophany are equivocal and ambivalent because their power is so startling. The experiences are disruptive of ordinary time and place, which is why they are so specifically remembered as happening on a particular day, a day like that, there, in that place. Experiences of kratophany can be especially ambiguous and especially startling because they lack cultural theological explanations. There may be no precedent at all to be found in our own lives for such wholly original events. One contemporary example may suffice to explain what happens in the face of kratophany, and how it is later remembered.

J. Robert Oppenheimer (1904–67), director of the Los Alamos, New Mexico, laboratory during the development of the atomic bomb, is credited with two statements[84] uttered at the time of the first successful test explosion, July 16, 1945, Alamagordo, New Mexico.[85] One statement is the one we remember; the other statement is now nearly forgotten. The Oppenheimer statement we remember is: "I am become Death, the destroyer of worlds;"[86] the one we have forgotten: "If the radiance of a thousand suns were to burst forth at once in the sky, that would be like the splendor of the mighty one."[87] The first statement evokes horror. It conveys a vehement proscription regarding the use of atomic weaponry. It resonates with value and is, therefore, memorable. The second statement is descriptive, not normative in any sense. In its context, "the splendor of the mighty one" means the bomb, and nothing else. We remember what means more.

Both statements are from the Bhagavad-gita and are, in their original theological context, cultural statements of theophany concerning Krishna. Used, however, in the context of the first atomic explosion, the first statement ("I am become Death, the destroyer of worlds") is a strong statement of kratophany. It tells us of our fears,[88] and enjoins us to be wary of the power of "death, the destroyer of worlds." Thus, it has religious content. The second statement is one we are more likely to read today only as an interesting literary allusion. The A-bomb site is a place of kratophany and, in fact, it has been described in just those terms: "it seems something of a pilgrimage to power."[89]

Animism

Kratophany is an ancient experience. It is not, however, a so-called primitive religious experience—although most recorded examples of it appear to have been written by ethnologists attempting to understand the religious beliefs of non-Western, small-scale cultures, particularly those evidencing visionary shamanic practices. Religious historians for

1a, 1b. Kathy Gillis
and Carolyn Davis
Labyrinth models, 1993

2. Kathy Gillis and Carolyn Davis Labyrinth floor model, 1993

3a-3c. Dawn Dale. "Snake Path Outaouais," 1993

3d. Dawn Dale. "Snake Path Outaouais," 1993

4a. David Harper
     "Shelterwood," 1992

4b.
Jean and Robert Rutka
"Ancestors," 1992

5. "Chantmarle, Somerset," photograph by Jennifer Dickson, R.A.

6. "Studley Royal, North Yorkshire," photograph by Jennifer Dickson, R.A.

7. Casino Garden, Villa Farnese, Caprarola, Latium,
photograph by Jennifer Dickson, R.A.

8. Villa Farnese, Caprarola, © Wayne Andrews/Esto

9. "Villa San Remigio, Pallanza," photograph by Jennifer Dickson, R.A.

10. "Star Axis." Artist: Charles Ross; photo: © Edward Ranney 2/25/89

11a–11b. Moose Mountain Medicine Wheel, Saskatchewan

12a–12b. Ancient lava flow, Oahu Island, Hawaii

13. Nancy Holt. "Sun Tunnel," 1973–1976. Courtesy
John Weber Gallery, New York

14. Walter De Maria. "The Lightning Field," 1977. All reproduction rights reserved. Copyright: Dia Center for the Arts. Photo credit: John Cliett

15. Robert Smithson. "Spiral Jetty," 1970. Photo: Gianfranco Gorgoni.
Estate of Robert Smithson. Courtesy John Weber Gallery, New York

16. Charles Ross. "Solar Burns Year Shape," 1971. © Charles Ross 1971

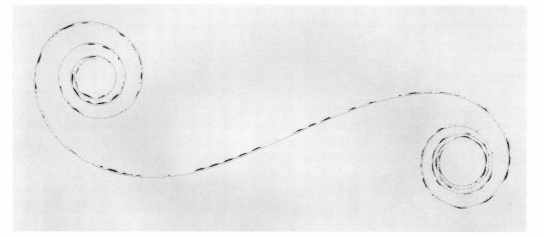

17. James Turrell. "Roden Crater," 1989, work in progress

their part have tended to lump various ethnological descriptions of personal experiences of kratophany together and cite them as examples of "animistic" beliefs, thereby defining animism as supposedly primitive religious beliefs that postulate the existence of innate "souls" in ordinary made things and natural phenomena.

Kratophany *is* related to animism, but the relationship must be spelled out carefully because the term "animism" is typically associated in religious history with the somewhat discredited evolutionary theories of the origin of religion attributed to Edward Tylor (who popularized the term) and R. R. Marrett (who refined Tylor's definition). There is no particular reason to burden ourselves with a weighted definition of animism that includes an evolutionary program of primitive-to-evolved (higher, more ethical, more monotheistic, more "white") religion. Similarly, we need not limit our use of the terms "animistic" or "animism" to the descriptions of non-Western, small-scale societies.

What I would like to propose is a consideration of animism in the context of kratophany that would enable us to apply the term to religio-aesthetic examples of it existent in contemporary Western society.

In religion, the notion that something inert (or something nonhuman) can be alive (in a rather human way) is what we call animism. Usually we mean things like rock, tree, bear. Sometimes we mean a made object. For example, if we are discussing sacred images, we might say a religious painting or sculpture is imbued with mana—that is, if we liked it. If the painting or sculpture made us anxious and we wanted to avoid it, we could say the object is taboo. Both mana and taboo are concepts linked to animism. They have been poorly formulated in their use by religious historians. Anthropologists today tend to use these terms only to describe the beliefs and practices of the cultures in which the words are actually used, those of the native religions of Oceania.

Religious historians, however, have taken the words mana and taboo out of their original context in order to use them more generally to name all powers recognized to be immanent in an object,[90] but somehow not a personal power,[91] instead, an "impersonal supernatural power."[92] This latter notion caused one anthropologist (George Murdock) to throw his hands up in dismay, saying he had never been able to find any primitive religion where the theoretical concept of mana was applicable.[93]

Religious historians have also considered mana and taboo to be ways of thinking peculiar to the "savage mind," mana and/or taboo being what the savage says creates a "wonder-working condition"[94] about that object. Mana has also been said to be a "substance or essence" that increases someone's natural abilities by conferring supernatural skills upon that person[95] (evidently something like Dorothy's red slippers) and leads to magical abilities, not to religious understandings.[96]

Both terms have fallen into disfavor today with many religious historians because, as Kees W. Bolle notes: "The term [mana] occurs as a rule in a far more complex context, as do words such as 'the sacred' or 'magic' with ourselves."[97]

The difficulty, it seems to me, with all of the above statements is the failed effort to render mana comprehensible as a diffused *outside* power that somehow gets *inside* something else. As discussed earlier, in traditional Amerindian beliefs, it is up to the beholder to determine whether something has power. That is also true for the contemporary artist and the artist's audience, which brings us back to my original point. Can we use the word "animism" properly to describe experiences of kratophany, power particularized to place?

We can, but we do not need the associated terms mana or taboo. It is simpler and more accurate to speak of some things as being "animated," vibrant, special in some way. In the following statement by Mircea Eliade, the word "animated" can be readily substituted for mana with no loss of meaning; in fact, the meaning is clarified for the general reader. As written by Eliade:

> Everything that *is* supremely, possesses *mana;* everything, in
> fact, that seems to man effective, dynamic, creative, or perfect[98]
> . . . all that *exists fully* has *mana*.[99]

And, as recast, Eliade's statement:

> Everything that *is* supremely, is *animated;* everything, in fact,
> that seems to humans effective, dynamic, creative, or perfect. . .
> all that *exists fully* is *animated*.

There exists good precedent outside religious history for the use of the word "animated" to mean "all that exists fully," and whatever is "effective, dynamic, creative, or perfect." In art history and art criticism, "animated" means the ability to create virtual space where there is none. Paint applied to canvas becomes a painting if it succeeds in creating a virtual space out of the inert material of paint and canvas; in other words, *if* it succeeds in *animating the picture plane.* If the picture plane is not animated, it is dead, lifeless.[100] The image does not work. It has no soul. And that is exactly, as discussed earlier, what artists will say about it: the painting is dead; it does not speak; it is a *dumb* composition.

Philosopher Susanne Langer argues that animated space, or virtual space, is space more real, made more real because it is organized space—space realized as a universe in which a symbolic form exists.[101] In other words, Langer is describing space as a set-apart place—one that is symbolically and physically created by the plastic arts. The artwork creates its own virtual space; thus it exists in an organized space, one that is bounded, centered, and approached in a particular way. The artwork has domain.

No one can describe a painting to someone else. It must be seen. The viewer must stand in front of it. Does this make the painting an experience of hierophany? It might. That would depend upon the viewer's perception and the viewer's understanding. The painting, however renowned, could be as far as the viewer is concerned a dead bore.

Mircea Eliade excludes no possible vehicle of hierophany. In theory, according to Eliade, anything can manifest the sacred—even the plastic arts. Generally, though, in Eliade's formulation there are three forms for hierophany that he terms cosmic, biological, and local hierophanies. The cosmic hierophanies include such manifestations as the sky, large bodies of water, the earth, stones; the biological hierophanies include events such as the lunar and solar cycles, change of season, puberty; and local hierophanies include consecrated places and temples.[102]

In *Patterns in Comparative Religion*, Eliade introduces the notion of "elementary hierophany"—a kratophany which is not yet known to be sacred because it has not yet been fitted into a system of belief—a system comprising features of ritual, myth, high gods, ethics.[103] The sacred character of an experience of kratophany must be demonstrated in order to be validated as sacred.[104]

In his later writing, however, Eliade drops the notion of elementary hierophany equivalent to kratophany, choosing instead to focus upon (as discussed earlier) a presentation of hierophany equivalent to theophany. Local hierophany thus becomes another form of theophany, not of kratophany.

Eliade retains the notion that kratophany comes in two forms—mana and taboo—but, because kratophany is an accompaniment of hierophany (and hierophany always means the appearance of a god), Eliade insists that mana and taboo are linked to systems of belief that include a high god of some sort.[105]

Eliade may have cut his own formulation of what constitutes a hierophany a bit too close to the bone. The concepts of elementary or local hierophanies are good ones to retain in the context of kratophany. If kratophany is defined instead as power particular to place, a power that must be experienced in that place, the word "kratophany" will name precisely and satisfactorily exactly those instances Eliade once called "elementary" or "local" hierophanies. These experiences are initially and originally experiences of kratophany. They can become experiences of theophany, but their value changes in important respects if they are fitted into a systematic belief structure and take on the encrustations of religion. The experiences become acculturated in their naming and understanding. Nevertheless, the original experiences yet remain ones of kratophany—be they ones of a lightning flash or the silence at the top of a low hill rise in Saskatchewan.

Alan L. Miller states it even more simply: "every kratophany must be, at the same time, a hierophany."[106] It is "an appearance of the sacred in which the experience of power dominates."[107] For Miller, the best examples of sacred power in religion are to be found in myths of origin because, as he notes:

> within cosmogonic myths everything that happens is a unique demonstration of creative power . . . (a power) to bring a world into being, to shape reality.[108]

In a true sense, an artist's work is one of shaping reality. That is the everyday work of artists. It is the everyday work of those with visions who have the confidence to shift shapes, and animate surface and plane. In their work as visionaries, they reveal deep structure and meaning in order to put the world together again, to bring the world into harmony.

The Center of the Universe

Characteristic of the experience of hierophany is the sense of having transcended ordinary time and place, of encountering straight-on a hyperreality, a suprareality, a truly mythic reality, mythic in the very sense that in the experience of hierophany time is experienced as cyclical, ever-regenerative, and *placed* here and now. The experience of reality is intensified and made intrinsically valid. Reality is animated, vibrant, powerful. It is time out of time and place rarefied. Reality is not a theoretical construct. It is experiential.

Of the three major categories of visual art—painting, sculpture, architecture—only one uses time as a formal element. Time, the fourth dimension, is the defining characteristic of architectonic space. Painting animates a flat plane and is two-dimensional; sculpture animates the immediate space about it and is three-dimensional. An animated architectonic space, if powerfully animated enough, may animate the entire world from wherever we are to the horizon line about us. We view architectonic space as a complete and essential place.

A powerful architectonic space absolutely requires that we enter it. We must enter from some other place. We must change our two irreducible axes of orientation, where we stand upon this earth and where we stand in relation to the horizon, in order to find a point of entry to that other place. In that bounded space our vertical and horizontal axes are predicated by the site itself, by the angle of vision prescribed for our stance. In that set-apart area we stand at the ready to know something else. There is a significance of place that makes our presence there something that we must attend to. We participate in that space. Architectonic space is therefore particularly suited for the plastic realization of cosmogonic myth, our stories of creation and origin. Is it any wonder then that our experience of centered space is one of having entered a sacred place? Of having experienced a hierophany?

A morphology of sacred place, thus, is not that difficult to establish. A sacred place can be described rather precisely, or as precisely as is necessary, in terms of its physical features: that is, in terms of its boundary, approach, point of entry, angle of vision, center, and domain. The question with which I opened this chapter asked how was it that Charles Ross knew he had found "the center of the universe," the place in which it was appropriate for him to build "Star Axis"?

The answer to my question rests in our very natural human ability to know ourselves as earth-centered people. That is part of what it means to be human, a meaning also conveyed in the ancient Indo-European root of the word "human"—*dhghem*—which means to be of the earth, of the land, earthly.[109] We have, as human beings, walked this earth for a very long time and in doing so have known many places of significance, of presence. That knowledge is our birthright.

Some people manage to be earth-centered a lot, whether by cultural orientation or by personal inclination. For other people it is a sometime thing. Nevertheless, because we can be (and perhaps have often been) earth-centered in our own visions, we can and do encounter and experience ancient places as loci of kratophany. We are able to do this *because we are already familiar with events of kratophany in our own lives, events that may have occurred in seemingly mundane places.* The sites themselves are various.

A wooded glade, a front lawn, a boat shed, a medicine wheel, a lava slope? Who would have thought that any one of those sites could be so special, would be so animated, for the people who were there? Yet each site was important in just that way for those people. Further, the importance of those sites is lasting for the people who were there. They remember the sites and they remember their visions there. The moment of vision and the person are variables. The place, however, is a constant and can be described. Wherever it was we were at the time, *there*, in *that* place, we felt our own capability to be earth-centered. *There*, in *that* place, the power of our own wholly original vision was evident. Such places, like all other ancient sacred sites, share a set of common physical attributes that comprise the descriptors needed for a morphology of sacred place.

Some of us are capable of clarifying cosmogonic vision in order that others may share some aspect of it. Those are the people we call artists. Religious historian Charles Long notes that art is "a correlate of the mythic apprehension;"[110] further, as Long writes, the "relationship of the cosmogonic myth and art objects is another way in which the sacramental nature of existence is realized."[111]

It may be useful to note, too, that just as the work of art historians is influenced by a scholarly reliance on still photographs of sacred sites so, too, are religious historians unduly influenced by written text. We are always *reading* myths. Seldom do we hear them told; seldom do we hear them told in the places where they happened, and happen again with each retelling. Seldom do we experience myth *in and of ourselves.* Artists, however, do. That appears to be why they are artists, and why Charles Ross was driving around New Mexico looking for a site so centered it was "the center of the universe." He found it. Its physical characteristics were those of boundary, point of entry, approach, a shift in normal angle of vision. Ross's apprehension of the site was this: the artist perceived the site as a uniquely organized space, as a place of particular power, as a place of particular animation. In this manner, the artist knew his site to be a *sacred place.* There, in that place he began to build "Star Axis."

5

The Earthwork—A Sacred Art

In the Four Corners region[1] and surrounding outlying areas of the American Southwest—a vast sprawl of desert, mountain, high plateau, salt flats, ancient lakes, and river beds—may be found today a number of stunning contemporary earthworks that have been built in the last twenty years. Some are completed, others are works in progress. Among the most renowned are Nancy Holt's "Sun Tunnels" (Utah, 1973–76); Walter De Maria's "Lightning Field" (New Mexico, 1974–77); Michael Heizer's "Complex One/City" (Nevada, 1972–76); Robert Smithson's "Spiral Jetty," (Utah, 1970, now submerged); Charles Ross's "Star Axis" (New Mexico, 1971–present); and James Turrell's "Roden Crater" (Arizona, 1977–present). The last two could be finished sometime during the 1990s.

Not one of the six sites is easy to get to. All are located in remote areas, and it is difficult to make arrangements to visit most of them. Permission is sometimes refused or written requests ignored.[2] Thus, what is generally known of the six earthworks is based upon the written descriptions and photographs of others.[3] Most of the descriptions have been written by art field cognoscenti—critics, historians, patrons, and other professional friends of the artists. Nevertheless, despite the expertise of those writing about the contemporary earthwork, the earthwork appears to resist being placed into an art historical framework. A bibliographic search through the *Art Index* for the last twenty years does not produce anything in the way of iconographical studies nor much in the way of formal problem analysis of form, material, and composition. Instead, what the reader finds are occasional articles written by arts professionals, but published for the general reader in newspapers and magazines.[4]

The 1969 "Earth Art" Exhibition

Initially, earthworks were called variously "earth art," "land art," "ecology art," "environmental art," or "earthworks." Art critics and art historians usually discussed the earthwork in terms of the material the artist used and whatever seemed novel about its installation. The earthwork was little discussed in terms of site specificity. That remains true today in the art-critical professional literature. The omission is startling.

A sited sculpture is a work that can be placed elsewhere. Just as it is possible to move framed pictures from wall to wall as need be, so too can outdoor sculpture be moved from one location to another, in principle. A site-specific architectonic work, however, cannot be relocated. Its origin lies in the response of the artist to the land itself. If the artist perceives the site to be a locus of kratophany, the choice of site is not discretionary. The artist is impelled to build the work there in order that others may know a similar vision.

The question of an earthwork's site specificity is answered partly in terms of physical descriptors—the work and its site, its placement, its materials, and the history of the site. Part of the answer also rests in the artist's statements concerning the site and the work. And, part of the answer may be discerned in the reactions of visitors to the site.

One of the earliest statements about earthworks is a curatorial essay[5] by Willoughby Sharp written in 1969 for an exhibition entitled "Earth Art" at Cornell University, New York. Nine artists were invited to construct earthworks on site—both interior or exterior to the university museum—for a six-week exhibition. All were sent site maps indicating what locations could be made available. Most of the artists chose to construct work on site; some, however, stayed home and sent instructions explaining how others could construct the work.

In his essay, Sharp did not discuss the interaction (or lack of interaction) of the nine artists with the sites they chose. Sharp never asked of the artists or of their work, "Why here, why not there?" Nor did he ask "why?" There were two other variables that intrigued Sharp more: *what* materials did the artists use and *how* did the artists construct their work?

The artists used odd materials indeed—dirt, grass, wood, snow, fiber, mirrors, and so forth. Their construction methods consisted of piling or placing material in and about the gallery's premises. For example, artist Hans Haacke dumped a mound of earth on the museum floor, then sowed it with winter rye. He called the work "Grass Grows." The rye grew and died within the allotted three weeks of the exhibition.

All nine projects were additive sculptures,[6] but not in the usual manner of being additive work. In fact, Sharp wrote:

> Nothing is *made* in the traditional sense; materials are allowed to subside into, or assume, their final shapes naturally without being coerced into a preconceived form.

That was true; moreover, none of the projects had a "finished" or permanent look. One reason for this effect was that none of the artists used a pedestal for the display of the work. (The pedestal, like the picture frame, is a formal, boundary-setting device in visual art.)

Although Sharp was enthusiastic about the work, he discussed all of the projects as though each were a three-dimensional *sculptural object* being placed by the artist (or the museum staff) into a *neutral space—* be it the museum's interior rooms or the wider, extended potential "sculpture garden" of the great outdoors of Ithaca in the winter. He did not discuss any of the work as time-focused architectonic structures comprised of a center element in a wider, activated, bounded discrete space of the cosmos. Nevertheless, the catalogue illustrations indicate a number of the earthworks built for the exhibition *were* architectonic installations—primarily those that were built at the outdoor sites.

Several of the outdoor sites were reformed into bounded sites with directed points of entry. For example, Jan Dibbet, one of the exhibition artists, walked on a snowy day in the woods for many miles until he found a large clearing next to a creek. In that clearing, Dibbet cut a large 30-degree angle, a "V" comprised of two straight shallow trenches, each one nearly 6 feet wide and almost 110 feet long. Dibbet called the work "A Trace in the Wood in the Form of an Angle of 30 Degrees Crossing the Path." According to the artist, both the snowfall *and* the walk through the woods were as much a part of the resultant work as the clearing, the creek, and the shallow cut Dibbet made in the clearing.

Unfortunately, because Sharp does not assess the work in terms of site specificity, he concluded that the purpose of the exhibition was to show the artist's concern for "elemental materials" and "to sharpen (the viewer's) sensory and intellectual perception." Sharp's conclusion never questions the gallery locale as a framing or organizing device for this work. In fact, he implicitly suggests that a gallery locale is the basic requirement—a gallery with enough surrounding land and a willing staff. Nothing more.

The "Earth Art" exhibition included an artists' symposium. Members of the audience could ask the participating artists what they were doing and why. Six of the nine artists[7] in the exhibition were present for the symposium and an edited transcript of the symposium was included in the exhibition catalogue. All of the artists quoted stated their intentions in constructing their "Earth Art" projects in terms that had little to do with formal art criteria. Instead, the artists spoke of other dimensions for their work, existential and religious dimensions of orientation to other levels of reality. For example, Robert Smithson stressed the importance of magnifying time changes because Smithson felt that people tended to believe a work of art is timeless, and that belief renders the artist "alienated from his own time." Richard Oppenheim, too, wanted to break down the barrier between artist and audience. He pleaded for

> an art that is inside our head and inside our total system so that it will be out of the caves of the Manhattan lofts and spread across a vaster area.

Hans Haacke followed an Oppenheim's point by arguing that it did not matter much what the work looked like, but what the viewer thought about when seeing it:

> I believe art is not so much concerned with the looks. It is much more concerned with the concepts. What you see is just a vehicle for the concept. Sometimes you have a hard time seeing this vehicle, or it might even not exist.

Neil Jenney was even more direct when he said,

> I don't care what my piece looks like. I'm not concerned with expanding the boundaries of good taste at all. If the thing has a certain amount of presence, then I think basically that's it.

Gunther Uecker did not even discuss the appearance of his work because, like the others, he maintained it was not his job as an artist to "make pretty" or "make beautiful work," to make work that could be called "fine art." Uecker said forthrightly that his intention as a working artist was to work in a cosmological and spiritual manner. He intended to make "zones, regions" for "spiritual self-realization" in order that we might

> not take to other planets ideologies which are the products of an outdated world consciousness. Let us use the earth itself to create a new spiritual awareness.

And, in response to a question from the audience about what the limits of his work as an artist were, Richard Long replied matter-of-factly and laconically, "I don't work with limitations."

Sharp concluded, almost as an afterthought, that the earthwork appeared to be calling

> for the radical reorganization of our natural environment; it offers the possibility of mitigating man's alienation from nature.

Sharp was right. His comment was prescient.

The "Earth Art" projects twenty-five years ago were magisterial prototypes of ahistorical directions in contemporary vision and perception—ahistorical because several of the artists' projects were mythic in intention; magisterial because several of the projects devolved from the artists' unique visions of kratophany.

Site Specificity and the Earthwork

By 1983, the body of extant earthwork was large enough to prompt a stylistic ordering of its forms that went beyond those first comments on the loss of the pedestal, the peculiarity of material, and concomitant construction technique. In a short essay written in 1983,[8] Mark Rosenthal set up five categories of form for the contemporary earthwork according to site specificity. Rosenthal noted that site specificity mattered in only two categories: one he called the "modest gesture in the landscape," the other he termed an "idealized landscape." In two other categories, Rosenthal argued that site-specific spatial considerations were incidental decisions. One of these categories he termed a "gesture in the landscape." It was not modest in scale. It was monumental and meant to be viewed from the sky. The other category Rosenthal termed "enclosure in the landscape." Work in both categories, Rosenthal argued, was not site-specific work: both required only *enough* outdoor space, not any particular outdoor place. The landscape gesture, for example, is a mark upon the land so large it is best viewed and photographed from the air.[9] The landscape enclosure category excludes the surrounding landscape. The viewer enters it and, once entered, the surrounding landscape is irrelevant. (We could call this the "anywhere-a-*sanctum-sanctorum*" category.) Finally, the fifth category in Rosenthal's schematic was one he called "nature for itself." These were "earthworks" made of so-called elemental, raw materials, but placed indoors. Hans Haacke's "Grass Grows" in the "Earth Art" exhibition is of this type. Nature-for-itself work requires only there be enough *indoor* space, not all outdoors. Thus, of the five categories, only the "modest gesture" category and the "idealized landscape" category were truly site-specific. The others could be sited anywhere if the patron or sponsor were willing.

Rosenthal's categories are important because they indicate that by 1983 site specificity was recognized as a key physical descriptor of the earthwork. Site specificity is, as noted, also part of the religious experience of kratophany. As a power particular to place, kratophany cannot be experienced just any place, it has to be experienced some place in that form, and in no other form.

Rosenthals's two categories in which site specificity is the whole of the formal content are also ones whose examples (as cited by Rosenthal in his essay) fit the typology of sacred space established in chapter 4. They are all architectonic spaces with features of boundary, pathway, point of entry, angle of vision, center, and domain.

As an example of a "modest gesture in the landscape," Rosenthal gives us the work of Richard Long and Michael Singer. Long usually places small stones or branches out of doors into rather fragile geometrical enclosures in natural clearings. (That is also what he did in 1969 in the Cornell exhibition.) Singer for his part often weaves thin sticks and grasses into fragile webs or temporary platforms and stations in out-of-the-way marshy clearings. Both artists usually exhibit only a photograph of their work as documentation that it once existed.

Singer's and Long's "gestures" are so modest, so seemingly by happenstance, that the viewer sometimes has to look quite closely at the exhibited photograph in order to see just what it was that the artist contributed to the place. Often, what the artist contributed was a marking or delineation of a natural boundary in a natural clearing. The clearings seem to be anonymous ones, ones that no viewer could hope to locate. The viewer can only know them through the artist's own photograph; and, no doubt by the time the artist's photograph was published, the viewer suspects that time, wind, and rain have erased the artist's modest gesture in the clearing. The photograph offers the viewer a printed memory of beautiful moment *and* a hint that there are other delicate places to be found one by one if you, the viewer, will walk softly alone and quietly in the world.

The "idealized landscape" form is the one Rosenthal suggests characterizes the work of several sculptors for whom the site determines *all* of their decisions, including the most important: to do the work at all. These artists are impelled to make their mark upon the land *there*, in *that* place. Their work is not concerned with "finding" a translucent moment in a place (as it is with Long and Singer), although that matters. Their work is much bolder. They seek to find in that place all that has gone before and will come to be in that place. Theirs is a vastly heroic vision.

Rosenthal discusses some of Robert Smithson's work as being of the "idealized landscape" form. In the "Earth Art" symposium, Robert Smithson laid out his personal methodological precepts for the idealized landscape. He called it a "site;" all other installations were "nonsites:" (As a result, Smithson's friends soon came to call him "siteseer"— a title now applied to his widow, the artist Nancy Holt.) In Smithson's dialectical rubric:

> The site is a place you can visit and it involves travel (i.e., time) as an aspect too. . . . The site is the physical, raw reality—the earth or the ground that we are really not aware of when we are in an interior room or studio or something like that. . . . My nonsites (i.e., the museum display) in a sense are like large, abstract maps made into three dimensions. You are thrown back onto the site.[10]

Thus, for Smithson, time processes—the rhythmic journey from here to there (and the journey back again with what you have learned)—are as much a key factor as site specificity.

How would the six earthwork examples cited at the beginning of the chapter fit into Rosenthal's schematic, and concomitantly into the general typology of sacred place established in chapters 3 and 4? What, if any, is their relationship to the specific typology of built forms developed by Amerindian peoples? None of the six earthworks are indoor installations. That leaves four possibilities in Rosenthal's scheme of which only two are site specific—the modest ground-level gesture in the landscape and the idealized landscape. The non-site-specific categories are the larger bird's-eye-view gesture in the landscape and the enclosed, anywhere-a-*sanctum-sanctorum* structure.

"Sun Tunnels," Nancy Holt

From published photographs, Nancy Holt's "Sun Tunnels" (see figure 13) appears to be an enclosed form that might have been built anywhere there was a flat desert plain—from Utah, where it is, to Uzbekistan, where it is not. It does not look to be site specific. The artist, however, argues that it is: "Sun Tunnels" is astrally aligned.

"Sun Tunnels" consists of four cast concrete tunnels, each one nearly 20 feet in length and almost 10 feet in diameter. The tunnels are placed at right angles to one another in a Greek cross formation with the center open where a small concrete circle has been sunk flush into the ground. Each tunnel has been aligned to the winter or summer solstice of the rising or setting sun. Each tunnel is also perforated with small holes of varying size that replicate the configuration of the four constellations, Capricorn, Draco, Columba, and Perseus. (I have found no explanation published for the selection of those four constellations.)

According to Holt, she first conceived the idea for "Sun Tunnels" while she was somewhere in the American Southwest,[11] thus, her claim for the work's site specificity. It is worth noting, however, that Holt was somewhere out in the desert—not actually at the "Sun Tunnels" site when she conceived the work. Site selection was an activity Holt undertook *after* she had the form of the project in mind.[12] She found her site in the Utah desert.

Holt made her tunnels of cast concrete. Is cast concrete a material particularly site-specific, one that is indigenous to the Utah desert? Holt claims it is, and she is right—in part. Concrete, a mixture of broken rock, pebble, clay, and water, was widely used by the Romans who called it *opus concretum* and perfected the technology needed for building with it. The concrete we build with today is the same sort of mixture used by the Romans. Concrete has not, however, been a traditional building material used in the Utah desert. For one thing, the indigenous people of the Utah desert lacked water to make a poured slag building mixture; moreover, they were nomads. The Apache, for example, built their wickiups and tepees from brush, saplings, and skins. Their structures were temporary ones, made of the materials readily at hand, structures that did not require gangs of laborers to construct them.

Holt intends no homage to the Apache or any other desert people in her choice of material, nor does she seek to invoke memories of any ancient solar structure,[13] Old World or New World. Her concern, as she notes, is only that the color and substance of "Sun Tunnels" be "the same as the land they are part of."[14]

Although the tunnels have been astrally aligned and carefully placed on the Utah desert floor, they might have been placed in a variety of flat plane surfaces. In her own photographs of "Sun Tunnels," Holt has tried to show that it is the view *through* the tunnels to the horizon line that matters most to the artist. If that is what really matters, then Holt's case for "Sun Tunnels" site specificity is stronger; on the other hand, visitors to the site do not appear to be concerned with views on the horizon line. They stress the view of dappled light *inside* the tunnels.

John Beardsley, however, looked to the horizon line and found the view through the pipes to it to be discomfiting. He felt the framing provided by the pipes increased the sense of distance one perceives between the centered tunnels and the horizon line.[15] Holt has stated she wanted the framing to make the distance more comprehensible to the viewer. In her view the purpose of the tunnels is to *mediate* a great distance for the viewer, not exacerbate the viewer's sense of distance. And of that view through the tunnels, Holt has said:

> The panoramic view of the landscape is too overwhelming to take in without visual reference points. The view blurs out rather than sharpens. Through the tunnels, parts of the landscape are framed and come into focus.[16]

Lucy Lippard had a more positive reaction to the framed horizon line seen through the pipes than Beardsley. Lippard felt the tunnels served to "expose and protect" the site visitor, and, Lippard felt, that was appropriate because the tunnels are in the desert and the "desert is the traditional geography of revelation—simultaneously empty and full."[17]

According to Holt, "Sun Tunnels"—like all of her work—concerns perception, inside and outside. She also states it has personal religious content that she is reluctant to discuss,[18] although she has said of "Sun Tunnels" that "day is turned into night, and an inversion of the sky takes place: stars are cast down to earth, spots of warmth in cool tunnels."[19]

"Sun Tunnels" has been much praised for its ability to focus the site visitor's perception on "the finite instant and the infinite passage of time."[20] "Sun Tunnels" has also been called a "pearl of simplicity."[21] It does not appear to be an architectonic form, however. From published photographs, it appears to be an effectively sited sculpture, a placed object on a flat plane, an object of industrial size and strength in a neutral space, one that will not roll away—but not a site-specific architectonic form.

"Complex One/City," Michael Heizer

Michael Heizer's "Complex One/City"[22] is difficult to comprehend through published photographs and written description, in part because the work is not completed and in part because photographs seldom convey scale effectively and scale is what seems to be most important to this work. When completed, "Complex One/City" will consist of several large structures of rammed earth arranged about a plaza; to date, only "Complex One" has been built. It is a "horizontal mound of earth bound within steel and concrete sides,"[23] and is located in the high desert of Nevada on a plot of land about 2 miles square. The mound itself is almost 23 feet high and about 155 feet long, shaped in the form of a trapezoid with a front face angled back at 45 degrees.[24] It is very big.

Many, although not all, of Heizer's works are enormous in size and have required the use of sophisticated construction techniques in their making. Heizer does not, however, consider any of his work to be outsized because, he says, all are small relative to the size of the earth or the cosmos.[25] Nevertheless, relative to human scale, some of Heizer's projects *are* outsized. In fact, their scale has posed particular dangers for him and his work crews. There have been several injuries sustained on site, and Heizer himself has said of "Complex One/City," "I'll die finishing this city myself."[26]

Heizer says his work is about the exchange of points of view.[27] Perhaps. What others have said is far more declarative. Robert Hughes describes "Complex One" as "minatory," and says it is rather like a bunker in its appearance.[28] Some people have criticized "Complex One" because they find its form too derivative to be worthy of the originality of an artist's vision. They note that "Complex One" by scale, siting, and material looks like a takeoff on a Mayan plaza or an Egyptian mastaba, a tomb. Heizer admits to all of these possibilities for the work, but that need not detract from it, he argues. If the cultural references seem too obvious, he states, it is only because the work is of this time and this place:

> What if an artist is so confused by his society that he reflects other cultures in his work? Perhaps the indication is that present society has finally opened to requiring an undifferentiated expression, or even more amazing, that time warps and does not extend indefinitely.[29]

For some visitors to the site, "Complex One/City" is not at all particularly monumental of size relative to the visual plane of the desert valley chosen by Heizer for the project. It is situated in a large valley near the Nevada AEC Testing Site. Rainer Crone describes the approach to the site:

> If one approaches "Complex I" from the entrance of the valley, it seems a mere dot on the vast desert horizon. The object soon begins to take on a rectangular shape. Yet, after a few more minutes of driving, the rectangle appears to be breaking up; concrete shapes contrast with transient abstract forms of shade on the mound.[30]

Elizabeth Baker, too, states that its form is really a fragile one. Its solidity, when seen from a distance of half a mile away, dissolves upon closer approach:

> the rectangular framing quite literally comes apart: light starts to slip between different segments of the horizontal and vertical parts, and between column sections and the main mound.[31]

Following Rosenthal's schematic, "Complex One/City"—although obviously made of earth—is problematic as a site-specific earthwork. Presently, it is not an enclosure; nor is it a gesture meant to be seen from the air. Indeed, the artist intends that the piece be viewed frontally—one might even say, hieratically—because he has left the back of it unfinished.[32] "Complex One/City" is certainly not a "modest gesture" despite Heizer's statement to the effect that size is a measure proportionate to the earth. It is not; size is proportionate to us. Like Nancy Holt's "Sun Tunnels," there appears to be only the loosest relationship of material and form to the indigenous history of the site. "Complex

One/City" is made of local earth, but its framing of steel is not from a material indigenous to the site, nor is its form one that is indigenous to the archaic history of the place (although as a "minatory" object, "Complex One/City" may be related to the nearby AEC Testing Site).

Despite the published descriptions that stress the fragile placement of "Complex One/City" in a landscape of ambient desert light, from its photographs the project just looks to be a *big*, booming, effectively placed, albeit site-imposed sculpture. At this point of its construction, "Complex One/City" is a monumental sculpture, not a site-specific architectonic space. Indeed, the frontality of its form reminds one of the nearby military airplane hangers. Robert Hughes's one-word assessment for "Complex One/City"—"minatory"—may prove yet to be the last word on the project. On the other hand, the site will change once all of the other structures Heizer plans for the plaza are built.

"Lightning Field," Walter De Maria

Walter De Maria's "Lightning Field" (see figure 14) fits neatly under the Rosenthal rubric of "modest gesture in the landscape," even though one unofficial estimate of the cost of "Lightning Field" is more than $1,000,000.[33] De Maria's "Lightning Field" celebrates the glory of lightning in a ritualized place of observance. "Lightning Field" calls out for all of the cosmos to come to bear upon that one valley. John Beardsley writes of it:

> The work is neither of the earth nor of the sky but is of both; it is the means to an epiphany for those viewers susceptible to an awesome natural phenomenon. Few leave the "Lightning Field" untouched by the splendid desolation of its setting and the majesty of its purpose.[34]

Published photographs of the work are convincing. Because the work is so linear in form, "Lightning Field" is comprehensible when photographed. Moreover, we can readily believe it to be a site of kratophany because we know what a lightning storm can be like; our own memories provide us with the scent of ozone, the tremor of discharged electrons.

"Lightning Field" consists of 400 stainless steel poles, sharpened to needle points. The poles are approximately 23 feet high and 2 inches in diameter. They have been erected nearly 250 feet apart on a grid that is approximately a mile in length east to west and about a half mile across north to south. The site itself is a high desert plateau ringed by distant mountains. The poles are intended to attract lightning, and perhaps three to thirty times a year they do.[35] John Beardsley describes the field as

> fugitive work, disappearing in the bright midday sun and becoming visible only at dawn and dusk when the entire length of each pole glows with reflected light.[36]

The regularity of the grid creates an optical illusion of an eternal progression that establishes for the viewer—with or without lightning—a sense that all of the world, all of the cosmos, is here and there, and everywhere in and out of this one place where everything is silent. Unless there be lightning. (The visitor's instruction sheet and claims waiver form warns that at the first crack of lightning you are to leave the field immediately and are never to touch the poles at any time. The absence of lightning, however, does not render the "Lightning Field" a hazard-free zone; there may be rattlesnakes and other venomous creatures.)[37]

What makes this work so obviously site-specific, unlike "Sun Tunnels" and "Complex One/City"? For one thing, the grid for "Lightning Field" has been laid out in an area known to be receptive to frequent, intense lightning storms. For another thing, the field itself has not been leveled or cleared. The number of poles and their placement were adapted to the requirements of the terrain, not the reverse (which would not have been difficult). De Maria's first plans called for shorter poles (less than 20 feet high), placed much closer together (about 210 feet apart);[38] and many more of them—600 in all.[39] In 1977 John Beardsley wrote that he himself first believed the site when built would have "little clear sense of form."[40] Instead, as Beardsley subsequently noted a decade later, what De Maria created with "Lightning Field" is a work of "dimensional, directional space with an understated, almost immaterial means."[41]

The work has form, although the grid does not dominate the site. It is truly a "fugitive work." "Lightning Field" is as fragile as Richard Long's and Michael Singer's thin sticks and small stones. De Maria's stainless steel poles do not reach to the heavens. There is no need to make the attempt. In the high desert the sky seems very close at hand. The poles are delicate pointers, not enclosures. The surrounding mountains are the boundary of the site. Brush grows within the grid and desert animals live there.

One site visitor, for whom there was no lightning strike that visit, described the effect of her overnight stay at "Lightning Field" in rhapsodic language:

> Morning was pure grace. Light breeze stirred fronds of grass still silver with dew. . . . "The invisible was real," wrote Walter De Maria about his work. He was right. It was not the array of poles alone that enthralled us, but the ordinary invisible motions and changes of air, light and life around it, drawn to our attention by it.[42]

"Spiral Jetty," Robert Smithson

"Spiral Jetty" is the lost work; yet like "Lightning Field" it lives as much, if not even more strongly, in a mythic sense of what it must have been like to be there. Its photographs are haunting.

Robert Smithson's "Spiral Jetty" (see figure 15) was built in 1970 of more than 7,400 tons of bulldozed earth, rough black basalt, and limestone—all materials found at the site, Rozel Point, the Great Salt Lake, Utah. Now fully submerged by the still rising waters of the lake,[43] the jetty extends in a grand spiral more than 1600 feet out under the surface of red, salty water. When the waters were first rising and receding over the jetty twenty years ago, people noticed that even the red salt crystals that formed on the jetty's surface (over 15 feet wide) were themselves spirally configured.[44]

Visitors to the site reported that "Spiral Jetty" was strongly animated, vibrant with intense heat waves and the flickering reflections of light on water, the movement of cloud across sun. Lawrence Alloway described a walk out along the jetty in these words:

> a breathless experience of horizontality. The lake stretches away, until finally there is a ripple of distant mountains and close around one the shore crumbles down into the water. . . . The spiral is a low trail of stones and rocks resting on the water like a leaf on a stream. It is a moist and earthy causeway with salt caking on the rocks and on the visitor.[45]

Following Rosenthal's schematic, one can easily argue for the site specificity of "Spiral Jetty." Oddly, however, Rosenthal takes a different tack. He himself has classified "Spiral Jetty" as a monumental "gesture in the landscape" because he states "Spiral Jetty" was intended to be seen from the air and is not really specific to the history of the site.[46] I disagree with Rosenthal's assessment for two reasons. Although the most reproduced photograph of the "Spiral Jetty" has been, indeed, an aerial view, Smithson also published photographs of the jetty at ground level and from hilltop. The work's site specificity was beautifully realized. Most site visitors saw "Spiral Jetty" from the land, not from the air. The work was made of local materials found on the site, and its form is one specific to the site's archaic mythos. Even more importantly, we have in Smithson's own words his eloquent description of the astounding vision he had at the site that inspired "Spiral Jetty."

Robert Smithson had read of lakes like the Great Salt Lake in which nothing grows but red algae. Wanting to see the phenomenon for himself, the artist drove down one hot summer's day into a valley on the northern end of the Great Salt Lake. He described the landscape when he arrived at Rozel Point as being "an impassive faint violet sheet held captive in a stoney matrix, upon which the sun poured down its crushing light."[47] As the artist stood in the harsh light, a vision arose from the lake itself. It was an experience of kratophany. Everything, he reported, began to spin before his eyes. In Smithson's own words:

> As I looked at the site, it reverberated out to the horizons only to suggest an immobile cyclone while flickering light made the entire landscape appear to quake. A dormant earthquake spread into the fluttering stillness, into a spinning sensation without movement. This site was a rotary that enclosed itself in an immense roundness. From that gyrating space emerged the possibility of the *Spiral Jetty*.[48]

Thus, using Rosenthal's schema, I would argue instead that "Spiral Jetty" is an "idealized landscape," and that it continues to be one even today because its memory is so evocative.

When the Mormons—the first nonnative settlers of the area—arrived at Great Salt Lake, they saw something odd in the lake, something like a whirlpool. Their explanation for the phenomenon was ingeniously mechanical, not at all religious; from time to time, thought the Mormon pioneers, the Great Salt Lake must be draining into the Pacific Ocean clear on the other side of the world.[49] So, rather like letting out the bathtub stopper, every now and then one might see a whirlpool in the lake, and that was all the Great Salt Lake's spiral meant. The spiral meant much more to Smithson. In his vision at Rozel Point, Smithson—like the first Mormons—saw a spiral. But for Smithson, the spiral was a revelation. The spiral made visible in graphic form the artist's long-standing concerns about entropy and time and the earth. In 1968 Smithson had written:

> The deeper an artist sinks into the time stream the more it becomes oblivion; because of this he must remain close to the temporal surface.... Floating in this temporal river are the remnants of art history, yet the "present" cannot support the cultures of Europe, or even the archaic or primitive civilizations; it (the present) must instead explore the pre-and post-historic mind; it must go into places where remote futures meet remote pasts.[50]

There is hardly a pictograph or emblem that could be devised to realize so perfectly in plastic form Smithson's beliefs as the figure of a single, monumental spiral drawn on the blasted site of dead land and blood-red sea. The spiral makes comprehensible Smithson's understanding of entropy, the belief that all order inevitably is transformed into disorder, to ruination. All order is intrinsically, inimicably, immanently chaotic—and then it forms itself again anew.

Smithson had been long concerned with wrecked landscapes, not with a sense of dismay, but with a harsh acceptance that people as well as nature both create and destroy. John Beardsley writes of the artist that "Smithson accepted signs of degeneration and the collapse of ordered systems as evidence of inevitable entropic change."[51] People were not outside nature nor necessarily disruptive of nature, they were part of nature. Smithson's point was that we needed to know all of that better than we did,[52] and that is why the artist was so often drawn to the throwaway site. It was more real, more organized, than the nonsite of the gallery installation. As Smithson said in 1969: "The site is a place where a piece should be but isn't."[53]

If Smithson found the spiral in that horrid place, it was because he had been readying himself for several years to encounter it in all its mythic proportions. In 1966 Smithson entitled one of his sculptures "Alogon I." In order that gallery visitors might understand the work better, he exhibited it with a lexical note explaining the meaning of the word "alogon" and the meanings that Smithson associated with it. He was not telling viewers what they *had* to see in the work; instead, he was providing them with confirmation of what they *could* see. Smithson's words were not intended to be esoteric. (Had he meant them that way, he would never have provided their definitions.) Smithson relied upon scientifically technical words because they were *precisely the words he needed to state the concepts that engaged him*. In this case, an alogon— as critic Lawrence Alloway explains—is a Pythagorean term for

> mathematical incommensurables, meaning the "unnameable" or "unutterable"; these were unaccountable imperfections in the numerical fabric of the universe, not mysteries which is why they were not to be named or discussed.[54]

(We retain this meaning today in our words "alogical" and "alogism."[55] Alogon and entropy are related concepts; both concepts are necessary for our comprehension of chaos.)

To return to our first question: is "Spiral Jetty" site-specific? Yes. One simply cannot imagine it elsewhere. Underwater it is still there insisting that we look at that place, insisting that we feel the salt upon our skin and the heat blinding our eyes, in front of us the lake and far away the mountains, connecting everything above and below, an archaic spiral of beautifully regular proportion, a spiral figure all center and no perimeter, a spiral amid swarming black flies and the stench of rotting pelican carcasses.[56]

Throughout the world in many times and many places, spirals have been incised upon the earth, considered in the eddying flows of streams and tidal pools. For all of our speculative thoughts about what these ancient spirals may have meant—labyrinth, birth canal, intestine, cave—in this case we know what was intended: The spiral records the vision that Robert Smithson had one blistering day at Rozel Point on the northern shore of the Great Salt Lake in Utah. The spiral is the record of that kratophany; the spiral "appears to decipher what it divines."[57]

"Star Axis," Charles Ross

The spiral has also been a figure of prime significance for Charles Ross. In 1964 he dreamed[58] of an odd contraption one night and all the next day the dream image haunted him. Finally, Ross sat down to sketch it out and realized he had, possibly, the plans for constructing a large standing prism. The artist took the plans then to a friend who was a mechanical engineer. The friend told him the "right" way to build a prism. Ross did, and it exploded. After sweeping the debris out of his studio, Ross built the prism again—this time following the instructions from his dream. *That* contraption worked.

Over the course of the next year Ross recorded solar burns, which he created by focusing sunlight through the prism onto wooden planks that he changed daily. At the end of the year, he placed the planks together and saw that the burns formed a single line that curled itself into a double spiral. Ross had unwittingly made a graphic record of the sun's movements throughout the year (see figure 16). According to Ross:

> Everything is now a continuum. Since that first dream about the prism in 1964, all my ideas have been carrying that one dream forward.[59]

"Star Axis" is a multimillion dollar project that has preoccupied Ross for almost fifteen years (see figure 10). The project is largely self-financed.[60] The money Ross earns from other sculptural installations— Ross is justly famed for his prism installations in public spaces—is poured directly into "Star Axis," which is within a few years of completion.[61]

When "Star Axis" is completed, its construction will enable site visitors to understand step by step—*literally* step by step—spatially and specifically how the earth's precession (the tilt of its axis) changes over time our earthbound view of the position of stars in the firmament. If that makes "Star Axis" sound like a prize-winning science fair display, then the reader is misled. The work is not that at all. Reality is scientific, and Ross believes we very much need to be able to understand it better than we can if we rely solely upon science's explanations—hence, the provocative images of Ross's art. All of Ross's work has stood "at the crossroads of science and mysticism, where he thinks much art exists."[62] In fact, Ross believes the reason we are always awed by starry, starry nights is because we

> carry a cellular memory of starlight in our very being. We are the stuff of which stars are made. . . . Our cellular memory is what provides us with a tremendous sense of connectedness.

These are feeling states, not just energy states. As humans we are the interface between the earth and the stars. We are the translation of that star stuff. We are the earth/sky connection.[63]

At the moment "Star Axis" is a dream, a set of drawings, and a construction site located high on a mesa in New Mexico, more than 7,000 feet above sea level. It is a very big hole in the ground. More accurately, it is a rock-lined cleft or shaft in the capstone of the mesa that is being readied for the insertion—of a stainless steel tunnel almost 220 feet long. The tunnel shaft will rise seven stories high through the mesa for a total distance of eleven stories, and be angled to Polaris. Upon entering the tunnel, the visitor will find that with each step taken to ascend to the end of the tunnel, the view of the night sky will enlarge and Polaris—our supposedly fixed North Star—will shift its position. Seen from within the tunnel, Polaris will appear to be a transitory phenomenon; so, too, will all the other stars of the firmament. The tunnel itself will not be visible at ground level. Local red earth and sand from the construction site will be used to cover it over completely. In short, "Star Axis" is a naked-eye observatory, an observatory without a telescope.

Leaving the tunnel, at the "place of emergence"—as it is labeled on Ross's drawings and which Ross explains is *not* intended to be an allusion to any of the Pueblo Indian origin myths[64]—the viewer will look out upon a broad apron of caliche.[65] The apron—rather like a proscenium stage, in fact—will be scraped clear to form a screen for sun-angled, seasonal shadow projections from a tower rising approximately 55 feet further into the sky from the place of emergence.[66]

Why should anyone bother to build a naked-eye observatory today? We have sent cameras and telescopes to the farthest reaches of our own galaxies. Our astronomers claim to be happily swamped with computer-generated data from recent space missions. Why bother with the starry view obtained through a simple sighting aperture in New Mexico? And what makes that view art? Ross argues that what is important about "Star Axis" is precisely that it focuses our attention directly, without any obvious technological mediation, upon the heavens above. How else, he asks, shall we understand our ancient connection to the stars unless we view them as others saw them once, and that is why, Ross explains, he is building "Star Axis" "in the tradition of ancient observatories."[67]

Charles Ross searched four years for the "Star Axis" site after first experiencing the dream, the vision, that inspired this particular work.[68] In his own words:

> I knew the site had to be the center of the universe, that I would have to feel that sense of centeredness in the site before I could build it. I looked for it in Utah, Arizona, Texas, a lot of different places. . . . One day we were driving around in the middle of ranchland. I didn't know exactly where I was at all. . . . That's how the site for "Star Axis" was located. It has turned out to be exactly right in every way. I've been guided in some ways to this place, I really have been. . . . Part of "Star Axis" has been calculated, part planned; but certainly part of it has been revealed. . . . It's important that "Star Axis" appear to grow out of the site, and it has actually grown that way. It is not a site-imposed work. It is the way it has to be.[69]

In other words, "Star Axis" most certainly seems to be an "idealized landscape," a site-specific work whose every decision in its making has been and continues to be generated by the given characteristics of the place itself.

"Star Axis" baffles some art historians. John Beardsley writes: "It is still anyone's guess what will be the precise effect of Ross's piece."[70] Lucy Lippard likens Charles Ross's effort to that of those long ago who incised star charts on rocks in Canyon de Chelly, sites still visited today by devout Navajos for ritual reasons.[71] "Star Axis," however is different from those earlier configurations. Although Ross has built star maps in the past, he is not seeking to learn the forms of the sky. He knows them already. "Star Axis" is an attempt to collapse, expand, change time zones—not by an hour or two or a day—but by eons. When completed, "Star Axis" will reach backwards 14,000 years for its starting point and forward 12,000 years for its terminus. That is scary, brilliant, and audacious.

Donald Kuspit, writing about Ross's earlier star charts, stated that however "comforting" Ross's abstract designs appear to be—after all, they do look like art when hung on gallery walls—moments later the inherent *scientific* chaos of Ross's visual images inevitably registers upon the viewer "and we are completely dislocated in and by it." In fact, Kuspit speaks of Ross's star charts as the "skin of the sky . . . flayed and hung as a trophy." He is troubled by Ross's work, and appears to think that if the images Ross presents are real, i.e., scientific (and they are), then the images cannot also be mythic, i.e., artistic.

Ross, however, has been careful to explain that none of his visual images are scientific breakthroughs. He says his job as an artist is "to make the invisible visible."[72] Many artists would agree with that job description of their work. Artists are always describing the importance of their work in terms of changing people's perceptions—to make the invisible visible. According to Ross:

> the reason for "Star Axis" isn't to demonstrate that the math is correct. We know what we need to know. There just isn't anything we need to figure out anymore; we just have to pay attention to what we know.[73]

In the Hopi, Dineh, Pueblo traditions of how humans came to be, there are many stories telling of the difficult passage of the first humans out of the ground to the surface of the earth. The first people are so weak and have so much to learn, but the world is beautiful. Sometimes they fail and are sent underground again. Then, when the world is made new, once more they are given permission to emerge into the sunlight.[74] The journey through the long tunnel of "Star Axis" may prove to be a daunting one. I can imagine a weak-kneed emergence for many at the end of the tunnel's long incline, the "place of emergence"; but then all liminal states are potentially frightening as was illustrated by the garden photographs discussed in chapter 2. Once, not that long ago, escaped American slaves found their way to Canada by remembering the words of a spiritual: "Keep your eyes on the prize, hold on." The words were geographic directions: the "prize" was the North Star, freedom.

By walking through the tunnel of "Star Axis," quite literally we will find ourselves walking among the stars. We will see the sky as others saw it in times past and as others will see it in times to come. "It is," Charles Ross has said, "being built as an act of pure faith."[75]

"Roden Crater," James Turrell[76]

There is another naked-eye observatory also under construction in the Southwest—James Turrell's "Roden Crater" project[77] (see figure 17). It, too, is being built as an act of pure faith, an act of sweeping personal vision. Not enough of the work has been completed for anyone to know all that James Turrell intends for it—although much has been done to date since Turrell first started the project in 1979.

The crater, a volcanic cinder cone about 650 feet high, which looks as though it came out of the ground precisely that way, did not. It has been completely reformed into crater qua crater. Every inch of that long-extinct volcano has been combed and smoothed and shaped by hand, and shovel, and backhoe.[78] As a result, the bowl of the crater is a more perfectly shaped parabola with sides that look as crisp-edged and clear as the rakings in a Zen sand garden. Now comes the hard part: Turrell is cutting a circular tunnel perhaps 12 feet wide and more than a thousand feet long within the cone[79] that will connect a number of rooms, enclosures, wherein will be a play of light—starlight and sunlight and all of it ambient light—projected naturally upon various reflecting surfaces (sand, snow, water). Each room will have a different light mist, a different image, in order to create for the viewer an enveloping perceptual environment within the room. Four of the rooms will be oriented to the cardinal directions. In addition, there may be several others with other astral orientations,[80] some of which would be frequently occurring orientations (e.g., semiannual solstices) and others of which would be more infrequent (e.g., 12,000 years from now when the North Star changes over from Polaris to Vega).[81]

When all is done, Turrell intends that no one seeing the crater from afar, on land or in the sky, would know that it is a constructed work—although someone climbing the crater and knowing nothing of its history "might guess it was a temple built thousands of years ago."[82] In Turrell's words: "*Roden Crater* is a work of art that is empowered by the movements of the sun and moon and starlight."[83]

The crater itself is one of hundreds of similar soft-edged parturient mounds that dot the San Francisco Volcanic Field in the high desert of the Four Corners area. These soft, rounded hills, soft as velvet in their appearance and colored gorgeously in plushy blacks, purples, reds, and creams, were once all active volcanos—some active as long ago as 2.4 million years and some active as recently as 700 years.[84] The Hopi call them "Loha-vutsotsmo" (testicle hills).[85] Part of the ancient migration trail of the first peoples cuts through these fields that lie east of the San Francisco Mountains and border on the territories of the Dineh and Hopi nations off to the west across the flatland of the Painted Desert. There are sacred eagle nests in some of the cinder cones.[86]

The Roden Crater itself is a little-known archaic site still sacred to the Hopi, whose ancestors, the Sinaqua and Anasazi, once lived on its slopes.[87] James Turrell did not know the site was holy when he first saw the crater. The previous owners of the crater may have known the site had religious importance, but that was not anything that mattered much to the Chambers family. The archaic importance of the land is something that matters to Turrell, who has sought and obtained the blessing of the Hopi elders for his work on the crater.[88]

Turrell looked long and hard for a site for the observatory. In one year, he logged 500 hours of flying time as he crisscrossed the North American West from Canada to Mexico in a small airplane. (Turrell is a professional pilot.) He sought an extinct volcano, or perhaps even a high mesa, which would be 6,000 feet or more above sea level, be on privately owned land (hence, it could be bought), and be already of a form that would enable its being worked into a recessed bowl of enormous proportion. Roden Crater fit every one of Turrell's specifications. It was difficult, however, to persuade the owners, a local ranching family, to sell the crater to a sculptor who wanted to make a naked-eye observatory out of it, a sculptor who expressed his notions about the crater by saying it was "an eye, something that is itself perceiving. . . . When you're there, it has visions."[89] Turrell's negotiations to buy the crater from the Chambers family took three years to complete. In the meantime, Turrell camped out on the crater's rim, learning from the site and meditating upon his vision.

All told, Turrell camped on the crater's rim seventeen months[90] during those three years,[91] flying in his supplies himself from nearby Indian villages. One morning walking about the sides of the cinder cone, Turrell noticed that a cloud had settled within the bowl of the crater. Fred Hapgood explains what happened when Turrell scrambled up to the crater's rim. The artist

> plunged into the cloud. It was different from thick seacoast fogs, in which the light level is quite low, he says. At this altitude, nearly 6,000 feet above sea level, sunlight penetrated all through, evenly lighting the suspended droplets. The whole space glowed: a homogenous field.[92]

This was a key event. In his earlier gallery works, Turrell had demonstrated that he was capable of creating a homogenous light field from artificial sources within the confines of a gallery, but here in front of him within the rim of the crater was a light field far more intense, which was occurring quite naturally, quite of its own accord.

Since the late 1960s, Turrell has been engaged in an experiential exploration of the properties of *Ganzfeld*, the perceptual phenomenon of light as light, of light without form, of light as a homogenous field. A *Ganzfeld* is rather like an Arctic whiteout. As we know, the experience of a severe Arctic whiteout is a dangerous one for anyone. Whiteouts can be so disorienting that hysteria and extreme angst are frequent reactions among individuals who are caught in one and fear for their lives. But, for some of those who survive one, the experience can be the locus of a vision of great power, a kratophany that changes their lives. Controlled laboratory experiments with *Ganzfelden* perception have produced similar powerful psychological reactions in volunteer subjects.[93]

The "Roden Crater" project concerns the production of various forms of *Ganzfelden*, but it concerns more than that. It concerns the production of site-specific, powerful trance states, experiences of kratophany. Oddly enough, the "Roden Crater" project has not been much discussed as either a sited work or a site-specific work. One would almost think that Turrell's choice of a volcano for this project was a value-free, neutral choice:[94] that is, as though any volcano at all might do.

Turrell has explained repeatedly to interviewers what he was looking for and how he found it, but he has not said why. The answer for his reticence may lie in his experience of the cloud cover that morning upon the crater's rim. Certainly the effect of the crater's cloud cover upon him, although uncommon, would not be unknown to the people of the area—the Hopi and the Dineh, who among other things also know that one does not talk of religious matters to those who do not know about them.

What spiritual importance do the Hopi attach to the crater's white-light mists? What importance does Turrell attach to those mists, or to the Hopi interpretations? Those are the questions one wishes someone would ask Turrell, who could still choose not to answer if asked.

Turrell complains that art historians, steeped in European art historical traditions of scholarship, may be missing the point of his work on this project. They may not, in fact, even be the audience for this work. Turrell has said that the audience he is addressing in this work "already has a spiritual vocabulary; it is important to approach the work without rhetoric; I will not talk about the spiritual content, but of course it has spiritual content."[95] The artist has said little about the crater's spiritual content, and the published quotes attributed to him tend to be rather prosaic ones describing why the Roden Crater itself is geologically and geographically a suitable site for his work, how the work has been funded to date, and—in part—what it will consist of when completed. Still, in one published interview, Turrell did state:

> Another reason I chose this crater is that I am interested in the state of mind engendered by looking into fire. It is not-thinking, it is a wordless thinking that is a pure, primal sort of thinking. I looked for spaces that are empowered by the kind of light-presence that has that quality. And so one of the settings I wanted was a place of geologic time. I like craters; they are definitely part of geology. . . . One feels as if one were in a time beyond ours. . . . There is that feeling of orienting to things beyond. . . . We can decide to see things a certain way, and then we can be shown that we can see them another way. . . . It is sort of what one has to do to be a twentieth-century shaman.[96]

The "Roden Crater" project has been written about and visited by many of the most prominent contemporary art critics and historians today. What they have written about has been the effect of their unaccustomed hike to the crater's summit and what they see when they get there—the sensation of the sky as a perfect vault arcing above, a vault that surrounds and envelopes without distance. This sensation is enhanced by resting prone on your back within the crater's bowl and facing the sky overhead. It is an uncanny sensation, one of tranquility and peacefulness, mostly because, within the crater itself, sound seems to disappear. Yet everything seems so potentiated, so very new. The world could begin in the next moment or two.[97]

Nevertheless, what anyone sees (or hears) at the top of Roden Crater is very much what could be seen or heard at the top of any of the other neighboring cinder cones, or when lying upon one's back in the middle of a mountain meadow. The Roden Crater project is meant to extend, complement, enhance, direct our attention to naturally occurring perceptual phenomena. Not very far down the road, in fact, is the Grand Canyon—a sight that brooks no visual competition.

John Russell, art critic of the *New York Times*, did not mince any words in his description of his visit to the Roden Crater:

> Access to this undertaking is possible only on foot—or in my case, on all fours—up a steep slope some 700 feet high. The terrain gives way at almost every step, and the ascent was made at

dusk. "Some way to earn a living!" I said to myself. . . . Yet no sooner did our little party stand on the rim of the crater—which is to the plateau below what the top of the Chrysler Building is to the street level of midtown Manhattan—than an exuberance beyond measuring took hold of us and we felt ourselves, as Emerson said on another occasion, "glad to the brink of fear."[98]

Russell's reaction is typical of those who see the journey to the crater (and the somewhat wearying ascent to its rim) in terms of pilgrimage and ritual. The Roden Crater provokes those responses. Mark Stevens, writing in *Newsweek,* calls Turrell "more shaman than magician, . . . an artist with a spiritual turn of mind."[99] And Craig Adcock wrote of his visit to the crater site:

> Standing on Roden Crater looking at the beautiful land by day and the myriad stars by night, one wants very badly for humans to be there while the cycles slowly revolve and those distant images are projected into Turrell's spaces. One wants someone to be there in 19,084.[100]

Or, as John Beardsley noted, what Turrell hopes to achieve is "an environment of rapture."[101]

In short, it is possible that James Turrell may succeed in creating with the "Roden Crater" project an "idealized landscape," in Rosenthal's terms. On the other hand, the site as Turrell well knows is of itself a powerful site, traditionally known as a place of kratophany. Perhaps all that need be done in the future is what is now being done by the Skystone Foundation staffers: take a few people by the hand to the site from time to time; tell them to lie on their backs and watch the clouds drift by; let them see moonrise and sunrise. Still, knowing there are light mists from time to time at the site, one also wants to see the mists. When Turrell finishes his refinement of the site's natural possibilities, occasional occurrences will be predictable ones. Turrell's work is complementary to the ancient meaning of the crater. That may be why he has a rapport with the Hopi. Perhaps they both see the same things in the same place.

Are Earthworks Sacred?

All six contemporary earthworks are simple forms, and all are freestanding with the exception of Charles Ross's "Star Axis." That one is a buried work. All six of the works do "weather" in some way. They are intended to change as the seasons change. Four of the six artists used material indigenous to the site in the construction of their work. Nancy Holt and Walter De Maria did not; however, they were aware that there were material dictates prompted by the site. Thus, Holt's tunnels are the color of the desert, and De Maria's steel poles are so slender they disappear in the noonday sun. The other four artists all used indigenous materials for their constructions—in whole or in part. Robert Smithson's "Spiral Jetty" is the only one of the six earthworks made solely of materials indigenous to the site; but when "Star Axis" and "Roden Crater" are finished, they will look as though they have been made of local materials. Michael Heizer's "Complex One/City" looks as though it will still retain its apparent composite features of having been constructed of imported and indigenous materials.

Thus, if we assess the contemporary earthwork in terms of its fidelity to archaic forms, many do exhibit a heritage of type. That does not necessarily make the contemporary earthwork sacred work. By no means are all contemporary earthworks sacred endeavors. Some fail. The artist may lack talent, or talent equal to the artist's vision. The artist may lack the simple opportunity to do the work. Some earthworks are just what their sponsors claim them to be—land reclamation projects, gardens, parks, playgrounds, or other sorts of outdoor sculptural installations.

In order to know if any of the six contemporary earthworks are sacred works of art, several questions remain unanswered: Do the sites themselves appear to have been places of kratophany, places of vision for the artists who made the earthworks? And are they now for site visitors? Does the earthwork itself succeed in mapping, defining the artist's vision so others may see some part of the power the artist experienced on site? May we take our questions further and ask: Has the work itself been done in a spirit of reciprocity with the earth? These questions are useful ones to ask of contemporary North American earthworks because they are also the ones researchers raise with regard to ancient Amerindian sites.

In the face of great stress, from early contact to present day, some indigenously native beliefs have persisted. One of these beliefs is an earth-centered reverence that permeates all native land use. Another is the importance of the sunwise circle. A third is the concept of reciprocity, of balance, harmony. Underlying all is the understanding of the importance of personal vision, the importance of transformation, the importance of rendering the invisible visible.

Michael Heizer's "Complex One/City" has *not* elicited rhapsodic descriptions from site visitors. From its published descriptions, it appears that visitors see what they expect to see, although they are confused by the scale of the work on its site and it is not always obvious to the visitor whether "Complex One/City" is a large work or a small work. "Lightning Field," "Spiral Jetty," and the "Roden Crater" have all prompted published statements indicating that for some people, quite unexpectedly, their site visits became unforgettable personal experiences of kratophany. "Sun Tunnels," too, usually elicits statements of admiration from its site visitors, but that may not be the same as calling it a potentiated locus of hierophany.

For Robert Smithson, James Turrell, and Charles Ross, there is published documentation confirming that for the artists themselves, come hell or high water, they have been *impelled* to undertake the making of their earthworks. Only when they found themselves standing in a specific physical place did their visions become comprehensible and compelling. Moreover, all three artists have indicated in their statements that the form of the earthwork was dictated by what they saw in the landscape—*there,* in *that* place. I have not located in my bibliographic search similar statements from Holt, De Maria, or Heizer.

The sacred place is described generally as an architectonic space that is enclosed or set aside in some way; it is a place that has a point of entry, requiring the visitor to go from here to there along some directed path. The sacred place is animated: it is a site where something important happens, where our everyday sense of time and place collapses.

All six contemporary earthworks are architectonic spaces. Each is located in a remote region that takes some doing to get to the site. Each one has a particular path that must be followed to get there, and each one has a directed point of entry to the site. Moreover, each artist's reputation is on the line: will the journey undertaken be a worthwhile one for the site visitor? Once one has invested that sort of time and energy to find the contemporary earthwork, the site visitor (like any pilgrim) is prepared to find meaning in the journey, which may explain why there has been little critical formal analysis of the contemporary earthwork by the art field cognoscenti who have made the journey. Many have found "environments of rapture" and they have said so. Others have kept their mouths shut. We do not know what everyone has found.

Does it matter that the site visitor may be predisposed to find something wonderful and important at the site (a.k.a. "the emperor's new clothes")? No, not really. Any journey *is* part of getting there. The devout of any faith make at least that much of a commitment to the possibility of hierophany just by walking into a church, a temple, a synagogue, a mosque, or whatever built space they associate with personal faith. If enough people want them, churches can be built on every city block. They will all be potentiated loci of hierophany, albeit in corporate terms, simply because the devout expect such sites to be loci of vision and miracle.

A similar dynamic of expectation also obtains for the journey to the contemporary earthwork. However, and importantly so, *what is expected is an "art experience"* (i.e., something that contemporary society usually defines as "nonreligious"). The site visitor does *not* expect to obtain an experience of hierophany at the earthwork site. Nevertheless, visitors sometimes do. In these instances, the artist appears to have found a form that conveys to others authentically some aspect of the artist's own visionary experience. The artist has indeed made the invisible visible to others. Certainly then, the artist's work is "sacred."

The use of physical descriptors, the use of a site typology, enables us to describe a sacred place—to say *what* it looks like *and* to make comparisons between sites. If we can describe a site, we can also begin to talk with some precision about *why* it looks this way. We can begin to identify the choices made in the site's architectonic setting. With care, we can begin to think symbolically about the site. Our eye widens, the site begins to unfold. Its possibilities become permutations, multivalent, clotting with possibility. We ask questions. It is in those moments when the artist's work succeeds—it is "working." The artist's work has prompted us to pay attention, to be still, to look, to query.

When we learn to ask good questions, we get better answers. The set-up is labyrinthine—one way in and one way out—because questioning is questing.

6

Seeing the Earth

The prefatory note in poet John Smith's book *Sucking-Stones* (1982) explains that in some cultures it is a traveler's custom to carry a small, smooth stone in the mouth. Sucking on the stone keeps the mouth moist, alleviates hunger, and, as Smith notes, such stones obtain a sacramental quality.[1] I have been thinking of late about sucking stones. Sucking stones come from the place left behind. A suckling is one too young to be weaned. The word "succor," to rescue, to comfort. The festival of Sukkoth, the harvest festival, the shelter of hope in the wilderness. The word "Sukkoth" has a different origin than "suck," but the sounds are the same. I think, too, of homeless people. Perforce and by force, there are more who are homeless now than ever before in the world.

Nomads appear to be homeless, but to be nomadic is not the same condition as being homeless. Homeless is to be without refuge. Nomads follow known trails, song lines of demarcation synchronized with the seasonal cycles of growing plants and migrating animals. Nomads know where they have come from and where they are going. Their landscapes are always being renewed and they know the stories of their landscapes. The homeless are the castaways of natural, political, personal disasters. They do not know how things may be or will be, or what it all will appear to be.

My own childhood was part homeless, part nomadic. We were a military family, and we moved often, generally in response to someone else's Cold War strategem. We traveled light. I owned no books. When I was seventeen, I left the overseas network of military camps to enter university. Arriving on campus, I became a castaway, alien in my own homeland, immigrant to a country I did not know. That first year of school,

I happened upon a small volume of poems by Rainer Maria Rilke, a book small enough to carry in my coat pocket. The poems became my sucking stones. I read them daily, sacramentally. In two lines particularly I took comfort: "Slowly, we make the world our own with words and pointing fingers" *(Wir machen mit Worten und Fingerzeigen / uns allmählich die Welt zu eigen).*[2] *Allmählich:* we grow into the world slowly.

Several years later, I lost the little book. I was never able to replace it, but I had made an accommodation with the city by that time (although not fully with the country). In any event, I no longer carried poems about in my pocket. As I organized the research for this book, I found myself spontaneously remembering lines from Rilke's poems. His words were pointing the way down old nomadic trails, and it was as though the little book were still in my pocket when I made appointments to meet with artists. I was remembering the long-ago ache of not knowing where I was and where I was going. This time, however, there were artists to meet who knew where I had come from (insofar as a university is a place to "come from"). Far better than I did, the artists also knew where my research would take me. We were all of us attempting to understand visionary experiences—earth-centered, sacred visions.

With Words and Pointing Fingers

It seems to me that wanting to be of the world, wanting to make the world our own, is the common note throughout the endeavors of the artists discussed in this study—whether the artists are those who marked the ancient sites or those who mark sites today.

As noted earlier, to be human is to be as often wanderer as settler. Wherever it is that we are, we strive to make the world our own, to clear a bit of ground, to find someplace where we may *be*. The question that follows from that observation is one of process and of premise (pun intended). Is the world our own? And can we claim it? One set of answers can be found in myths of origin—how we speak of the world *and* how we look at the world—"*mit Worten und Fingerzeigen.*"

We speak of the world in our myths of origin. Origin stories bring the world into being. They shape our perception of reality. Through these stories, we orient ourselves in relationship to what we are and what we are not. The Cahuilla story mentioned in chapter 2 tells how the creator god, Muhat, is poisoned by the people he made. He dies a bloody death, leaving "places of power where his blood—hematite—

dropped."[3] These "places of power" are sites for visions; the god is metaphorically in the earth; the god is the earth. His blood (the hematite) confirms that for the Cahuilla people. Further, their story explains why Muhat cannot be beseeched specifically; he has given his power to coyote.

Genesis, the Western myth of origin, is a different story. The creator god is outside the earth. Genesis tells of beginning. Beginnings assume ends. The world was made once; it is purposeful; there is some hereafter reckoning point when humans and the world are no longer. The story implies that humans, because they are human, are aware of this and animals are not. Humans, therefore, have an enhanced—if not superior—relationship to an inevitable process of progression from start to finish. That there is an end implicitly signals some other stage than the earth itself follows.

Genesis, the story we all know, serves to explain some features of our lives, but not all. It is hard, for example, to maintain human superiority to animals when, as a general category, all the beasts of land, sea, and air are superior to humans in every important quality needed for survival. Animals hunt better, shelter themselves better, maturate faster, and reproduce with more ease. Typically, non-Western stories of the first peoples explain better the relationship of human and animal in terms of actual observed fact than does Genesis.

Of the several interpretations of Genesis current in our culture, one of them concerns our own importance as "self-conscious" beings. We sometimes credit the difference between ourselves and the beasts to human "self-consciousness," claiming thereby that animals have not a clue what it means to be self-conscious (as if we would know if they did). Self-consciousness seems to me to be a poor peg upon which to hang any claim to superior difference. An argument might, however, be made for territoriality because all species are territorial to the extent that any one of them is found someplace, and not some other place.

The activities of any nonhuman animal take place within a territory that is smaller than human territory. We have, as a species, wandered all of the earth, and some of the solar system. Other animals have not, unless we have brought them with us. Perhaps our range as human became one so far and wide because from an early time we were able to adapt certain animal features to our own purposes. We sewed skins together and became furry like bears; we made canoes and paddled like ducks; we learned to fly like birds and dive like dolphins; and we have become over time wonderfully omnivorous. Most recently, we flung ourselves right up there with the stars. We have put our satellites and telescopes far into the firmament. In so doing, we managed to extend our range beyond that of the natural animal world. For the first time, we have put ourselves someplace where there are no animals to show us what we need to know in order to survive. We are truly on our own. Is it any wonder there is such a popular resurgence of interest in angels?

In 1959, Frederick Kiesler, one of the more influential artists of the 1950s, wrote: "God save the moon from man."[4] Ten years later, man was on the moon. Some have suggested that the human activity of space exploration is engendering today a profound revisioning of Western mythos.[5] Daniel Noel is one of those scholars. In his 1986 study *Approaching Earth*, Noel argues that "our earth, newly visible from above and beyond, is the most important discovery of our space efforts so far."[6] I agree.

Microcosm and Macrocosm

We have not yet understood what this iconic image of the earth means although we are beginning to understand that it suggests the cosmos is actually something both micro and macro. For example, the 1992 United Nations Conference on the Environment and Development quickly became known everywhere as the "Earth Summit." No popular expression better captured the urgent hope so many have.

There is a photograph of the earth that needs no label. In the time span of a generation, all have come to recognize the image of a disc swirled blue and white, sharp-edged against a black field, as a photograph of our "earth." Now that we can see the world as a whole, we begin to think of it in worldwide terms. The justly famous United States National Aeronautics and Space Administration photograph of the earth enables us to find the words more easily.

Not surprisingly then that UNESCO has begun to monitor both natural and "cultural landscapes" (a new category) on its list of World Heritage sites. In 1993, cultural landscapes were defined as those that "illustrate both specific land-use techniques and a spiritual communion with nature."[7] According to the UNESCO guidelines, cultural landscapes may include gardens and parks. The category is intended to include sites with "powerful religious, artistic, or cultural associations of the natural element, rather than material cultural evidence."[8] I note with interest and satisfaction the inclusion of the words "artistic" and "spiritual" in the guidelines. The UNESCO guidelines mean sacred places everywhere are all part of our world heritage. The guidelines suggest that artists have a role to play in the identification of these sites.

Artists do have an eye for places that matter. Naturalist Joseph Kastner recently discovered that. He became interested in a vacant lot on the lower east side of Manhattan island, New York, surely one of the most densely populated neighborhoods of the world. In five years time, sixty different plants—trees, bushes, flowers—grew there.[9] The lot was vacant because the gas station that had occupied it had been torn down and an economic recession had hindered the building of anything new upon it. Kastner watched the lot—an arid patch of concrete rubble. He documented the plants that grew there. Initially, the plants were tough ones—for example, fast-growing plantain and ailanthus tree. The plantain came over from Europe with the first colonists. The ailanthus tree was initially imported from China. Later came the indigenous plants— evening primrose, daisy, aster, goldenrod. No one particularly cared for the lot, people threw all sorts of things into it. The lot flourished anyway. Eventually, though, along with the butterflies and woodpeckers came rats. The neighbors complained and, in 1993, the city bulldozed the lot to clear the rats away.

Not to worry. The lot has begun to reseed itself. There is no lack of seed in the neighborhood because not far away are a score of new gardens. Kastner discovered when he walked around the neighborhood that, for some time, local artists have been reclaiming empty lots. They are making gardens. The artists call themselves the "Green Guerillas" and they mean eventually to reclaim all of New York's empty lots for nature.[10] They mean to reshape the urban environment into one that acknowledges its indigenous roots—nature, the earth, the world—as well as its human history. Again, just as I have observed in Ottawa, here is a body of successful, professional artists who are working outside the commercial gallery art distribution system. Their reasons have nothing to do with commerce or limited display space. In Ottawa, the number of artists and art galleries may be limited, but in New York City the numbers of both are seemingly limitless. Artists often have other motivations for their work besides fame and fortune.

Geo-Metaphors

The artists for whom earth is the central subject are searching new and renewed metaphors for place in order to bring us home again. These artists are pointing to the world, to the earth, to nature. They are seeking places where all the world is there, in that place. These are sacred visions and sacred landscapes. The metaphors they use could be called "geo-metaphors," a useful word coined by scholar Daniel Noel. Geo-metaphors have an ancient history everywhere.

The artists' religio-aesthetic search is important, more important than perhaps we know or are willing to credit because love of the earth, topophilia, has its dark side too. Everywhere today in the world there are bloody surges of tribalism, ethnic-based nationalism, and violent attempts to bring bloodline-based political states into being, thereby displacing others that once lived in these places, too. Yi-Fu Tuan cautions that the mix of topophilia with ethnicity as a religious stance (one he terms "geo-piety") often breeds intolerance towards strangers.[11] That is true. As anthropologists tell us, most indigenous people call themselves "people," they do not call strangers "people." Sometimes strangers are not-quite human. Sometimes they are enemy.

In the traditions of the native peoples of this land, the earth is holy—but the expressions are many and various, and not at all well understood. Oftentimes, those expressions are in visual forms. When the signs and symbols used are visual ones, there is no written text to analyze, and the language needed, obviously, is a grammar of visual forms. As a visual form, the earthwork bridges archaic native traditions and the secular circumstance of contemporary art. To some extent, so does the garden. All are geo-metaphors.

The meaning of this body of earth-imaging work is one of "finger-pointing," to make the world our own. What we call it is another problem, another concern. Naming must be as carefully done as placing. As Rilke cautioned, *allmählich*, go into it slowly, by degrees.

Word shaping to shape the world is powerful; finger pointing is even more powerful. The artist's preferred medium is not self-conscious words. The artist uses finger pointing to create order with outward signs. Finger pointing requires that we use *all* sensory receptors if we are to see what is being shown. In order to see, the artist creates a way in which to see, a composition.

Compositions are ordered images within experiential grids. Compositions exist in states of tension. That is where their energy comes from, and that is what makes the composition animated (if the work is successful). For example, beginning art students sometimes draw from photographs instead of live models. This is a false economy. A photograph is a photograph. It is an image on a two-dimensional plane. It is not what was photographed (usually an object in a three-dimensional plane). The art student cannot draw well from a photograph; the student can only copy and/or reinterpret the flat image. The creative problem is different, and much harder, to render the lights and darks of three dimensions onto a two-dimensional plane. In order to do that the artist transforms in several dimensions (space *and* time) what the artist sees to what *can* be shown. When the student copies the photograph, the student has only copied another artist's (in this case, the photographer's) answer. In other words, as John Dixon notes, the work of an artist is "fundamental thinking about fundamental ideas."[12]

The work of an artist is transformation, the transformation of space and time, the creation of order, the creation of a *new* space and time—a place. Thus, reading about James Turrell's "Roden Crater" is not the same as being there. The work is completed when seen and, one hopes, seen as it is intended by the artist. If the work is genius (in every sense of the word), the perceptions of the viewer feed back into the work and extend its meaning further. When the work is genius, we can carry it away in our minds *as an eidetic image*. That is why a work of genius has a powerful accuracy beyond that of any curatorial written description. Robert Smithson's "Spiral Jetty" is work with that sort of mythic power.

Sacrality—the apprehension of some feature of the world as particularly, vividly animated—is a matter of individual perception *and* of orientation, as we saw in the explicit precision of Jennifer Dickson's garden photographs. Individual perceptions are changeable, mutable, just as are all other forms of the world. There are many possible site-reckoning points and many myths of explication. Their common features can, however, be adumbrated because all hold one image in common—the world—and all are *human* signs and symbols. All are metaphors of orientation and explication.

Out in Space

The encounter of the Old World with the New World was only 500 years ago. When Columbus sailed into the gray Atlantic, his proposal for a westward voyage included finding gold. Gold was wanted in order to fund a definitive crusade for the recapture of Jerusalem. No clearly articulated statement exists for the continuation of exploration out in space now that the old one of "beating the Russians" is defunct given the recent implosion of the Soviet Union.

The orientation problem space presents is an obvious one. Once we are out there in space, we lack all necessary proportion and scale, all sense of place. These are serious physical and psychological losses. Two coordinates, at a minimum, are necessary to fix a point. Our own verticality, obtained by earth's gravity, is one of those coordinates. Where, in space, is the horizon line to fix the second? Where is the earth to fix the first?

The concern of so many contemporary artists for the earth is tremendously provocative. Their insistent use of earth imagery appears to signal a paradigmatic shift in our understanding of who we are and what we are about as North Americans at the close of the century. If so, the buildup towards this shift began about 500 years ago and can be traced in the history of the landscape as a motif in Western art.

The landscape has not been an important subject until rather recently. Although art history students dutifully learn that there are examples of landscape painting on the walls of Roman villas and the frescos of Egyptian tombs, examples are few until the class reaches the Renaissance. Even then, there are not many: Leonardo's misty mountains and foliage in the backgrounds of the *Mona Lisa* and *Ginevra de'Benci* are typically presented as protolandscapes. In the seventeenth- and eighteenth-centuries, the landscape becomes a far more important subject for artists and it dominates much of nineteenth-century painting because artists begin to view nature symbolically, in religio-aesthetic terms. In the twentieth-century, the landscape continues to be an important motif—not just in painting, but also in photography and, as we have seen, in architectonic space. In fact, the history of landscape painting parallels that of the garden and, indeed, has influenced garden and park design right into the twentieth-century.[13]

I do not think the process of revisioning—of searching geo-metaphors, of becoming earth-centered—means, however, that artists are turning their backs on outer space exploration.[14] Quite the opposite. I suspect the artist's focus on earth is one of bringing the earth and ourselves into a better mythic alignment with all that there is—and that includes everything "out there." Charles Ross, for example, speaks of his work as one of providing us with a way to realize we are *also* made of star stuff.[15] Frederick Kiesler thought in those terms, too. He felt that even our thought processes were "concocted by the forces of the universe."[16] Those are mythic thoughts, indeed. To think of ourselves as "star stuff" and as embodiments (pun also intended) of universal forces is a very different way of thinking than to think of ourselves as lowly creatures of the earth, of the ground, as self-conscious human animals.

Seeing the Earth

Daniel Noel believes that the image space exploration has given us of the earth has had two identifiable effects upon our collective human psyche. First, we have shifted from a bird's-eye view (mountaintop, balloon, or airplane) to a god's-eye view of the planet, and secondly, we are shifting to a "*mythic* (or more precisely, a *neo-mythic*) *way of seeing*"[17]—shifting away from an emphasis on linear, Apollonian logic to one more intuitive, Dionysian. The god's-eye view, Noel feels, is feminine and one that he describes in terms of "geometaphors grounded in Gaia."[18]

Mostly I agree with Noel's observations, but not completely. For one thing, as important an image as the NASA photograph of the whole earth is in and of itself, it remains a documentary photograph. It is not interpretative; therefore, it is not metaphorical or mythical. The photograph is a machine-made image—not one composed by a photographer—and I can and do know that with my own eyes. Other people do, too. NASA especially. That is why from time to time NASA has invited artists to propose projects for outer space. The agency hopes thereby to find some way to make its mission better understood by the general (tax-paying) public.[19]

To understand the earth as Gaia is certainly interpretative, metaphorical, mythical. And, I confess, it pleases me to say the word "Gaia." I like its sound, I like the way my mouth moves when I say "Gaia." Still, my feeling is that if the viewer finds a goddess in a garden or at an earthwork site in North America, it is because the viewer brought her there instead of letting the land tell its own story. I cannot help but wonder, too, whether much is gained by a seeming see-saw replacement of an all-inclusive patriachial image with yet another high god, this one in a matriarchial guise.

I note also that in other cultures the incomprehensible notion might be the one of a "god's-eye view." For example, the Ojibway know the Thunderbird is not a god; thunderbirds are mythical birds, beings of great powers whose flight is surely not restricted to certain heights. Thunderbird's vision is a "bird's-eye view," mythically yes, but still a bird. Similarly, anthropologist Marie-Françoise Guédon tells a story of accompanying an old Dene woman long resident in the Alaskan bush to the hospital by airplane for the first time, along with all her family. They settled the old woman into her hospital bed and turned on the television—just in time for the first moon walk. Everyone understood exactly what the images showed—there, that minute, there was a human being on the moon. No one said anything, then the old woman spoke: "I think it will be all right. You see, he is dancing."[20]

Secondly, the more powerfully original and important the vision, the more important is the artist's skill, training, and discipline in transforming and reifying it. If, as a whole, the collectivity of humanity is shifting from Apollo to Dionysus in its psychic structure, the artist is unlikely to be part of that shift. The artist's work is one of harmonizing both metaphorical stances. The artist's work is more than a Dionysian experience. Apollo is an intrinsic, necessary part also. Or else the work does not get done, and all that remains is frothy bits of blood and bone along a spiraling pathway. Every spiral in is also a way out. The artist's work is one of finding the visual metaphors to carry the significance of the vision to others.

It is true that contemporary earthworks, as a North American phenomenon, are coeval with the opening of the space age. But I wonder if there are not two more contributing factors fostering the expanded and enhanced use of geo-metaphors by artists: the continuing wars of this century (with all the subsequent displacements of people) *and* the opening of the nuclear age (with its even greater potential for displacement of people).

The artists of this study are all of an age to remember classroom bomb drills and fallout shelters. They are also of an age to remember when ecological disasters were regional events, not global. Once, not long ago, one would not have known that a volcanic explosion in the Philippines was likely the source for a long, hard winter a year later in subarctic Canada. On the other hand 500 years ago, when one walked into a walled town in Europe greeted by bodies swinging from gibbets, there were people who knew the names of those who hung there dead. We do not know the names of the dead this week in Soweto, Bosnia, or Chiapas. Artists often speak of their fear that we are destroying ourselves and our planet. These issues may be interrelated.

The incremental contemporary despoliation of urban life is certainly one of the reasons artists are more and more willing to work out of doors, to take on public commissions (work which they often do at an out-of-pocket deficit), to give lectures, to educate the public's eye. It is one of the reasons, for example, artist Peter Hutchinson's garden in Provincetown, Rhode Island, is registered with the Commonwealth of Massachusetts as a "natural wildlife habitat." Hutchinson, in fact, does not speak of himself as a sculptor, but as a "dedicated gardener" who is sheltering birds and insects.[21] Jennifer Dickson, too, regards her work as an artist striving to create beauty as part and parcel of her (to date) fruitless struggle with the City of Ottawa regarding the degraded streetscape of the downtown core.[22]

The Buffalo Commons

The garden and the earthwork are geo-metaphors realized in the land. Another geo-metaphor has been brought forth recently by two American professors—one a geographer, the other an urban planner. In the same region of the United States where several of the earthworks discussed in chapter 5 are located, Frank and Deborah Popper propose there be a "Buffalo Commons." They want to return the land to its original grasslands state, a place of indigenous flora and fauna, and of indigenous peoples. They argue it is time to give the Great Plains back to the buffalo (and the Indian). Their proposal is intended to renew the Great Plains and heal old, suppurating wounds—the wounds of war, betrayal, broken treaty, and land grab, wounds of displacement.

Frank and Deborah Popper are Rutgers University (New Jersey) faculty members. Frank Popper is head of the urban studies department and Deborah Popper is a member of the geography department. Their argument, first voiced in 1987, is being heard and it is succeeding. By 1998 grazing fees, for example, on United States federal lands will become three-times higher than in 1993 in order to effect the return of vast tracts of grazing land to its prefrontier state, Secretary of the Interior Bruce Babbitt recently explained.[23] The Poppers and Babbitt are natural allies.

Babbitt knows what he wants, as a recent *New York Times Magazine* article[24] profiled: He wants to be the first Secretary to ever blow up a federal dam, he wants to rid the United States of its wealthy "welfare cowboys," he wants to end the federal giveaways of public resources. Babbitt was born and raised in Arizona, he knows the land of which he speaks and he cares for it deeply, religiously.[25]

The Poppers' discovery of the Great Plains was very different. They were on holiday and were exploring a part of the country they did not know. The discovery of its beauty and its tragedy proved haunting. The towns were empty or emptying. Many of the "settlements" had populations that had peaked in 1930 or 1920 or even in 1890.[26] Maps were deceptive. Towns were marked where there was no one there, and in many places there had not been a population for decades because once too many people tried to live on a land that could not support them, and could not support cattle ranching and wheat farming. Hence, the Poppers' dramatic insight that the land should be permitted to return to its original land-use state—the land of buffalo and Indians.

The Poppers land-use proposal covers an area that encompasses much of ten American states and three Canadian provinces along the 98th meridian, a north-south line intersecting Texas and Manitoba, everything in between eastward to the prairies and westward to the Rockies. They arrived at their 1987 proposal through careful analysis and computer modeling of 1980 land-use data using six variables for the ten American states that constitute the Great Plains. Recently, they updated their study by using 1990 census data and they have begun to look at Canadian data. They learned that the population base was dropping even faster than they had anticipated.[27] Again, they concluded that it makes no sense to try to reverse the effects of relentlessly depressed economies and dwindling populations on the Plains.

The better question, the Poppers say, is what should follow? To their surprise, they learned that the implementation of the proposal they called in 1987 the "Buffalo Commons" is well under way—albeit in an imaginatively revised and more appropriate form. In 1987 they had argued that the United States federal government should purchase outright more than 139,000 square miles of private land already adjacent to federal land, relocate the nonnative people living there, and turn the whole thing into a wildlife refuge managed by native peoples. In short, give the land back to the buffalo (and the Indian). In 1987, the Poppers imagined the people of the native reserves (part of the federal land base in their calculations) would engage in ecotourism, recreational hunting activities, and land-sparing traditional uses of the region.[28] The Poppers discussed none of this with either a native or nonnative resident of the region. When they finished their calculations, they wrote a short article that was published in 1987 in a Chicago-based professional journal on planning. Almost overnight, they were famous and notorious.[29]

The protests were immediate and strong, as one may imagine, to the thought of reversing "more than 100 years of American history."[30] Nevertheless, things began to happen, planned and unplanned, that pointed to the need for new thinking *now*. Population decline worsened for a number of new and old reasons. There were serious droughts in 1988–92; military base closings increased in North and South Dakota, Montana, and Wyoming; deregulation of the transportation and communication industries further isolated small communities; some federal farm subsidies were decreased for the first time ever; soil erosion worsened; and health-conscious people began to eat less beef. In fact, one mathematician seriously proposed blowing up the moon in order to change the tilt of the earth's axis and shift weather patterns.[31] His evil proposal has gained no support.

Instead, the Buffalo Commons proposal began to gain support from a mixed bag of scientists, academics, local people, government officials, and, very much so and not surprisingly either, from the Lakota nation. The Poppers traveled throughout the region explaining their ideas, listening to objections, worrying about the emergence of gambling and landfill sites as the new growth industries in the region.[32]

But when the Poppers looked at the 1990 data, they saw something unexpected. The buffalo had returned—not in great number, but in rapidly increasing numbers.[33] A hundred years ago in all of Canada and the United States, there were perhaps 1,000 buffalo. Today there may be 126,000. Not a lot compared to the estimates of 75 million that once roamed the Plains, but a start. In 1975, fourteen ranchers formed the American Bison Association. Today, the ABA has 1,100 members raising buffalo and they estimate there are over 100,000 head in the United States. In Canada, the Canadian Bison Association has grown to 275 members and 26,000 beasts in the same period of time. There is a third buffalo-raising group: the twenty-four-member Intertribal Bison Cooperative with 5,000 head of buffalo. In addition, in the United States, private land conservation foundations have begun to buy land in order to return it to wilderness, buffalo included; and in Canada federal and provincial governments appear to be engaged upon the creation of a new national park for the buffalo.

Thoughtful people are beginning to understand there is simply not enough money around to continue to underwrite beef and wheat production in an arid, barren sector. As writer Andrew Nikiforuk bluntly notes, "On both sides of the border, half the net farm income in former bison haunts now comes out of taxpayers' pockets. The great frontier has become a thinly disguised welfare state."[34] Other ideas are needed. The Buffalo Commons is one of those.

Three things make the Poppers' land-use proposal worth tracking: one, the Poppers are receiving a wide public hearing for their ideas; two, they are listened to respectfully at every level of American government and are beginning to be heard in Canada (one-third of the Great

Plains is Canadian); and, three, at its heart, their proposal is about an earth-centered mythos of harmony and reciprocity.

The Poppers have come to realize the specificity of their first proposal extolling the federal purchase and maintenance of private lands was wrong and misplaced. When the Poppers speak of the Buffalo Commons now, they describe it as a "metaphor for a large-scale, long-term restoration project . . . an appeal for rethinking Plains possibilities."[35] They tell their audiences that "'Buffalo' symbolizes less intensive and more diverse ways of working with the land . . . while 'Commons' refers to local communities taking better care of their futures."[36]

Importantly, their work and the reactions to their work have religious and artistic meaning, although the Poppers themselves were initially unaware of this and say they do not fully understand it now.[37] Perhaps I do. If I am correct, *the power of their proposal is in its metaphorical strength*, not in its reasoned argument. "With words and finger pointing," the Poppers identified a key geo-metaphor—the mythic buffalo. In their almost accidental and surely ironic juxtaposition of "buffalo" and "commons"—wild beast and village green—these two scholars created a powerful religio-aesthetic metaphor, indeed a geo-metaphor, that breaks through the ice floes of jammed old-style thinking. The strength of their metaphor is its fusion of word with image and with place. The metaphorical Buffalo Commons connotes and denotes a sacrality of land, of earth-based vision. It speaks of a holy place of harmony, a place of reciprocity for human and beast, a centering place.

The great visionary and holy man Black Elk could have told them that they share similar goals with the Lakota. So might any number of contemporary artists for whom the earth, too, is an altar of sacred places and events. Black Elk was nine at the time of his first vision, a vision that occurred during a buffalo hunt. The power of his vision, however, rested until he was old enough to make a public statement, a ceremony, from the vision. The vision itself was words and pictures, and Black Elk said of it:

> I did not have to remember these things; they have remembered themselves all these years. It was as I grew older that the meanings became clearer and clearer out of the pictures and the words; and even now I know that more was shown me than I can tell.[38]

Artists, like all visionaries, work metaphorically to find ways to point to what is true. More than is perhaps readily understood, the artist's work of visual transformation is about a perception of reality as movement, not stasis. Visionary states are not unlike watching waves at the seashore or watching the northern lights. It is not possible to watch a single wave form, roll, and break. The wave is always changing, always an ebb and flow, always the pull of the moon, the pulse of the sun, the solar wind, and *always* the earth, centered. The rhythms are ceremoniously *placed*. Knowing that is one thing; finding a way to map it for others still another; and marking the place of sacred site—earthwork, garden, and buffalo—yet another. All are ways home.

Notes

Chapter 1. Introduction

1. Kathy Gillis, artist, personal communication, Ottawa, August 9, 1993.

2. Ibid.

3. Gallery 101, Ottawa, and Galerie Axe-Neo 7, Hull. Outside/Ex-Site, July 9–August 31, 1993, was curated by Richard Gagnier and Cindy Deachman. The exhibition included site-specific sculptures installed at five sites by Dawn Dale, Mary Faught and c.j. fleury, Geoffrey Wonnacott, Diane Genier, and Michael Robinson. The sixth site was used for the projection of photography on an outdoor screen by Anne-Marie Zeppetelli, Richard Nigro, Pierre Dalpe, Justin Wonnacott, and Andre Martin.

4. The artists who participated in the Art Terre '92 exhibition, August 15–October 11, 1992, L'Ange-Gardien, Québec, included Mary Faught, Jean and Robert Rutka, c.j. fleury, Thoma Ewen, Dawn Dale, and David Harper. The dancer was Sandy Rowlatt.

5. There were no gardens in the settlements of Oceania or sub-Saharan Africa according to Derek Plint Clifford, "Garden and Landscape Design," *Encyclopaedia Britannica*, 15th edition (Chicago: Encyclopaedia Britannica, Inc., 1984), Macropaedia, vol. VII, p. 900.

6. Ibid., p. 891. George B. Tobey, Jr. in *A History of Landscape Architecture: The Relationship of People to Environment* (New York: American Elsevier Publishing Company, Inc., 1973), p. 28 presents a plan for a Theban estate, which shows a walled garden entered via a pylon gate and containing a fish and duck pond, plus date and palm trees.

7. See for example, Alan Sonfist, ed., *Art in the Land: A Critical Anthology of Environmental Art* (New York: E. P. Dutton, Inc., 1983).

8. The phrase "patterns of power" is one I have borrowed from the title of an exhibition catalogue by Ruth B. Phillips—*Patterns of Power: The Jasper Grant Collection and Great Lakes Indian Art of the Early Nineteenth Century*, Kleinburg, Ontario: The McMichael Canadian Collection, 1984. Phillips writes (p. 12): "The objects in the Indian cabinet are enriched with images and designs. We can think of these as patterns of power, making visible the forces which, according to Indian belief, pervade the natural world."

9. Rick Bartow, artist, interview notes, July 24–25, 1989.

Chapter 2. Jennifer Dickson's Gardens

1. Jennifer Dickson, interview notes, July 5, 1989.

2. Yi-Fu Tuan, *Landscapes of Fear* (New York: Pantheon Books, 1979).

3. Jennifer Dickson, interview notes, July 21, 1993.

4. Dickson, ibid., July 5, 1989.

5. Lelde Muehlenbachs, "Mixture of print and art is jarring and distracting," *Edmonton Journal*, October 29, 1980, np.

6. Sol Littman, "Delights of a Female Voyeur," *Sunday Star*, Toronto, October 22, 1978, p. B-6.

7. Jennifer Dickson, artist's statement, "Through a Glass Darkly," an exhibition, November 8–December 6, 1967, Arts Centre, University of Sussex.

8. Ivy A. Harding, "South Africa's First Woman A.R.A.," *Personality*, August 27, 1970, pp. 69–73.

9. Terry Kirkman and Judy Heviz, "Mortality is the Message," *Montreal Star*, December 2, 1972, np.

10. Dickson, ibid., July 5, 1989.

11. Dickson, ibid., July 21, 1993.

12. Ibid.

13. Ibid.

14. Ibid.

15. Ibid.

16. Ronald Sweetman, Jennifer Dickson's husband.

17. Jennifer Dickson, interview notes, July 22, 1993.

18. Ibid.

19. Ibid.

20. Haddon Hall, seat of the Duke of Rutland, an old terraced garden in Derbyshire, England; Chatsworth, also in Derbyshire; and Castle Howard, in North Yorkshire.

21. Jennifer Dickson's recollection is this may have been either the artist Evergon—who was working with color xerography then—or it may have been curator Martha Langford.

22. This portion of *"Il Paradiso Terrestre"* was curated by Pierre Dessureault.

23. See, for example, the reviews of Virginia Nixon, "Dickson's Creations Express Opposites," *Montreal Gazette*, May 24, 1980, p. 113; Bruce Paton, "Paradise Expedition Comes to NFB," *Ottawa Revue*, January 8–14, 1981; Carol Poser, "The Earthly Paradise," *Vanguard*, vol. 9, nr. 1, February 1980.

24. Rosalie Smith McCrea, "Art Photographs Use Myth to Test Belief," *The Ottawa Citizen*, December 6, 1980, p. 35.

25. Jennifer Dickson, interview notes, September 7, 1993.

26. Ibid.

27. Ibid.

28. Ibid.

29. Philip Yorke, 2nd Earl of Hardwicke (1720–90), as quoted by John Dixon Hunt and Peter Willis, eds. in *The Genius of the Place: The English Landscape Garden 1620–1820* (London: Elek Books Ltd., 1975), pp. 237–239.

30. Dickson, ibid., September 7, 1993.

31. Ibid.

32. Yorke, ibid.

33. Dickson, ibid., September 7, 1993.

34. Jennifer Dickson, "Some Gardens of the Ile de France," public lecture 3 of "Grace and Favor: Architecture and Gardens in the Old and New Worlds," Ottawa Art Gallery, November 2, 1993: "I don't think you can have too many statues in a garden: you can have too many people, but not too many statues."

35. Dickson, ibid., September 7, 1993.

36. Ibid.

37. Arthur Cotterell, *A Dictionary of World Mythology* (Suffolk: Oxford University Press, 1991), pp. 154–55.

38. Dickson, ibid., September 7, 1993.

39. John Fleming, Hugh Honour, and Nikolaus Pevsner, *The Penguin Dictionary of Architecture* (Harmondsworth, Middlesex: Penguin Books, 1966), p. 234.

40. Jennifer Dickson, artist's statement, "The Garden of Mystery" (1992).

41. Jennifer Dickson, "The Evolution of the Italian Garden," public lecture, National Library of Canada, Ottawa, April 14, 1993.

42. Derek Plint Clifford, "Garden and Landscape Design," *Encyclopaedia Britannica Macropaedia* (Chicago: Encyclopaedia Britannica, 15th edition, 1984), vol. 7, p. 894. The date of the villa's completion appears to be in doubt. John Shearman, in *Mannerism* (Harmondsworth, England: Penguin Books, 1967), p. 199, dates its construction to 1559–73, noting further of the villa: "Begun c. 1515 as a fortress by Antonio da Sangallo the Younger, completed by Vignola as a villa for Cardinal Alessandro Farnese. A fish-pond placed by Vignola between the oval ramps, has been removed; the loggia above the main door was originally open."

43. Dickson, ibid., September 7, 1993.

44. Today, the Farnese name is familiarly attached by art historians to a number of important examples of Western art once part of the family holdings—for example, the "Farnese Hercules," the "Farnese ceiling," the "Farnese globe."

45. Shearman, ibid., p. 19. According to Elizabeth Holt (*A Documentary History of Art*, vol. II, 1958, pp. 62–65), Mannerism's excesses in the depiction of religious imagery earned it the distinction of being the first artistic style condemned by the Council of Trent—an event that occurred in the council's last session of 1563. The impact of the Council of Trent declarations upon the subsequent secularization of the Mannerist style in particular and visual arts in general is a subject that remains to be studied.

46. Nikolaus Pevsner, *An Outline of European Architecture* (Harmondsworth, England: Penguin Books, 1968), p. 223.

47. Jennifer Dickson, "Evolution of the Italian Garden," public lecture, National Library of Canada, Ottawa, April 1, 1993.

48. From an official notice, September 1685, quoted by Yi-Fu Tuan in *Landscapes of Fear* (Minneapolis: University of Minnesota Press, 1979), p. 135: "This year in Rome, we have seen more heads of bandits on the Ponte Sant'Angelo than melons in the marketplace."

49. Dickson, ibid., September 7, 1993.

50. Ibid.

51. Pevsner, ibid., p. 225: "For the garden of the sixteenth century is still walled in. It may have long and varied vistas, as you also find them at the Villa Este in Tivoli or at Caprarola, but they do not stretch out into infinity as in the Baroque at Versailles. Neither do the low colonnades on the ground floors of Mannerist buildings . . . indicate infinity—that is, a dark, unsurveyable background of space, like a Rembrandt background. Back walls are too near."

52. Dickson, ibid., July 21, 1993.

53. Ibid.

54. Ibid.

55. Ibid. Jennifer Dickson also explains that the garden walks are solitary activities because the relationship is ". . . a direct one between the natural world and oneself."

56. Ibid.

57. Ibid.

58. Dickson, ibid., July 5, 1989.

59. Ibid.

60. Dickson, ibid., July 22, 1993.

61. Dickson, ibid., September 7, 1993.

62. Ibid.

63. Artist Carla Whiteside first expressed this idea in a conversation with me a few years ago. She was explaining her reluctance to document her artwork: Carla Whiteside, interview notes, July 12, 1989, Ottawa.

64. Jennifer Dickson, lectures 3 and 5 of "Grace and Favour: Architecture and Gardens of the Old and New Worlds," five illustrated lectures, The Ottawa Art Gallery, Ottawa, October 19–November 16, 1993.

65. Hunt and Willis, ibid., p. 18.

66. Ibid.

67. Kirkpatrick Sale, *The Conquest of Paradise: Christopher Columbus and the Columbian Legacy* (New York: Alfred A. Knopf, 1990), pp. 74–91.

68. Sale, ibid., p. 101–6.

69. Sale, ibid., p. 289.

70. Lowell John Bean, "Menil (Moon), Symbolic Representation of Cahuilla Woman," *Earth and Sky: Visions of the Cosmos in Native American Folklore*, ed. by Ray A. Williamson and Clair R. Farrer (Albuquerque, New Mexico: University of New Mexico Press, 1992), pp. 162–83.

Chapter 3. To Speak of the Earth—Ancient Landscape Markers

1. For a quick review of current theory regarding the dating of human migration from Asia to North America, see Donald J. Ballas, "Historical Geography and American Indian Development," in Thomas E. Ross and Tyrel G. Moore, eds., *A Cultural Geography of North American Indians* (Boulder, Colorado: Westview Press, 1987) pp. 13–31. The land bridge routes from Asia, as Ballas notes, may have been as long ago as 145,000–155,000 years ago, but conservative estimates for the Beringia approach are nearer 55,000–65,000 years ago. Alice B. Kehoe in *North American Indians: A Comprehensive Account* (Englewood Cliffs, NJ: Prentice-Hall, 1981), pp. 1–10, reviews what she terms the "radical, liberal, and conservative" schools of thought regarding dates of human entry into North America and concludes the date of entry is "at least twenty thousand years ago, very possibly earlier." No doubt that is so. Some sites in both North and South America have yielded artifacts estimated to be 24,000 years in the Yukon, 33,000 years old in Chile, and 45,000 years old in Brazil (John Noble Wilford, "What Unearth Is Going On?" *Ottawa Citizen*, June 18, 1989, p. E-7.) At the Sheguiandah site in Ontario, artifacts (worked stones) whose age has been estimated to be 30,000 or more years old have been found. For more information, see Franklin Folsom and Mary Elting Folsom, *America's Ancient Treasures* (Albuquerque: University of New Mexico Press, 1983), pp. 358–59. Some scholars think approaches via the sea from the southern Pacific were also possible. For example, Japanese pottery, 5,000–6,000 years old, has been found in Ecuador. A summary of current arguments is found in John Barber, "Oriental Enigma," *Equinox*, January–February, 1990, pp. 83–95.

It is important, too, to remember that many Amerindian religious beliefs center on the construct that the first peoples of the New World have *always* inhabited the New World. Of necessity, this leads to a harsh stand-off between faith and science, and sometimes between science and politics. Alice Kehoe cogently summarizes (*North American Indians*, pp. 1–2) the problems that arise from studies of origin by noting her study "lies within the anthropologists' universe of discourse [and] readers looking for explanations derived from myth or revelation must turn to books discoursing on the spiritual universe."

2. Edward Sapir, *Time Perspective in Aboriginal American Culture: A Study in Method* (Ottawa: Canada Department of Mines, Geological Survey, 1916), p. 17.

3. The notion of there being an evolutionary social continuum of human development from "primitive" to "evolved" or "civilized" is not a useful one—although it persists insidiously and continues to taint Western intellectual scholarship today. The survival of any ancient social structure or belief into our own time should suggest to us that there is probably nothing maladaptive, unaccomplished, or simple-minded about that structure or belief. In other words, such structures and beliefs are not "primitive"; they are merely long-lasting. Often they are non-Western and, in that way, they are indeed "different."

4. For example, Paula Gunn Allen in "Grandmother of the Sun," the first essay in her study, *The Sacred Hoop* (Boston: Beacon Press, 1986), posits close connections—if not equivalences—between the tribal genetrix, Thought Woman of the Keres Pueblo, and other goddess figures found among the Hopi, Lakota, Iroquois, and Cherokee. In so doing, Allen (herself a Keres Pueblo scholar) attempts to discuss the history and traditions of a number of peoples from four quite different language groups—Keresan, Iroquoian, Siouan, and Uto-Aztecan—scattered clear across the continent from the eastern woodlands, to the plains, to the southwest as though they were one people with one tradition. There is little in the archaeological record to support her discussion. If, in fact, there were several migrations from Asia to the New World, migrations separated by millennia, then it seems more likely there would be several different myth systems operative in North America. A female-centered Ur-system of native belief true for all New World peoples would be possible only if there had been one migration or no migration at all. Scientific evidence in the New World points to multiple origin stories and many peoples, not just one people with one story.

5. Joseph Campbell, for example, often used the stories of indigenous peoples in his commentary on the psychological centrality of myth to explain neolithic and paleolithic motifs continents and light years away. Daniel Noel has recently edited a critical study of Campbell's popular and scholarly contributions, bringing together 12 perceptive essays by leading scholars in religious studies—Daniel C. Noel, ed., *Paths to the Power of Myth: Joseph Campbell and the Study of Religion* (New York: Crossroad, 1990).

6. The vision of Black Elk (1863–1950) is perhaps the best known of all recorded Amerindian visions. Black Elk told his story to John Neihardt in 1931 because he felt it was his duty, Neihardt relates, to "save his Great Vision for men." Black Elk was 9 when he had his great vision, but he did not speak of it until he was 16. He feared that in telling his vision, he would give away its power, and perhaps even his own life's power. Finally, however, Black Elk confided his vision to an elder. In John G. Neihardt, *Black Elk Speaks: Being the Life Story of a Holy Man of the Oglala Sioux as Told through John G. Neihardt (Flaming Rainbow)* (Lincoln, Nebraska: University of Nebraska Press, 1979), pp. 204–12, we read that Black Elk realized he had to speak of his vision in order to justify his ability to heal and to lead his people. Even then, Black Elk did not tell the full story of the vision, just "all he [Fox Belly, the elder] needed to know that he might help me." Fox Belly confirmed the authenticity of Black Elk's boyhood vision, saying, "My boy, you had a great vision, and I can see that it is your duty to help the people walk the red road in a manner pleasing to the Powers." Fox Belly then performed a ceremony. Importantly, the purpose of ceremony was to make a visual mark upon the earth, "a picture of the relation between the people and the bison and the power was in the meaning." First an appropriate place, a sacred site was selected, then a sacred tepee

erected. Within that enclosed place was made "a circle of the four quarters." In other words, the world itself was visualized both macrocosmically and microcosmically. It was all centered upon Black Elk who wore the buffalo horns because it was in the first instance *his* personal, private vision that was being realized in terms other people could now understand. And as Black Elk recounts: "It is from understanding that power comes; and the power in the ceremony was in understanding what it meant; for nothing can live well except in a manner that is suited to the way the sacred Power of the World lives and moves."

7. Christian Norberg-Schulz, *Genuis Loci: Towards a Phenomenology of Architecture* (New York: Rizzoli International Publications, 1979), pp. 25–26.

8. Neihardt, *Black Elk Speaks*, p. 43.

9. "Navaho" is an older spelling of "Navajo." In their own language, the nation is called *Dineh*, "the people."

10. Åke Hultkrantz in *Native Religions of North America: The Power of Visions and Fertility* (San Francisco: Harper & Row, 1987), p. 25, like other religious studies scholars who have not studied the Dineh first-hand, identifies the sacred mountains specifically as Big Sheep Peak in the north, Pelado Mountain in the east, Mount Taylor in the south, and the San Francisco Mountains in the west. A recent field study by Rik Pinxten, Ingrid van Dooren, and Frank Harvey—*Anthropology of Space: Explorations into the Natural Philosophy and Semantics of the Navajo* (Philadelphia: University of Pennsylvania Press, 1983)—was able to confirm only two of the above four named mountains as ones universally regarded by their informants to be indubitably the sacred mountains.

11. Pinxten, van Dooren, and Harvey, *Anthropology of Space*, pp. 24–25.

12. Blessingway is the sequence of ceremonial stories and ritual underlying all Dineh traditions, a sequence of stories and ritual that re-create the world and the house of the ritual.

13. Sam Gill, *Native American Religious Action: A Performance Approach to Religion* (Columbia, South Carolina: University of South Carolina Press, 1987), p. 19.

14. Ruth Landis, *Ojibwa Religion and the Midewiwin* (Madison: University of Wisconsin Press, 1968), pp. 106–8: In the midéwiwin journey, bear emerges from layers within the earth, travels east to the sunlight, then to the ocean for the manito-migis shell, and then to the Ojibway. When bear emerges from the center of the earth, he is white as snow (equivalent to the north wind), then yellow as a growing thing (equivalent to the west wind), then red as a growing thing (equivalent to the south wind), then black as a dead thing (equivalent to the east wind). He travels north-west-south-east, the opposite of a sunwise direction. Moreover, when he arrives at east, the beginning of life, he is black. Why? One must assume this is because bear is from the spirit world. All things are opposite there although the direction chosen is still a sunwise direction, even if reversed. In the ghost midéwiwin, the orientation of the midéwiwin lodge is north-south, not east-west. Nevertheless the journey is still a sunwise journey because the purpose of the journey is to enable one to become part of the sun and the stars—Earle H. Waugh and K. Dad Prithipaul, eds., *Native Religious Traditions* (Waterloo: Canadian Corporation for Studies in Religion, 1979), p. 38. Both forms of the midéwiwin ceremony require the sacrifice of a white puppy in lieu of bear. Why white? Perhaps because in death the white puppy turns black (as do all living things when dead). In that case then, the circle of life begins anew—white (puppy alive) to black (puppy dead) to red to yellow (growing things) to white. Bear's journey on earth (as started by the surrogate, a sacrificed white puppy) is sunwise, earthly. The journey restores harmony and balance between all the layers of the cosmos.

15. Frida Deising, Haida, interview notes, July 15, 1989.

16. For example, in a recent study by M. A. Brown, "Grave Orientation: A Further View," *Archaeological Journal*, vol. 140 (1983), pp. 322–28, of neolithic, early Christian, and mediaeval grave orientation in England, the same axial orientation was found predominant for all graves: Christian and non-Christian alike attempted to bury their dead with feet pointing to the rising sun.

17. Peter Nabokov and Robert Easton, *Native American Architecture* (New York: Oxford University Press, 1989), p. 35.

18. "Land claims," however, is probably not the best phrase to use. It bespeaks too many years of frustrated effort by people consigned to reservations, consigned—it appears—to parley endlessly for more equitable treatment with those who put them there. "Entitlement" with its connotations of moral dignity and human worth might be the better word.

19. Patricia Albers and Jeanne Kay, "Sharing the Land: A Study in American Indian Territoriality," in Thomas E. Ross and Tyrel G. Moore, eds., *A Cultural Geography of North American Indians* (Boulder, Colorado: Westview Press, 1987), p. 56.

20. Bruce Trigger, in *Natives and Newcomers: Canada's 'Heroic Age' Reconsidered* (Kingston and Montreal: Queen's University Press, 1985), carefully documents the various options explored by the Algonkian and Iroquoian peoples in their efforts to come to terms with the trading possibilities presented by English, Dutch, and French colonizers. Most were unsuccessful because none of the Europeans shared the same notions of land use as the native peoples.

21. Yi-Fu Tuan, *Topophilia: A Study of Environmental Perception, Attitudes, and Values* (Englewood Cliffs, NJ: Prentice-Hall, 1974), p. 146.

22. Christian Norberg-Schulz, *Intentions in Architecture* (Cambridge, Massachusetts: MIT Press, 1965), pp. 32–49.

23. Folsom and Folsom, *America's Ancient Treasures*, pp. 16, 17.

24. Cheryl Nickel, "The Semiotics of Andean Terracing," *Art Journal*, Fall 1982, pp. 200–203.

25. Ibid., p. 201.

26. Joseph Epes Brown, *The Spiritual Legacy of the American Indian* (New York: Crossroad, 1987), pp. x–xii.

27. Yi-Fu Tuan, *Topophilia*, p. 132.

28. Peter Nabokov, "Native American Architecture: Preserving Social and Religious Life," *Four Winds*, Spring-Winter 1981, p. 47.

29. Enrico Guidoni, *Primitive Architecture* (New York: N. Abrams, 1978), p. 8.

30. William M. Gardner, "The Palaeoindians of the Shenandoah Valley, Virginia," *Archaeology*, May/June 1986, pp. 28–34.

31. Among the Papago and Pima peoples of today, a story exists that says the building of Casa Grande, a Hohokam structure probably built between c.e. 1350 and 1450, was at the direction of a "man who came from the south," but he proved to be cruel, so one day the people simply moved away. Indeed, the structure is different from those of other known Hohokam sites according to Folsom and Folsom, *America's Ancient Treasures*, p. 16. The Papago and Pima trace their ancestry to the ancient Hohokam, a Pima word meaning "they are used up." Anthropologists—according to Kehoe, *North American Indians*, pp. 102–12—generally agree that the Hohokam were a conduit of cultural influence from Mexico into Arizona and that the Pima and Papago are descendants of the Hohokam.

32. According to Nabokov and Easton, *Native American Architecture*, p. 55, the confederacy may have included as many as 30 different tribes comprising almost 200 villages. The confederacy did not survive the European incursion into the lands of south-

central United States, falling apart after its defeat in 1645 under the leadership of Powhatan's brother, Opechanacanough (Kehoe, *North American Indians*, p. 200).

33. Campbell, *Historical Atlas of World Mythology*, vol. 1, part 2, pp. 220–21.

34. Thomas E. Ross and Tyrel G. Moore, "Indians in North America," in Thomas E. Ross and Tyrel G. Moore, eds., *A Cultural Geography of North American Indians* (Boulder, Colorado: Westview Press, 1987), p. 3: "Recent findings suggest that *some* Indian cultures were not in harmony with nature, but were, in fact, exploitive of their natural surroundings to such a degree that their groups, in some cases, disappeared from the earth because the physical environment became so depleted that it could no longer support life." Archaeologists are fairly certain that is what happened to many of the ancient precontact Pueblo and mound-building groups.

35. William R. Iseminger, "Excavations at Cahokia Mounds," *Archaeology*, Jan/Feb. 1986, p. 59.

36. In the 17th century, European-introduced diseases took a horrifying toll among the Eastern Woodlands peoples. Some population groups suffered losses in excess of 90 percent, a terror that was repeated on the Plains and along the Northwest Coast in the 19th century. We do not know what the precontact population for the New World was. Older estimates of only 8 million for both North and South America combined have been replaced by current estimates running as high as 100 million for North America. According to David K. Ellades, 50 million is a safe estimate—"Two Worlds Collide: The European Advance into North America," in Thomas E. Ross and Tyrel G. Moore, eds., *A Cultural Geography of North American Indians* (Boulder, Colorado: Westview Press, 1987), p. 35—and that is, in fact, the estimate for the 1492 population from the arctic regions to central America that Kehoe presents in *North American Indians*, p. 1. The larger estimates may prove out because current scholarship keeps pushing back the dates of human habitation everywhere in the New World as scientists look more closely at the archaeological data. No new study that I know of has brought the initial New World entry dates forward, nor decreased any pre-or protocontact tribal population estimate. See also Trigger, *Natives and Newcomers*, chapter 5, "Plagues and Preachers," for a review of current estimates and the problems they present scholars.

37. Among the most notable of the protocontact drawings are Jacques LeMoyne's 1564 drawings of the Timucuas villages in Florida; John White's 1585 watercolors of Algonkian villages in the Carolinas; the drawings, c. 1535, made from Jacques Cartier's written descriptions of Hochelaga, an Iroquois village near present-day Montreal; Karl Bodmer's 1833–34 watercolors of the Mandan, and George Catlin's watercolors and oils, also from the same time period, of a number of the Prairie groups, including the Mandan: Paul Kane's watercolors, c. 1845, of a Kiowa village near Lake Huron: Henry B. Brown's drawings in 1852 of a California Wintu village; and John Webber's watercolors from 1770 of Captain Cook's explorations among the Nootka of the Northwest Coast and Alaska. Many of these drawings and watercolors have been widely published.

38. The only comprehensive study of the indigenous architectural forms of North America is the superb 1989 study by Nabokov and Easton, *Native American Architecture*. It is richly illustrated with historic photographs and diagrams and describes how the architectonic structures were made, the mediating factors of climate and economy, social structure, history, and the religious meanings of these structures for their makers. In addition, a few scholarly monographs or articles have been written to date on the architecture of individual tribal groups as religious architecture. One of the best, now out of print, is by Vincent Scully, *Pueblo: Mountain, Village, Dance* (New York: The Viking Press, 1975). Others include a study by George MacDonald, *Haida Monumental Art* (Vancouver: University of British Columbia, 1983); and an essay by Stephen C. Jett, "The Navajo

Hogan," in Thomas E. Ross and Tyrel G. Moore, eds., *A Cultural Geography of North American Indians* (Boulder, Colorado: Westview Press, 1987), pp. 243–56. Unfortunately, too many summary descriptions of North American native architecture fail by starting with the presupposition that there really is little to be had because there are so few examples of "big" structures, or at least structures made of long-lasting stone. Jamake Highwater, for example, one of the better-known interpreters of Amerindian art today, writes in *Arts of the Indian Americas: Leaves from the Sacred Tree* (New York: Harper & Row, 1985), p. 259: "The only Native American structures in the United States which might be given the status of architecture are the multiple dwellings created by the Pueblo Indians and Cliff Dwellers, as well as the earthworks produced by the Ohio and Mississippi Mound Builders." This is arguable. I think Guidoni's approach is a far more useful and inclusive one. As Guidoni notes in *Primitive Architecture*, p. 9: "By bringing into the purview of architecture the problems connected with spatial conceptions and social functions, we underscore the architectonic quality of *every active interpretation of the physical environment* (my underlining), the significance of spatial models as mediation between social structure and constructional typology, and the symbolism underlying architectural organization, which belongs to the historical-mythical patrimony of a people." This, indeed, is the approach taken by Nabokov and Easton, which is why their study is recommended.

39. Nabokov and Easton, *Native American Architectures*, p. 355.

40. Joseph Epes Brown, *Spiritual Legacy of the American Indian*, pp. 3–4.

41. Nabokov and Easton, *Native American Architecture*, p. 17.

42. Pinxten, van Dooren, and Harvey, "Appendix B: 'The Device': A Synoptic and Revised Edition of the Universal Frame of Reference for Spatial Analysis," *Anthropology of Space*, pp. 183—225. In 1975, anthropologist Rik Pinxten devised a cumbersome typology system of 245 descriptive entries based on these three categories (Euclidean, topological, projective) of spatial relationships. Pinxten's Universal Frame of Reference (UFOR) is designed to be used by field anthropologists in order to standardize their spatial descriptions of physical space, sociogeographical space, and cosmological space.

43. Folsom and Folsom, *America's Ancient Treasures*, p. 310.

44. Ibid., p. 358.

45. Robert W. Neuman and Nancy W. Hawkins, *Louisiana Prehistory: Anthropological Study nr. 6* (Baton Rouge: Louisiana Department of Culture, Recreation, and Tourism, 1982), p. 10.

46. Anthony F. Aveni, "The Nazca Lines: Patterns in the desert," *Archaeology*, July/August 1986, p. 33. The Nazca lines are the best known, but there are many other similar patterns, or geoglyphs, throughout Peru. For example, as David J. Wilson notes, in "Desert Ground Drawings in the Lower Santa Valley, North Coast of Peru," *American Antiquity* 53(4), 1988. pp. 794–804, ground drawings in more than 50 other river valleys in Peru have been studied to date.

47. Joan Vastokas and Romas K. Vastokas, *Sacred Art of the Algonkians: A Study of the Peterborouqh Petroglyphs* (Peterborough, Ontario: Mansard, 1973), p. 25.

48. "Geographica," *National Geographic Magazine*, vol. 177, nr. 6 (June 1990), np.

49. Joseph Epes Brown, *Spiritual Legacy of the American Indian*, pp. 10–24.

50. Linda B. Eaton, "Nora Naranjo-Morse: Santa Clara Sculptor," *A Separate Vision* (Museum of Northern Arizona, *Plateau*, vol. 60, nr. 1, 1989), p. 14.

51. Sam D. Gill, *Mother Earth: An American Story* (Chicago: University of Chicago Press 1987) pp. 8–39. Gill argues that there is good reason to believe Tecumseh would not have stated his claim in this language. Among other evidences, Gill notes that the statement is not published until 1821 and is cited as having been said during 1811

meetings, not 1810 meetings. Further, Gill suspects Henry Schoolcraft is the source for the story, a story Gill posits as one more legend than historical fact.

52. "You ask me to plow the ground. Shall I take a knife and tear my mother's breast? Then when I die she will not take me to her bosom to rest. You ask me to dig for stone. Shall I dig under her skin for bones? Then when I die, I cannot enter her body to be born again. You ask me to cut grass and make hay and sell it, and be rich like white men. But how dare I cut off my mother's hair? It is a bad law, and my people cannot obey it. I want my people to stay with me here. All the dead men will come to life again. We must wait here in the house of our fathers and be ready to meet them in the body of our mother." Speech of Smohalla (Nez Percé), in Jay David, ed., *The American Indian: The First Victim* (New York: William Morrow, 1972), pp. 85–86. Smohalla was the leader of the Dreamers, a 19th-century religious resistance movement that had wide currency among the Nez Percé people of the Columbia River valley.

53. Joel Sherzer, "Areal Linguistics in North America," in Thomas A. Sebeok, ed., *Current Trends in Linguistics* (The Hague: Mouton, 1973), pp. 749–95, and Esther Matteson *et al.*, *Comparative Studies in Amerindian Languages* (The Hague: Mouton, 1972), pp. 23–24, 28.

54. For example, in Cree, the very same object may be declined as animate one minute and as inanimate the next—by the same speaker—as noted by Brian Craik in his study, "The Animate in Cree Languages and Ideology," in William Cowan, ed., *Papers of the 14th Algonquian Conference* (Ottawa: Carleton University Press, 1982), pp. 31–32.

55. B. Rachel Levy, *Religious Conceptions of the Stone Age and Their Influence upon European Thought* (New York: Harper & Row, 1963) p. 54. In this carefully documented, albeit wide-ranging study—first published in 1948 as *The Gate of Horn*—Levy draws examples of what she supposes to be palaeolithic survival motifs from cultures as diverse as the Australian aborigines, Pima Indians, and the Blackfoot to explicate Aurignacian and Magdelenian visual imagery. This is its primary weakness. Nevertheless, Levy's assessment of in situ goddess material of the palaeolithic and neolithic cultures of Old Europe is carefully done.

56. Mircea Eliade, *Myths, Dreams, and Mysteries: The Encounter between Contemporary Faiths and Archaic Realities* (New York: Harper Torchbooks, 1960) p. 168.

57. Ibid.

58. Sam Gill, *Mother Earth: An American Story* (Chicago, University of Chicago Press, 1987), pp. 107–28.

59. Annette Kolodny, *The Lay of the Land: Metaphor as Experience and History in American Life and Letters* (Chapel Hill: University of North Carolina Press, 1975), p. 146.

60. Ibid., pp. 4–5.

61. Ibid., p. 147.

62. Fr. Daryold Winkler, Ojibway native, personal communication, Ottawa, January 1989.

63. Gill, *Mother Earth*, pp. 129–50.

64. Joseph Epes Brown, *The Spiritual Legacy of the American Indian*, p. 4: "A presiding characteristic of primal people is a special quality and intensity of interrelationship with the forms and forces of their natural environment. As nomadic hunters or gatherers, or as agriculturalists, dependence upon natural resources demanded detailed knowledge of all aspects of their immediate habitat. This accumulated pragmatic lore was, however, always interrelated with a sacred lore; together these could be said to constitute a metaphysic of nature."

65. Kehoe, *North American Indians*, p. xii.

66. Wallace L. Chafe, "Siouan, Iroquoian, and Caddoan," in *Languages of the Americas*, edited by Thomas A. Sebeok (New York: Plenum Press, 1976), vol. 1, p. 561.

67. Harold E. Driver, *Indians of North America* (Chicago: University of Chicago Press, 1969), p. 25.

68. Alan D. McMillan, *Native Peoples and Cultures of Canada: An Anthropological Overview* (Vancouver: Douglas & Mcintyre, 1988), pp. 3, 6.

69. Driver, *Indians of North America*, p. 33.

70. Ibid., p. 29.

71. Ibid., p. 27. It is probably more accurate to say that many or even most people do not speak English with a high degree of fluency or precision—a matter more of their own limitations in the use of English grammar and vocabulary than of any structural defect in the language itself.

72. Benjamin Whorf, "Language, Thought, and Reality," in *Exploring the Ways of Mankind*, edited by Walter Goldschmidt (New York: Holt, Rinehart, and Winston, 1960), p. 106.

73. Ibid., pp. 106–7.

74. Victor Barnouw, "Language and Cognition," *An Introduction to Anthropology: Ethnology* (Homewood, Illinois: Dorsey Press, 1971), p. 70.

75. Ibid., p. 69.

76. Ronald Wright, "Beyond Words," *Saturday Night*, April 1988, p. 45.

77. Harry Hoijer, "The Nature of Language," in *Exploring the Ways of Mankind*, edited by Walter Goldschmidt (New York: Holt, Rinehart, and Winston, 1960), p. 81.

78. Driver, *Indians of North America*, p. 37.

79. Werner Müller, "The Passivity of Language and the Experience of Nature: A Study in the Structure of the Primitive Mind," in *Myths and Symbols: Studies in Honor of Mircea Eliade*, edited by Joseph M. Kitagawa and Charles H. Long (Chicago: University of Chicago Press, 1969), p 228.

80. Ibid., p. 230.

81. Ibid., p. 231.

82. Ibid., p. 233.

83. Ibid., p. 237.

Chapter 4. The "Look" of a Sacred Site

1. Charles Ross, interview notes, September 12, 1989.

2. Ibid.

3. Mircea Eliade arguably insists that almost all primitive or indigenous peoples everywhere have some sort of a belief in a "Supreme Being, creator, omnipotent, dwelling in the heavens and manifesting himself by epiphanies of the sky," even if, as he notes, this Supreme Being is no part of ordinary daily life—*Patterns in Comparative Religion* (New York: New American Library, 1958), pp. 24–25. Perhaps the reason the god went away is that there was no god there in the first place. There could be other attributions possible for sky epiphanies, attributions that escaped the notice of the ethnographer recording the information or the religious historian interpreting it.

4. In *Genius Loci: Towards a Phenomenology of Architecture* (New York: Rizzoli International Publications, 1979), pp. 24–48, Christian Norberg-Schulz argues that the "simplest model of man's existential space is . . . a horizontal plane (the earth) pierced by a vertical axis (the sky)" (p. 40). In forested areas where there is no vast expanse of cloudless sky above, earth is the dominant axis. In the desert, the sky is very big, prompting a vertical orientation in spatial organization and intellectual construct that gives rise to religious beliefs centered on one god—a sun god, a superior god. Therefore, in

Norberg-Schulz's view, animism and/or chthonic emphases in religion are more likely to be found in wooded and mountainous areas because these provide an appropriate setting for the establishment of religions of many gods, many tree and rock spirits, and much individuation of belief and religious experience. Norberg-Schulz recognizes a third type of landscape, which he calls "classical." In this type, the effects of sky and earth are evenly balanced: the earth "receives light without losing its (the earth's) concrete presence" (p. 45).

5. W. R. Lethaby, *Architecture, Mysticism, and Myth* (1891), reprinted (New York: George Braziller, 1975); Sir Joseph Norman Lockyer, *The Dawn of Astronomy: A Study of the Temple Worship and Mythology of the Ancient Egyptians* (nd), reprinted (Cambridge, Massachusetts: MIT Press, 1964).

6. Vincent Scully, *The Earth, the Temple, and the Gods: Greek Sacred Architecture* (New York: Frederick A. Praeger, 1969).

7. See further the two anthologies edited by Anthony Aveni: *Native American Astronomy* (Austin: University of Texas Press, 1975) and *Archaeoastronomy in Pre-Columbian America* (Austin: University of Texas, 1975); also, P. Clay Sherrod and Martha Ann Rolingson, *Surveyors of the Ancient Mississippi Valley* (Arkansas Archaeological Survey Research Series, nr. 28, 1987); and Ray A. Williamson, *Living the Sky: The Cosmos of the American Indian* (Norman, Oklahoma: University of Oklahoma Press, 1984).

8. Vincent Scully, *Pueblo: Mountain, Village, Dance* (New York: Viking Press, 1975). Others include Belden C. Lane, *Landscapes of the Sacred: Geography and Narrative in American Spirituality* (New York: Paulist Press, 1988); and Maureen Korp, *Sacred Geography of the American Mound Builders* (Lewiston, New York: Edwin Mellen Press, 1990).

9. Kees W. Bolle, "Speaking of a Place," in *Myths and Symbols: Essays in Honor of Mircea Eliade*, edited by Joseph M. Kitagawa and Charles W. Long (Chicago: University of Chicago Press, 1969), pp. 137–38.

10. Ibid., p 131.

11. Norberg-Schulz, *Genius Loci*, p. 13.

12. Ørnulv Vorren, "Sacrificial Sites, Types, and Function," in *Saami Religion*, ed. by Tore Ahlbäck (Uppsala: The Donner Institute for Research in Religions and Cultural History, 1987), pp. 94–109.

13. Tadehiko Higuchi, *The Visual and Spatial Structures of Landscapes* (Cambridge, Massachusetts: The MIT Press, 1983).

14. Ibid., pp. 98–181. The types are recognized by paradigmatic examples of each from which Higuchi derives his typology, specifically: the Akizushima-Yamota type (a compact bowl or valley nestled among green mountains and oriented to the east); the eight-petal lotus blossom type (a valley enclosed within a mountainous perimeter of jutting peaks, the directionality overall is up); the Mikumari shrine type (a crescent-shaped mountain valley having both low and high peaks and a river rolling down into the valley from the back and across, an up-and-down directionality); the secluded valley type (a narrow mountain valley with high peaks on both sides, a river running straight through creating a sense of looking down and into); the Zofu-Tokusui type (mountains at the north, a river or flowing water south, and a configuration involving all four cardinal directions); the sacred mountain type (a pyramidal mountain standing alone and set off by a river); and the domain-viewing mountain type (a mountain to be climbed in order to see the surrounding flatlands).

15. Ibid., pp. 182–89.

16. Unfortunately, to date Christian Norberg-Schulz has not chosen to write much about tribal architecture because, apparently, as he maintains in *Intentions in Architecture* (Cambridge, Mass.: MIT Press, 1965), p.49, the person he calls "primitive": "does

not master his surroundings satisfactorily, as his ability of abstraction is very limited," a limitation Norberg-Schulz ascribes to an inability to see the environment in any other than animistic ways. It would be difficult to cite any "primitive" group for whom this statement upon close examination would hold true; and it is surely not true for any collectivity.

17. Norberg-Schulz, *Genius Loci*, p. 185.

18. Ibid., p. 12.

19. Ibid., p. 5.

20. Christian Norberg-Schulz, *Meaning in Western Architecture* (New York: Praeger Publishers, 1975), p. 5.

21. Norberg-Schulz, *Genius Loci*, p. 13.

22. Ibid., pp. 17, 56.

23. Michael Pollan, "Why Mow? The Case against Lawns," *New York Times Magazine*, May 28, 1989. pp. 23–26, 41–42, 44.

24. Ibid., p. 41.

25. Ibid., p. 42, 44.

26. Ibid., p. 44.

27. Ibid.

28. E. V. Walter, "A Shelter for Dreams," *New York Times Book Review*, May 21, 1989, pp. 1, 52.

29. Ibid., p. 52.

30. Ibid.

31. Ibid.

32. Ibid.

33. Norberg-Schulz in *Genius Loci* writes (p. 17) that people can only build what they have seen: "Where nature suggests a delimited space, he builds an enclosure; where nature appears centralized, he erects a *Mal* (a centering point); where nature indicates a direction, he makes a path."

34. Pollan "Why Mow?" p. 44.

35. Ibid.

36. In fact, E. V. Walter criticizes the presentation of *The Most Beautiful House in the World* for having insufficient illustrations: "The illustrations, often critical in an architectural book, are disappointing. Mr. Rybczynski claims the sketches are his graphic record of an inner conversation and offers 14 drawings by his own hand. Unfortunately, they are tiny, but they are compensated for by lucid, eloquent word pictures and the inner conversation keeps the reader charmed to the last page"—Walter, "Shelter for Dreams," p. 52.

37. John W. Dixon, "Towards an Aesthetic of Early Earth Art," *Art Journal*, Fall 1982, p. 195.

38. Ibid., p. 197.

39. Ibid., p. 196.

40. The symbolic nature of this structure is discussed in John E. Pfeiffer, *The Creative Explosion: An Inquiry into the Origins of Art and Religion* (New York: Harper & Row, 1982); also in E. V. Walter, *Placeways: A Theory of the Human Environment* (Chapel Hill: University of North Carolina Press, 1988), pp. 91–95.

41. The basic feature of the Kurgan culture, for example, is its use of a round burial mound, covering a house-like tomb. The Kurgan culture arose in the middle and lower Volga river area in 7000 B.C.E. For further information, see Marija A. Gimbutas, *The Prehistory of Eastern Europe: Part I, Mesolithic, Neolithic, and Copper Age Cultures in Russia and the Baltic Area* (Cambridge, Massachusetts: Peabody Museum, 1956); and

Marija Gimbutas, *The Language of the Goddess* (San Francisco: Harper & Row, 1989). In the New World, the Poverty Point culture of Louisiana produced a number of burial mounds and other related earthworks that have been dated to 2000 B.C.E. See also Robert W. Neuman and Nancy W. Hawkins, *Louisiana Prehistory* (Baton Rouge, Louisiana: Department of Culture, Recreation and Tourism, Louisiana Archaeological Survey and Antiquities Commission, Anthropological Study nr. 6, June 1982); Jon L. Gibson, *Poverty Point: A Culture of the Lower Mississippi Valley* (Baton Rouge, Lousiana: Department of Culture, Recreation and Tourism, Lousiana Archaeological Survey and Antiquities Commission, Anthropological Study nr. 7, 1983).

42. Dixon, "Towards an Aesthetic of Early Earth Art," p. 196.

43. Ibid., p. 199.

44. *Patterns in Comparative Religion* (1958) is the English translation of *Traite d'Histoire des Religions* (1949).

45. Mircea Eliade, *Patterns in Comparative Religion* (New York: New American Library, 1958), p. 367.

46. Ibid., p. 24.

47. Ibid., p. 368.

48. Ibid., p. 369.

49. Ibid., pp. 370–73.

50. Ibid., p. 375.

51. Ibid., p. 369.

52. Ibid., p. 368.

53. Ibid., p. 380.

54. Ibid., p. 385.

55. Mircea Eliade, "Sacred Space and Making the World Sacred," *The Sacred and the Profane: The Nature of Religion* (San Diego: Harcourt Brace Jovanovich, 1959), pp. 8–65.

56. Ibid., p. 26.

57. Ibid., p. 21.

58. Ibid., p. 30.

59. Ibid.

60. Ibid., p. 64.

61. Ibid., p. 51.

62. Lane, *Landscapes of the Sacred*, p. 6.

63. Ibid., p. 12.

64. Ibid., p. 14.

65. Ibid., p. 15.

66. Ibid.

67. Ibid., p. 14.

68. Margaret Dyment and I have discussed this story and her subsequent visit to Moose Mountain medicine wheel on a number of occasions since 1988. The quotes that follow are from a taped interview, August 9, 1990.

69. Margaret Dyment, "The Sacred Trust," published initially by *Canadian Fiction Magazine* in the winter of 1990 and reprinted in the prestigious *Second Journey Prize Anthology* (Toronto: McClelland and Stewart, 1990).

70. World War II, the Korean War, the Vietnam War and, since the winter of 1989 when I was on Oahu, the Persian Gulf War.

71. Dixon, "Towards an Aesthetic of Early Earth Art," p. 195.

72. John Michell, *The Earth Spirit* (London: Thames & Hudson, 1975); also *City of Revelations: On the Proportions and Symbolic Numbers of the Cosmic Temple* (London: Garnstone Press, 1972); *A Little History of Astro-Archaeology: Stages in the Transformation*

of a Heresy (London: Thames and Hudson, 1977); and, *The New View over Atlantis* (San Francisco: Harper & Row, 1983).

73. An unpublished essay by Ottawa freelance writer Michael Davidson, "The Spiritual Geometry of Ottawa," August 12, 1987, describes efforts of several groups of people to demonstrate a "complex of three lines and a circle defining an apparent flow of geo-astral forces within the earth" centered on Parliament Hill and Victoria Island. In July 1990, the National Capital Commission, a federal agency, agreed in principle to acknowledge the claim of the Algonquin Indians to Victoria Island, a site the Algonquin consider sacred. The Ottawa Friends of the Earth and Seasons and the New Alchemists of Ottawa, both neo-Druid groups, had hoped to erect standing stones and other mesolithic-type structures on Victoria Island, but as Davidson writes: "These plans have been unanimously condemned as occultism and foolishness by all other groups studying the lines." *The Ottawa Citizen* paid Davidson a small honorarium for writing the article in 1987, but did not publish it.

74. Christopher Chippendale, "Stonehenge Astronomy: Anatomy of a Modern Myth," *Archaeology*, Jan/Feb. 1986, p. 52.

75. Walter, *Placeways*, p. 74.

76. Erich von Daniken, *Chariots of the Gods? Unsolved Mysteries of the Past* (London: Souvenir Press, 1969).

77. Barry Fell, *America B.C.: Ancient Settlers in the New World* (London: Wildwood House, 1976); also *Saga America* (New York: Times Books, 1980).

78. Joseph Epes Brown, *The Spiritual Legacy of the American Indian* (New York: Crossroad, 1987), pp. x, 2.

79. Franz Boas, *Primitive Art*, 1927 (New York: Dover Publications, 1955), p. 1.

80. Ibid., p. 10.

81. Brown, *The Spiritual Legacy of the American Indian*, pp. 3–4.

82. Andy Fabo, interview notes, June 17, 1989.

83. Marilyn Bridges, "Serpent Mound, Adams County, Ohio, 1982," *Aperture*, nr. 98 (spring 1985), p. 62.

84. John Bartlett, ed., *Bartlett's Familiar Quotations* (Boston: Little, Brown & Company, 1982), p. 94.

85. According to W. J. Frank, "Nuclear Weapons," *Encyclopaedia Britannica*, 15th edition (Chicago: Encyclopaedia Britannica, 1984), Macropaedia, vol. 13, pp. 325–26, the test explosion was expected to release 1,000–5,000 tons energy equivalent of TNT; instead it release an equivalent of 20,000 tons TNT.

86. Bhagavad-gita, chapter 11, v. 32.

87. Bhagavad-gita, chapter 11, v. 12.

88. Kenneth Bainbridge, another witness to that first nuclear explosion, is reported to have said, "Now we are all sons-of-bitches." Quoted by Johnathan Green, ed., *Says Who: A Guide to Quotations of the Century* (Essex, England: Longman Group, 1988), p. 600.

89. Larry O'Connor "Where the World Changed," *The New York Times*, December 9, 1990, section xx, p. 41. Closely supervised tours of the testing site are now available to the general public.

90. Alan L. Miller "Power," *Encyclopedia of Religion*, edited by Mircea Eliade (New York: Macmillan, 1987), vol. 11, p. 468.

91. Ibid., p. 470.

92. George Peter Murdock, *Our Primitive Contemporaries* (New York: Macmillan, 1934), p. xiii.

93. Ibid., pp. xiii–xiv.

94. R. R. Marrett, *Faith, Hope and Charity in Primitive Religion* (New York: Benjamin Blom, Inc., 1972), p. 9.

95. Guy E. Swanson, *The Birth of the Gods* (Ann Arbor, Michigan: University of Michigan Press, 1960), p. 6.

96. Edward Burnett Tylor, *Religion in Primitive Culture*, 1873 (New York: Harper & Row, 1958), p. xv.

97. Kees W. Bolle, "Animism and Animatism," *Encyclopedia of Religion*, edited by Mircea Eliade (New York: Macmillan, 1987), vol. 1, p. 299.

98. Eliade, *Patterns in Comparative Religion*, p. 20.

99. Ibid., p. 24.

100. Susanne K. Langer, *Feeling and Form: A Theory of Art* (New York: Charles Scribner's Sons, 1953), p. 79: "Nothing demonstrates more clearly the symbolic import of virtual forms than the constant references one finds, in the speech and writings of artists, to the 'life' of objects in a picture (chairs and tables quite as much as creatures), and to the picture plane itself as an 'animated' surface. The life in art is a 'life' of forms, or even of space itself."

101. Ibid.

102. Eliade, *Patterns in Comparative Religion*, p. xv.

103. Ibid., p. 30.

104. Ibid., p. 24.

105. Ibid., p. 30. Very often, in fact, in those cultures where the concepts of mana and taboo do exist, they are linked to beliefs in high gods. It would be more consistent if Eliade were to call them instances of theophany—not kratophany because they make manifest some attribute of some named deity. As theophanies, they are not instances of power immanent in a particular place. They are instances of power transmitted to a place.

106. Miller, "Power," p. 468.

107. Ibid.

108. Ibid.

109. William Morris, ed., *American Heritage Dictionary of the English Language* (Boston: Houghton Mifflin Company, 1978), p. 1513.

110. Charles H. Long, *Alpha: The Myths of Creation* (New York: George Braziller, 1963), p. 28.

111. Ibid., p 28.

Chapter 5. The Earthwork—A Sacred Art

1. The area where the state boundaries of New Mexico, Arizona, Utah, and Colorado intersect at right angles to one another.

2. From published sources, I located the names of artists or museums and foundations with curatorial responsibility for all six sites mentioned and wrote to all requesting information and permission to visit the sites. Of the six sites, at the date of this writing only Walter DeMaria's "Lightning Field" can be said to be accessible to the public, and only for part of the year. When completed, Charles Ross's "Star Axis" will be accessible year round by paved road.

3. There are several histories of the contemporary earthwork. They include: John Beardsley, *Probing the Earth: Contemporary Land Projects* (Washington, DC: Smithsonian Institution Press, 1977); John Beardsley, *Earthworks and Beyond* (New York: Abbeville Press, 1989); Willoughby Sharp, *Earth Art* (Ithaca: Cornell University Press, 1969); Alan Sonfist, ed., *Art in the Land: A Critical Anthology of Environmental Art* (New York: E. P. Dutton, 1983); and, in part, Peter Davies and Tony Knipe, eds., *A Sense of Place: Sculpture*

in *Landscape* (Tyne and Wear, England: Ceolfrith Press, 1984); Elinor W. Gadon, *The Once and Future Goddess: A Symbol for Our Time* (San Francisco: Harper & Row, 1989); and Lucy R. Lippard, *Overlay: Contemporary Art and the Art of Prehistory* (New York: Pantheon Books, 1983).

4. For example, one of the more complete articles was one written by an artist— Eleanor Munro. The article, however, appeared in the travel section of the *New York Times*, not in the newspaper's arts and entertainment section: Eleanor Munro, "Art in the Desert: Seeking Signs of Cosmic Coherence on a 3,200 Mile Pilgrimage to Earthworks in the Southwest," *New York Times*, December 7, 1986, pp. 9, 38.

5. Willoughby Sharp, "Notes toward an Understanding of Earth Art," *Earth Art* (Ithaca, New York: Andrew Dickson White Museum of Art, Cornell University, 1969), unpaged.

6. The two basic forms of sculpture are subtractive and additive. Subtractive sculpture is that which is carved, e.g., a woodcarving, a marble statue. Additive sculpture is that which is put together, e.g., a welded construction of steel beams, a mobile.

7. The six who participated in the symposium include Hans Haacke, Nell Jenney, Richard Long, Dennis Oppenheim, Robert Smithson, and Gunther Uecker. Jan Dibbets, David Medalla, and Robert Morris did not participate.

8. Mark Rosenthal, "Some Attitudes of Earth Art: From Competition to Adoration," *Art in the Land: A Critical Environmental Art*, edited by Alan Sonfist (New York: E. P. Dutton, 1983), pp. 60–71.

9. Ibid., p. 64.

10. Robert Smithson, quoted in Beardsley, *Probing the Land*, p. 81.

11. Diana Shaffer, "Nancy Holt: Spaces for Reflections or Projections," *Art in the Land: A Critical Anthology of Environmental Art*, edited by Alan Sonfist (New York: E. P. Dutton, 1983), p. 171.

12. Ibid.

13. Ted Castle, "Nancy Holt, Siteseer," *Art in America*, March 1982, p. 90.

14. Nancy Holt quoted in Shaffer, "Nancy Holt," p. 175.

15. Beardsley, *Earthworks and Beyond*, p. 63.

16. Nancy Holt quoted in Shaffer, "Nancy Holt," p. 171.

17. Lippard, *Overlay*, p. 106.

18. Castle, "Nancy Holt, Siteseer," p. 91.

19. Nancy Holt quoted in Beardsley, *Earthworks and Beyond*, p. 34.

20. Shaffer, "Nancy Holt," p. 177.

21. Eleanor Munro, "Art in the Desert," *New York Times*, December 7, 1986, p. 38.

22. Michael Heizer will not allow a photograph of "Complex One/City" to be included here. Letter from J. Mackiewicz (writing for M. Heizer) to M. Korp, July 12, 1995.

23. Rainer Crone, "Prime Objects of Art: Scale, Shape, Time," *Perspecta*, vol. 19, p. 17.

24. Elizabeth C. Baker, "Artworks on the Land," *Art in the Land: A Critical Anthology of Environmental Art*, edited by Alan Sonfist (New York: E. P. Dutton, 1983), p. 78. Robert Hughes gives the dimensions of "Complex One" as forty meters long, thirty-three meters wide, and seven meters high in *The Shock of the New: Art and the Century of Change* (London: British Broadcasting Corporation, 1980), p. 395.

25. Michael Heizer quoted in Crone, "Prime Objects of Art," p. 19: "Man will never create anything really large in relation to the world—only in relation to himself and his size. The most formidable objects that man has touched are the earth and the moon. The greatest scale he understands is the distance between them, and this is declaring nothing compared to what he suspects to exist."

26. Michael Heizer quoted in Crone, "Prime Objects of Art," p. 17.

27. Michael Heizer, "Earthworks," *Michael Heizer* (Essen: Museum Folkwang Essen, 1979), p. 13: "As the physical deteriorates, the abstract proliferates, exchanging points of view."

28. Hughes, *The Shock of the New*, p. 395.

29. Heizer, "Earthworks," p. 36.

30. Crone, "Prime Objects of Art," p. 17.

31. Baker, "Artworks on the Land," p. 77.

32. Ibid.

33. Jeffery Deitch, "The New Economics of Environmental Art," *Art in the Land: A Critical Anthology of Environmental Art* (New York: E. P. Dutton, 1983), p. 89.

34. Beardsley, *Earthworks and Beyond*, p. 62.

35. Lippard, *Overlay*, p. 130.

36. Beardsley, *Earthworks and Beyond*, p. 62.

37. All visits to "Lightning Field" must be scheduled through the Dia Art Foundation, 155 Mercer Street, New York, New York, USA 10012. Site visitors are taken in small groups by truck to the field and stay overnight in a rough cabin on site. The cost in 1989 was minimal, $65 per person. Visits are only permitted between mid-May and October because road conditions render the site inaccessible at other times of the year.

38. Carol Hall, "Environmental Artists: Sources and Directions," *Art in the Land: A Critical Anthology of Environmental Art*, edited by Alan Sonfist (New York: E. P. Dutton, 1983), p. 19.

39. Beardsley, *Probing the Earth*, p. 20.

40. Ibid.

41. Ibid., p. 19.

42. Munro, "Art in the Desert," pp. 9, 38.

43. Beardsley, *Probing the Earth*, p. 88: "While the water table is known to have cycles of rising and subsiding, the length of these cycles is unknown, so it is difficult to predict when *Spiral Jetty* will emerge again."

44. Beardsley, *Probing the Earth*, p. 27.

45. Lawrence Alloway, "Robert Smithson's Development," *Art in the Land: A Critical Anthology of Environmental Art* (New York: E. P. Dutton, 1983), p. 139.

46. Rosenthal, "Some Attitudes of Earth Art," pp. 64, 70–71.

47. Robert Smithson quoted in Beardsley, *Earthworks and Beyond*, p. 20.

48. Robert Smithson quoted in Beardsley, *Probing the Earth*, p. 86.

49. Hughes, *The Shock of the New*, p. 395.

50. Robert Smithson quoted in Lippard, *Overlay*, p. 77.

51. Beardsley, *Probing the Earth*, p. 25. In a series of roundtable discussions held in New York City from December 1968 to January 1969, and published as "Discussions with Heizer, Oppenheim, Smithson," *Avalanche*, Fall 1970, p. 67, Robert Smithson explained these ideas further when asked if there were "elements of destruction" in his work: "It's already destroyed. It's a slow process of destruction. The world is slowly destroying itself. The catastrophe comes suddenly, but slowly . . . You know one pebble moving one foot in two million years is enough action to keep me really excited. But some of us have to stimulate upheaval, step up the action. Sometimes we have to call on Bacchus. Excess. Madness. The End of the World. Mass Carnage. Falling Empires."

52. Beardsley, *Probing the Earth*, p. 28.

53. Smithson, "Discussions with Heizer, Oppenheim, Smithson," p. 67.

54. Alloway, "Robert Smithson's Development," p. 126.

55. *Alogical*: outside the bounds of that to which logic can apply; *alogism*: 1: any-

thing that is contrary or indifferent to logic: specifically, an irrational statement or piece of reasoning; 2: a view that denies thought a place in the valid and final apprehension of reality (*Webster's Third New International Dictionary*).

56. Beardsley, *Probing the Earth*, p. 85.

57. Donald B. Kuspit, "The Pascalian Spiral: Robert Smithson's Drunken Boat," *Arts Magazine*, October 1981, p. 82.

58. Charles Ross, interview notes, September 12, 1989. Ross states that his work is usually guided by dreams, a phenomenon that began in 1964: "I'd been working on some lattice-work sculpture. It was near the end of 1964, Thanksgiving weekend I think, when I dreamed the plan for a large prism. I didn't know that was what I'd dreamed actually. I thought it was some sort of another lattice. My initial reaction to the dream upon awakening was that I was not interested in building that thing. But the dream was insistent. The images from the dream were like gauze drawings and they stayed with me all day long. So I sat down about 4 p.m. and sketched it out. *Then* I saw what I had drawn was a prism. I ran out and bought the materials; however, not being sure of the plans I'd drawn, I went to see a mechanical engineer to find out how to build a prism. The advice he gave me was bad advice concerning the thickness of the prism. It blew up. So I swept the studio clean, threw everything out I had been working on to that date, went back to my notes from my dream—those notes were right—and I built the first prism that way. Since then, prisms have led me into everything."

59. Ibid.

60. "Star Axis" is funded in part by the New Mexico Arts Division, the Santa Fe Council for the Arts, and the National Endowment for the Arts. Contributors to "Star Axis" include the David W. Berman Foundation, the Frost Foundation; the William H. and Mattie Wattis Harris Foundation, and the New York Center for World Game Studies. The project has also received funding from the Museum of Modern Art, Contemporary Arts Council and from private individuals, including Virginia Dwan, Ted and Barbara Flicker, Ray Graham, Meg Heydt, and Dian Woodner. (Funding information supplied by Charles Ross, 1990.)

61. Charles Ross, personal communication, August 2, 1990.

62. Donald B. Kuspit, "Charles Ross: Light's Measure," *Art in the Land: An Anthology of Environmental Art*, edited by Alan Sonfist (New York: E. P. Dutton, 1983), p. 160.

63. Ross, interview notes, September 12, 1989.

64. Ibid.

65. Caliche is a hard white clayey rock found just inches below the surface throughout much of the southwestern desert. The rock is a traditional building material found at many archaic sites.

66. Ross, personal communication, August 2, 1990.

67. Ross, interview notes, September 12, 1989.

68. Ibid.

69. Ibid.

70. Beardsley, *Earthworks and Beyond*, p. 39.

71. Lippard, *Overlay*, p. 105.

72. Ross, interview notes, September 12, 1989.

73. Ibid.

74. According to Frank Waters, *Book of the Hopi* (New York: Penguin Books, 1977), pp. 103–4: the double spiral petroglyph, with its varying number of turns found throughout the Southwest, records the divers migrations of the first peoples, some of whom had completed more of their requisite sunwise journeys than others, according to the ancient

Hopi traditions. The double spiral, of course, is related to the labyrinth and sometimes represented as one—one way in; one way out.

75. Munro, "Art in the Desert," p. 38.

76. On March 24, 1989, I talked with James Turrell by telephone. I had called the Skystone Foundation offices in Flagstaff to finalize the arrangements for my visit to the "Roden Crater" project site the following Monday, March 27, 1989 with Giovanni di Panza, a member of the staff. Turrell abruptly canceled my permission to visit the site. Then just as abruptly when I explained my purpose in being there Turrell relented. My site visit was limited to one short afternoon. The artist explained: "You are the very last person Giovanni is going to take out to the site; the site is supposed to be closed to visitors." Turrell would not allow me to interview him. Nevertheless, he did answer my impromptu questions candidly and completely during our telephone conversation. I scratched notes as we talked and filled in my jottings immediately afterwards. The quotes attributed to him by me from that conversation are, I believe, accurate.

77. The name "Roden Crater" is not a misspelled homage to the sculptor Auguste Rodin. The crater was named after a local pioneer family. Dorothy A. House, in "Recent Dwellers in the Cinder Hills," *Roden Crater* (Flagstaff, Arizona: Museum of Northern Arizona, 1988), p. 23, comments further: "Ironically, although the Roden cattle operation dominated the country around it. Roden Crater itself never belonged to the family. It was part of a government land grant to the A&P Railroad (later the Santa Fe). They sold it to the Chambers family of Flagstaff, who ran cattle on its slopes until James Turrell convinced them Roden Crater served a loftier purpose."

78. Giovanni di Panza, personal communication, March 27, 1989.

79. James Turrell, "Roden Crater Project," unpublished prospectus, 1989.

80. Dorothy A. House, "A Modern Skywatcher," *Roden Crater* (Flagstaff, Arizona: Museum of Northern Arizona, 1988), p. 26: "He [Turrell] is reshaping the bowl at the summit to form a flatter, more perfect parabola; carving several small chambers, or spaces, out of the surface; boring at least three tunnels from the bowl through to the outer flanks; and constructing a series of walkways to connect the spaces and offer views of the surrounding panorama."

81. Turrell, personal communication, March 24, 1989. James Turrell has been working closely with E. C. Krupp, Director of the Griffith Observatory and Richard Walker of the U.S. Naval Observatory, Flagstaff, for a number of years on the mathematical calculations and alignments that would be possible to construct in a naked-eye observatory.

82. Fred Hapgood, "Roden's Eye," *Atlantic Monthly,* August 1987, p. 52.

83. James Turrell quoted in Janet Saad-Cook, "Touching the Sky: Artworks Using Natural Phenomena, Earth, Sky and Connections to Astronomy," *Leonardo,* vol. 21, nr. 2, p. 130.

84. Dorothy A. House, "Born of Fire," *Roden Crater* (Flagstaff, Arizona: Museum of Northern Arizona, 1988), p. 11. The Roden Crater is dated to the Tappan Age 600,000–175,000 years ago. According to Giovanni di Panza, writing as Director of Development, Skystone Foundation, in a fund-raising letter, March 28, 1989: "Potassium-Argon (K-Ar) radiometric dating of the volcanics has determined that the eruption of the Roden Crater occured [sic] 358,000 years ago."

85. Dorothy A. House, "Prehistoric Man in the Cinder Hills," *Roden Crater* (Flagstaff, Arizona: Museum of Northern Arizona, 1988), p. 20.

86. Ibid. The eagles are an integral part of the Hopi ceremonial year. Young eagles are captured in the winter months and sacrificed—by being smothered in cornmeal—in late July. In the intervening months they have kept watch over the Hopi. Now their

spirits fly away to the Chiefs of the Four Directions to tell them that the Hopi have been devout and have done all that they should do and are prayerful and hopeful that the rains will come for their cornfields. For more information, see Jake Page, "Hyeouma," *Native Peoples*, Summer 1990, pp. 30–36.

87. House, "Prehistoric Man in the Cinder Hills," p. 15.

88. James Turrell, personal communication, March 24, 1989. In response to my blunt question concerning his relationship with the native people of the area, the artist said his work has been blessed by Hopi elders; moreover, I should not be surprised if Gene Sesaquapti, a Hopi elder from nearby Hopiland should appear on the site when I was there because he sometimes did when there were visitors. Sesaquapti, the artist assured me, would be pleased to tell me about the Sinaqua and Anasazi ruins on the crater slope. According to Turrell, the area has not been much studied because "archaeologists are always looking for *treasure*, they've overlooked the fact that the site itself is the treasure." The ancient ruins themselves, at first glance, when I found them, appear to be little more than gentle rubble.

89. James Turrell quoted in Hapgood, "Roden's Eye," p. 52.

90. Giovanni di Panza, personal communication, March 27, 1989.

91. Hapgood, "Roden's Eye," p. 52. The purchase of 1,100 acres was concluded in 1977. Roden Crater was sold to the Dia Art Foundation for $64,000. The property has since then been transferred to the Skystone Foundation, a nonprofit organization established by Turrell to finance the completion of the crater project. Additional funding has come from the National Endowment for the Arts, the MacArthur Foundation, the Museum of Northern Arizona, and many private contributions. Giovanni di Panza, Turrell's chief fund-raiser, is the son of Count Giuseppe di Panza di Biumo of Italy, a long-time friend and patron of Turrell's. Giovanni di Panza, like many of Turrell's staffers on the project, is a volunteer.

92. Hapgood, "Roden's Eye," p. 51.

93. Hapgood, "Roden's Eye," p. 49: "[T]he human retina refuses to believe in homogeneous fields. When exposed to one, it tolerates the phenomenon for a few moments and then begins casting about for other possibilities. Different retinas produce different theories. The most common report was of 'swimming in a mist of light which becomes more condensed at an indefinite distance.' . . . There were reports of memory activation, time distortion, and other hallucinations . . . Sometimes the objects seem to vanish, leaving subject uncertain as to whether their eyes were even open. Aftereffects included extreme fatigue, great lightness of body, dizziness, and impaired motor coordination, sense of balance, and time perception. Sometimes subjects appeared intoxicated."

94. For example, articles written by Jeff Kelley, "Light Years," *Art Forum*, November 1985, pp. 73–75, and Craig Adcock, "Anticipating 19,084: James Turrell's *Roden Crater Project*," *Arts Magazine*, May 1984, pp. 76–85, were both concerned with the perceptual problems of depicting "celestial vaulting" and the divers ways in which our perceptions of the sky could be configured. Both articles stress the performance art qualities of Turrell's oeuvre, its effect as curiosity and novelty, rather than why these effects should matter or what they might explain. Adcock's essay, however, does devote attention to what he terms the "iconography of the volcano." Adcock twins the volcano with meteoric craters and presents both as ancient symbols of the chaos of life around us and the importance of the solace of order to be found in the skies above. Ancient peoples, however, did not usually split the difference in this way. Many ancient cosmogonic story cycles recognize naturally occurring places of order on the earth (for example, the seasonal migrations of animals worldwide) and naturally occurring moments of disorder

in the heavens (eclipses, for example) as complementary. A balance is what is sought not an obliteration.

95. Turrell, personal communication, March 24, 1989.

96. James Turrell quoted in Saad-Cook, "Touching the Sky," pp. 130–31.

97. Inside the crater's rim, the visitor is presented with a visionary sense of intense quietude. It is hard to leave. For example, Hapgood in "Roden's Eye," p. 52, described his reaction to seeing the sky from the bottom of the crater's bowl as he lay on his back in these words: "The walls of the crater had drawn into the sky, and the sky had descended to lie across them. The illusion of being sealed inside was so strong that my brain felt compelled to manufacture the sound, faint but unmistakable, of metal sliding over metal." John Russell in "James Turrell, *New York Times*, 1986," *Reading Russell: Essays 1941–1988 on Ideas, Literature, Art, Theater, Music, Places, and Persons* (New York: Harry N. Abrams, Inc., l989), p. 125, described his experience of lying on his back in the crater's bowl in almost similar terms: "What happens then is that we experience the universe as a perfect sphere, with the rim of the crater—more than 1,000 feet in diameter—as its terrestrial frontier. Above that rim, the sky hovers over us, boundless and immaterial. To an extent not paralleled in other places, all that is contingent or superfluous is abolished. As far as is possible on earth, movements and noise do not exist." When I visited the site, March 27, 1989, and lay down on my back inside the crater's rim, one word floated, quite actually floated, into my mind—"birthing."

98. Russell, "James Turrell, *The New York Times*, 1986," p. 124.

99. Mark Stevens, "Turrell's 'Celestial Vault,'" *Newsweek*, February 10, 1986, p. 71.

100. Adcock, "Anticipating 19,084," p. 84.

101. Beardsley, *Earthworks and Beyond*, p. 39.

Chapter 6: Seeing the Earth

1. John Smith, *Sucking-Stones* (Dunvegan, Ontario: Quadrant Editions, 1982).

2. Rainer Maria Rilke, *Die Sonnette an Orpheus*, I, 16.

3. John Lowell Bean, "Menil (Moon): Symbolic Representation of Cahuilla Women," *Earth and Sky: Visions of the Cosmos in Native American Folklore*, edited by Ray A. Williamson, Claire R. Farrer (Albuquerque, New Mexico: University of New Mexico Press, 1992), p. 162–83.

4. Frederick Kiesler, *Inside the Endless House, Art, People, and Architecture: A Journal* (New York: Simon and Schuster, 1966), p. 119.

5. On the other hand, perhaps the space exploration program is no break in Western history. Robert Brockway, *Professor Emeritus* of Brandon University, Manitoba, drew my attention to the metaphorical implications implicit in the municipal twinning of Cape Canaveral, Florida, home of the American space program, with Sagres, Portugal. In the 15th century Henry the Navigator gathered together at the port of Sagres the Western world's experts in cartography, seamanship, and shipbuilding, charging them with the discovery of the world's limits. Brockway, personal communication, May 1990.

6. Daniel Noel, *Approaching Earth: A Search for the Mythic Significance of the Space Age* (Amity: New York: Amity House, 1986), p. vi.

7. World Heritage Newsletter (World Heritage Centre, UNESCO, Paris) February 1993 nr. 1—electronic mail transmission via ANTHRO-L@UBVM.bitnet, May 19, 1993.

8. Ibid.

9. Joseph Kastner, "My Empty Lot: The Natural History of an Urban Patch" *New York Times Magazine* October 16, 1993, pp. 22–25, 41–44.

10. Ibid., p. 43.

11. Yi-Fu Tuan, "Geo-Piety: A Theme in Man's Attachment to Nature and to Place,"

in *Geographies of the Mind: Essays in Historical Geography in Honor of John Kirkland Wright*, edited by David Lowenthal and Martyn J. Bowden (New York: Oxford University Press, 1976), pp. 11–39.

12. John Dixon, *Art and the Theological Imagination* (New York: Seabury Press, 1978), pp. 23–24: ". . . the inability of the non-art people to see that art deals with fundamental issues. It is considered an enrichment of the human life, an extension of the forms of feeling, a symptom of movements of the mind (and, therefore, a diagnostic instrument), a reflection or illustration of ideas. It is not often considered a fundamental thinking about fundamental ideas."

13. See for example, Patricia Johanson's monograph, *Art and Survival: Creative Solutions to Environmental Problems* (North Vancouver, B.C.: Galerie Publications, 1992). This interconnection is also brought out in several studies of Frederick Law Olmsted's contributions to landscape architecture. See, for example, Julius G. Y. Fabos, Gordon T. Milde, and V. Michael Weinmayr, *Frederick Law Olmsted, Jr.: Founder of Landscape Architecture in America* (Boston: University of Massachusetts Press, 1968) and John Emerson Todd, *Frederick Law Olmsted* (Boston: Twayne Publishers, 1982). Recently, the Museum of Modern Art, New York City, sponsored an exhibition of the Brazilian and French garden designs of artist Roberto Burle Marx. The curator went to some pains to discount any possible "theological or mystical narrative recast as a modern garden" despite what the artist might say: William Howard Adams, *Roberto Burle Marx: The Unnatural Art of the Garden* (New York: Museum of Modern Art, 1991), p. 36.

14. Kiesler, *Inside the Endless House*, p. 404: Writing on February 14, 1961, Kiesler, noted: "The term 'outer space' is wrong, misleading. There is no outer space as far as the universe is concerned—it is all part and parcel of the same composition. To speak of outer space is to return the aspect of the cosmos to the pygmy perspective of man."

15. Charles Ross, interview notes, September 12, 1989.

16. Kiesler, ibid., p. 135: "Man's greatest invention has been constant since the beginning of time: the idea of immortality. However, no man can evolve an idea which isn't concocted by the forces of the universe itself and is put into us as computers of human visions. Because we are made of the same stuff the cosmos is made of."

17. Noel, ibid., p. 193.

18. Ibid.

19. Tal Streeter, interview notes, September 17, 24, 1989. Since the death of seven in the 1986 Challenger space shuttle explosion—including one nonprofessional "astronaut," an elementary school teacher—these initiatives have been halted. NASA now solicits projects and sponsorships from business and industry rather than the educational and cultural communities.

20. Marie-Françoise Gúedon, Ph.D., University of Ottawa, Ottawa, Canada, personal communication, 1989.

21. Peter Hutchinson, interview notes, July 27, 1989.

22. Jennifer Dickson, interview notes, July 21, 1993: "I find in my personal, day-by-day life a continual bleeding. All I have to do is look out my studio window and the irony of this is increasingly asserting itself. I am standing *inside* the walls of my studio painting pictures of European gardens—landscapes of profound beauty with all sorts of levels of meaning, of symbolism—and I am looking *out of* the window and seeing every form of degradation it is possible to see."

23. CNN World News, August 9, 1993.

24. Timothy Egan, "The (Bruised) Emperor of the Outdoors: With Little Help from his Boss, Bruce Babbitt Challenges the Old Politics That Have Shaped the New West," *New York Times Magazine*, August 1, 1993, pp. 21–23; 49–52.

25. Ibid., p. 50. Edward Abbey—naturalist, writer, and mystic—is one of the important influences upon Babbitt.

26. Frank J. Popper and Deborah E. Popper, "The Future of the Great Plains," *Forum for Applied Research and Public Policy*, to be published, 1994 (draft paper in typescript, p. 5).

27. Popper and Popper, ibid., p. 7: "In all Plains states most Plains counties lost population during the 1980s—for instance, 50 of Nebraska's 52 Plains counties, 38 of North Dakota's 41 and 22 of Oklahoma's 23."

28. Anne Matthews "The Poppers and the Plains" *New York Times Magazine*, June 24, 1990, pp. 24–26, 41, 48–49, 53.

29. Jon Margolis, "Them's Fightin' Words," *Chicago Tribune*, January 7, 1993, section 5, p. 1.

30. Matthews, ibid., p. 25.

31. "Periscope," *Newsweek*, May 6, 1991, p. 21: Alexander Alian: "From the earliest traces of primate fossils some 70 million years ago, no one, but no one, has ever raised the finger of defiance to the celestial organization. We have been like blind slaves obediently being rotated without our consent."

32. Andrew Nikiforuk, "Where the Buffalo Roam: Was the Settling of the Great Plains a Mistake That Is Now Being Corrected," *Harrowsmith Country Life*, July/August, 1993, p. 28.

33. The information in this paragraph is taken from two related articles by Andrew Nikiforuk, "Wild about Buffalo: The New West Might Look as Untamed as the Old," *Harrowsmith*, December 1992, pp. 46–52; "Where the Buffalo Roam: Was the Settling of the Great Plains a Mistake That Is Now Being Corrected?," *Harrowsmith Country Life*, July/August 1993, pp. 22–26; and Clifford D. May, "The Buffalo Returns: This Time as Dinner." *New York Times Magazine*, September 26, 1993, pp. 30–34.

34. Nikiforuk, "Wild about Buffalo," p. 49.

35. Popper and Popper, ibid., pp. 11–12.

36. Nikiforuk, "Where the Buffalo Roam," p. 27.

37. Professor Frank J. Popper, Department of Urban Studies, Rutgers University, personal communication, July 22, 1993: "There is a very distinct art-and-religion side to our work and the reaction to it. Last night, for example, I read a long piece on Sioux buffalo theology by a University of Colorado Native American scholar that argued the Buffalo Commons is, from the Lakota perspective, a theological concept. Fascinating stuff."

38. John G. Neihardt, *Black Elk Speaks*, (Lincoln: University of Nebraska Press, 1979, 1932), p. 49.

Bibliography

Adams, William Howard. *Roberto Burle Marx: The Unnatural Art of the Garden*. New York: Museum of Modern Art, 1991.

Adcock, Craig. "Anticipating 19,084: James Turrell's *Roden Crater Project*," *Arts Magazine*, May 1984. pp. 76—85.

———. "The Big Bad: A Critical Comparison of Mount Rushmore and Modern Earthworks," *Arts Magazine*, April 1983, pp. 104—7.

Albanese, Catherine L. *Nature Religion in America from the Algonkian Indians to the New Age*. Chicago: University of Chicago Press, 1990.

Albers, Patricia and Jeanne Kay. "Sharing the Land: A Study in American Indian Territoriality." In *A Cultural Geography of North American Indians*, eds. Thomas E. Ross and Tyrel G. Moore. Boulder, Colorado: Westview Press, 1987. pp. 47—92.

Allen, Paula Gunn. *The Sacred Hoop*. Boston: Beacon Press, 1986.

Alloway, Lawrence. "Robert Smithson's Development." In *Art in the Land: A Critical Anthology of Environmental Art*, ed. Alan Sonfist. New York: E. P. Dutton, 1983. pp. 125—141.

Amaya, Mario. "Land Reform: New Monuments by Michael Heizer," *Studio International*, vol. 198, nr. 1009 (1985). pp. 18—22.

André, Carl. *Carl André*. The Hague: Gemeentemuseum, 1969.

Assunto, Rosario. "Demythization: The End of Nature and the Death of Art (from a Schellingian perspective)," *Flash Art*, issue 96/97 (March—April 1980). pp. 11—14.

Austin, M. R. "A Coloured State of Grace," *British Journal of Aesthetics* vol. 19, nr. 4 (Fall 1979). pp. 352—60.

Aveni, Anthony F. *Archaeoastronomy in Pre-columbian America*. Austin: University of Texas, 1975.

———. *Native American Astronomy*. Austin: University of Texas, 1975.

———. "The Nazca Lines: Patterns in the Desert," *Archaeology*, July//August 1986. pp. 32—39.

Baker, Elizabeth C. "Artworks on the Land." In *Art in the Land: A Critical Anthology*, ed. Alan Sonfist. New York: E. P. Dutton, 1983. pp. 73—84.

Ballas, Donald J. "Historical Geography and American Indian Developments." In *A Cultural Geography of North American Indians*, eds. Thomas E. Ross and Tyrel G. Moore. Boulder, Colorado: Westview Press, 1987. pp. 15—31.

Barbar, John. "Oriental Enigma: Controversial Evidence Suggests Asian Sailors Explored the New World Centuries before the First Europeans," *Equinox*, July/August 1990. pp. 83—95.

Barnouw, Victor. "Language and Cognition." In *An Introduction to Anthropology: Ethnology*. Homewood, Illinois: Dorsey Press, 1971. pp. 65—75.

Barrie, David. "Religion, Science, and Art," *Apollo*, vol. 79, nr. 327 (May 1989). pp. 313—16.

Bartlett, John, ed. *Bartlett's Familiar Quotations*. Boston: Little, Brown & Company, 1982.

Bartow, Rick. Interview, by telephone, South Beach, Oregon, July 24, 1989.

Bean, Lowell John. "Menil (Moon), Symbolic Representation of Cahuilla Woman," *Earth and Sky: Visions of the Cosmos in Native American Folklore*, ed. by Ray A. Williamson and Clair R. Farrer. Albuquerque: University of New Mexico Press, 1992.

Beardsley, John. *Earthworks and Beyond*. New York: Abbeville Press, 1989.

———. *Probing the Earth: Contemporary Land Projects*. Washington: Smithsonian Institution Press, 1977.

———. "Traditional Aspects of New Land Art," *Art Journal*, Fall 1982, pp. 226—32.

Benson, Timothy O. "Mysticism, Materialism, and the Machine in Berlin Dada," *Art Journal*, Spring 1987. pp. 46—55.

Berry, Thomas, *The Dream of the Earth*. San Francisco: Sierra Club Books, 1988.

———. "The Earth: A New Context for Religious Unity." In *Thomas Berry and the New Cosmology*, eds. Anne Lonergan and Caroline Richards. Mystic, Connecticut: Twenty-third Publications, 1987. pp. 26—40.

———. "Economics: Its Effects on the Life Systems of the World." In *Thomas Berry and the New Cosmology*, eds. Anne Lonergan and Caroline Richards. Mystic, Connecticut: Twenty-third Publications, 1987. pp. 5-26.

———. "Our Future on Earth: Where Do We Go from Here?" In *Thomas Berry and the New Cosmology*, eds. Anne Lonergan and Caroline Richards. Mystic, Connecticut: Twenty-third Publications, 1987. pp. 103—6.

———. "Twelve Principles: For understanding the Universe and the Role of the Human in the Universe Process." In *Thomas Berry and the New Cosmology*, eds. Anne Lonergan and Caroline Richards. Mystic, Connecticut: Twenty-third Publications, 1987. pp. 107—8.

Bletter, Rosemarie Haag. "Global Earthworks," *Art Journal*, Fall 1982. pp. 222—25.

Boas, Franz. *Primitive Art* (1927). New York: Dover Publications, 1955.

Bolle, Kees W. "Animism and Animatism." *Encyclopedia of Religion*. Edited by Mircea Eliade. New York: Macmillan, 1987.

———. "Speaking of a Place." In *Myths and Symbols: Studies in Honor of Mircea Eliade*, ed. Joseph M. Kitagawa and Charles H. Long. Chicago: University of Chicago Press, 1969. pp. 127—39.

Brennan, Margaret. "Patriarchy: The Root of Alienation from the Earth?" In *Thomas Berry and the New Cosmology*, eds. Anne Lonergan and Caroline Richards. Mystic, Connecticut: Twenty-third Publications, 1987. pp. 57—63.

Brenson, Michael. "When Nature Became God, Art Changed," *New York Times*, March 11, 1990. sec. H, pp. 39, 42.

———. "Sculpture for Troubled Places," *New York Times*, October 15, 1989. sec. 2, pp. 1, 42.

Breuil, Abbe Henri. "The Palaeolithic Age." In *Larousse Encyclopedia of Prehistoric and Ancient Art*, ed. Rene Huyghe. New York: Prometheus Press, 1962. pp. 30—39.

Bridges, Marilyn. "High Overview, Newark, Ohio, 1982," *Aperture*, issue 98 (Spring 1985). unpaged.

———. *Markings: Aerial Views of Sacred Landscapes.* New York: Aperture Foundation, 1986.

———. "Serpent Mound, Adams County, Ohio, 1982," *Aperture*, issue 98 (Spring 1985). unpaged.

Brockway, Robert. Personal communication, May 1990.

Brown, Dee. *Bury my Heart at Wounded Knee: An Indian History of the American West.* New York: Holt, Rinehart & Winston, 1970.

Brown, Joseph Epes. "The Question of 'Mysticism' within Native American Traditions." In *Understanding Mysticism*, ed. Richard Woods. Garden City, New York: Image Books, 1980. pp. 261—69.

———. *The Spiritual Legacy of the American Indian.* New York: Crossroad, 1987.

Brown, Karen McCarthy. "The Power to Heal: Reflections on Women, Religion, and Medicine." In *Shaping New Vision: Gender and Values in American Culture*, eds. Clarissa W. Atkinson, Constance H. Buchanen, and Margaret R. Miles, Ann Arbor, Michigan: UMI Research Press, 1987. pp. 123—41.

Brown, M. A. "Grave Orientation: A Further View," *Archaeological Journal*, issue 140 (1983). pp. 322—28.

Campbell, Joseph. *Historical Atlas of World Mythology.* Vol. 1: *The Way of the Animal Powers.* Part 1: *Mythologies of the Primitive Hunters and Gatherers.* Part 2: *Mythologies of the Great Hunt.* New York: Harper & Row, 1989.

———. *Masks of God: Primitive Mythology.* New York: Penguin Books, 1984.

Cardinal-Schubert, Joanne. "In the Red: Safeguarding the Legacy of Canada's First Nations," *Artscraft*, vol. 2, nr. 1 (Spring 1990). pp. 4-21.

Castle, Ted. "Nancy Holt, Siteseer," *Art in America*, March 1982. pp. 84–91.

Chafe, Wallace L. "Siouan, Iroquoian, and Caddoan." In *Native Languages of the Americas*, vol. 1, ed. Thomas A. Sebeok. New York: Plenum Press, 1976. pp. 527–72.

Chafee, Katherine Smith. "Charles Ross," *Artspace*, Fall 1981. pp. 24–27.

Chatwin, Bruce. *Songlines.* New York: Viking Penguin, 1987.

Chippendale, Christopher. "Stonehenge Astronomy: Anatomy of a Modern Myth," *Archaeology*, January/February 1986. pp. 48–52.

Clark, Kenneth. *Landscape into Art* (1949). Boston: Beacon Press, 1961.

Clay, Grady. "King County's Earthworks Symposium Breaking New Ground with Land Reclamation as Sculpture," *The Arts (Earthworks): Newsletter of the King County Arts Commission*, vol. 8, nr. 7 (July 1979). pp. 1–6.

Clifford, Derek Plint. "Garden and Landscape Design," *Encyclopaedia Britannica*, 15th edition. Chicago: Encyclopaedia Britannica, Inc., 1984. Macropaedia, vol. VII, pp. 884–901.

CNN World News, August 9, 1993.

Coffin, David R. *The Villa in the Life of Renaissance Rome.* Princeton: Princeton University Press, 1979.

Corbitt, David Leroy, ed. *Explorations, Descriptions, and Attempted Settlements of Carolina, 1584–1590.* Raleigh, North Carolina: State Department of Archives and History, 1948.

Cotterell, Arthur. *A Dictionary of World Mythology.* Suffolk: Oxford University Press, 1991.

Craik, Brian. "The Animate in Cree Languages and Ideology." In *Papers of the 14th Algonquian Conference*, ed. William Cowan. Ottawa: Carleton University Press, 1982. pp. 29–35.

Critchlow, Keith and Graham Challifour, eds. *Earth Mysteries: A Study in Patterns.* Hammersmith, England: Research into Lost Knowledge Organization (RILKO), 1977.

Crone, Rainer. "Prime Objects of Art: Scale, Shape, Time," *Perspecta*, issue 19. pp. 14-35.

Crum, Robert. "Home on the Range," *Rutgers Magazine*, vol. 71, nr. 4, pp. 24—29.

Dalton, Deborah W. "Still Life in Quarry," *Landscape Architecture*, May/June 1985. pp. 66—69.

Von Daniken, Erich. *Chariots of the Gods? Unsolved Mysteries of the Past*. London: Souvenir Press, 1969.

David, Jay, ed. *The American Indian: The First Victim*. New York: William Morrow, 1972.

Davidson Michael. "The Spiritual Geometry of Ottawa." Ottawa, 1987. Unpublished manuscript.

Davies, Peter and Tony Knipe, eds. *A Sense of Place: Sculpture in the Landscape*. Tyne and Wear, England: Ceolfrith Press, 1984.

Deising, Frida. Interview, by telephone, Terrace, British Columbia, July 13, 1989.

Deitch, Jeffrey. "The New Economics of Environmental Art." In *Art in the Land: A Critical Anthology of Environmental Art*, ed. Alan Sonfist. New York: E. P. Dutton, 1983. pp. 85—91.

Dickson, Jennifer. "The Evolution of the Italian Garden," two illustrated lectures, National Library of Canada, April 1, 14, 1993.

———. "The Garden of Mystery" (artist's statement), 1992.

———. "Grace and Favour: Architecture and Gardens in the Old and New World" five illustrated lectures, Ottawa Art Gallery, October 19—November 16 , 1993.

———. *The Hospital for Wounded Angels*. Erin, Ontario: The Porcupine's Quill, 1987.

———. Interviews, in person, Ottawa, July 5, 1989; July 21, July 22, September 7, 1993.

———. "Through a Glass Darkly" (artist's statement), Arts Centre exhibition, November 8—December 6, University of Sussex, 1967.

Dillenberger, John. "Visual Arts and Religion: Modern and Contemporary Contours," *Journal of the American Academy of Religion*, vol. 56, nr. (Summer 1988) pp. 199—212.

Dillistone, F. W. *The Power of Symbols in Religion and Culture*. New York: Crossroad, 1986.

"Discussions with Heizer, Oppenheim, Smithson," *Avalanche*, Fall 1970. pp. 48—70.

Dissanayake, Ellen. "Aesthetic Experience and Human Evolution," *Journal of Aesthetics and Art Criticism*, Winter 1982. pp. 145—55.

Dixon, John W. *Art and the Theological Imagination*. New York: Seabury Press, 1978.

———. "Towards an Aesthetic of Early Earth Art," *Art Journal*, Fall 1982. pp. 195—99.

Dotson, Esther Gordon. "Shapes of Earth and Time in European Gardens," *Art Journal*, Fall 1982. pp. 210—16.

Driver, Harold E. *Indians of North America*. Chicago: University of Chicago Press, 1969.

Dwan, Virginia. "Reflections on Robert Smithson," *Art Journal*, Fall 1982. p. 232.

Dwyer, Gary. "Mea Culpa, My Fault: A Report on an Earthwork in Progress," *Leonardo*, vol. 19, nr. 4 (1986). pp. 285—87.

———. "The Power under Our Feet: Mea Culpa (My Fault): A Work in Progress," *Landscape Architecture*, May/June 1986. pp. 65—68. (Response: July/August 1986, p. 9)

Dyment, Margaret. Personal communication, Ottawa, August 9, 1990.

Eaton, Linda B. "Nora Naranjo-Morse: Santa Clara Sculptor." *A Separate Vision*. Flagstaff, Arizona: Museum of Northern Arizona, *Plateau*, vol. 60, nr. 1, 1989.

Eaton, Ruth. "Earth Architecture: Building in Mud," *Studio International*, vol. 196, nr. 999 (April/May 1983). pp. 44—48.

Egan, Timothy. "As Easterners Try to Save West, Westerners Blanch," *New York Times*, August 29, 1993, p. 1, 24.

———. "The (Bruised) Emperor of the Outdoors: With Little Help from His Boss, Bruce Babbitt Challenges the Old Politics That Have Shaped the New West," *New York Times Magazine*, August 1, 1993. pp. 21—23; 49—52.

Eliade, Mircea. "Brancusi and Mythology (1967)." In *Symbolism, the Sacred, and the Arts*, ed. Diane Apostolos-Cappadona. New York: Crossroad, 1986. pp. 93—102.

———. "Cultural Fashions and the History of Religions," *Occultism, Witchcraft, and Cultural Fashions*. Chicago: University of Chicago Press, 1976. pp. 1—17.

———. "A Dialogue with Marc Chagall (1963)." In *Symbolism, the Sacred, and the Arts*, ed. Diane Apostolos-Cappodona. New York: Crossroad, 1986. pp. 86—92.

———. "Divinities: Art and the Divine (1961)." In *Symbolism, the Sacred, and the Arts*, ed. Diane Apostolos-Cappodona. New York: Crossroad, 1986. pp. 55—63.

———. "Mythologies of Death," *Occultism, Witchcraft, and Cultural Fashions*. Chicago: University of Chicago Press, 1976. pp. 32—46.

———. *Myths, Dreams, and Mysteries: The Encounter between Contemporary Faiths and Archaic Realities*. New York: Harper Torchbooks, 1960.

———. "The Occult and the Modern World," *Occultism, Witchcraft, and Cultural Fashions*. Chicago: University of Chicago Press, 1976. pp. 47—68.

———. *Patterns in Comparative Religion*. New York: New American Library, 1958.

———. "The Sacred and the Modern Artist (1964)." In *Symbolism, the Sacred, and the Arts*, ed. Diane Apostolos-Cappodona. New York: Crossroad, 1986. pp. 81—85.

———. *The Sacred and the Profane: The Nature of Religion*. San Diego: Harcourt Brace Jovanovich, 1959.

———. "Sacred Architecture and Symbolism (1978)." In *Symbolism, the Sacred, and the Arts*, ed. Diane Apostolos-Cappodona. New York: Crossroad, 1986. pp. 105—29.

———. "The World, the City, the House," *Occultism, Witchcraft, and Cultural Fashions*. Chicago: University of Chicago Press, 1976.

———, and Laurence E. Sullivan. "Hierophany." In *Encyclopedia of Religion*, ed. Mircea Eliade. Chicago: University of Chicago Press, 1987, vol. 6, pp. 313—17.

Eliades, David K. "Two Worlds Collide: The European Advance into North America." In *A Cultural Geography of North American Indians*, eds. Thomas E. Ross and Tyrel G. Moore. Boulder, Colorado: Westview Press, 1987. pp. 33–44.

Evans, Karen. "Walking through Rainbows: A New Trip at the San Francisco Airport," *Image*, May 10, 1987. p. 29.

Fabo, Andy. Interview, in person, Ottawa, June 17, 1989.

Fabos, Julius G. Y., Gordon T. Milde and V. Michael Weinmayr. *Frederick Law Olmsted, Jr.: Founder of Landscape Architecture in America*. Boston: University of Massachusetts Press, 1968.

Farb, Peter. *Man's Rise to Civilization as Shown by the Indians of North America from Primeval Times to the Coming of the Industrial State*. New York: E. P. Dutton & Co., 1968.

Farris, James. "Redemption: Fundamental to the Story." In *Thomas Berry and the New Cosmology*, eds. Anne Lonergan and Caroline Richards. Mystic, Connecticut: Twenty-third Publications, 1987. pp. 65—71.

Faulstich, Paul. "Pictures of the Dreaming: Aboriginal Rock Art of Australia," *Archaeology*, July/August 1986. pp. 18—25.

Fedorick. Joy Asham. "Fencepost Sitting and How I Fell off to One Side," *Artscraft*, vol. 2, nr. 3 (Fall 1990). pp. 9—14.

Feest, Christian F. "From North America." In *Primitivism in 20th Century Art: Affinity of the Tribal and the Modern*, ed. William Rubin. New York: Museum of Modern Art, 1984. pp. 84—97.

Fell, Barry. *America B. C.: Ancient Settlers in the New World*. London: Wildwood House, 1976.

———. *Saga America*. New York: Times Books, 1980.

Fleming, John; Hugh Honour and Nikolaus Pevsner. *The Penguin Dictionary of Architecture*. Harmondsworth, Middlesex: Penguin Books, 1966.

Folsom, Franklin and Mary Ellen Folsom. *America's Ancient Treasures: A Guide to Archaeological Sites and Museums in the United States and Canada*. Albuquerque: University of New Mexico Press, 1983.

Frank, W. J. "Nuclear Weapons," *Encyclopaedia Britannica*, 15th edition. Chicago: Encyclopaedia Britannica, 1984. Macropaedia, vol. 13, pp. 325—26.

Frankfort, Henri. *Before Philosophy*. New York: Penguin Books, 1974.

Freed, Stanley A. "Dwelling Places," *Natural History*, July 1989. pp. 56—59.

Fry, Edward. *Robert Morris/Projects*. Philadelphia: Institute of Contemporary Art, 1974.

Fuller, Peter. "Carl André," *Art Monthly*, issue 16/17 (1978). pp. 5—11.

Gablik, Suzi. "Making Art as if the World Mattered," *Utne Reader*, issue 34 (July/August 1989). pp. 71—76.

Gadon, Elinor W. *The Once and Future Goddess: A Symbol for Our Time*. San Francisco: Harper & Row, 1989.

Gardner, William. "The Palaeoindians of the Shenandoah Valley, Virginia," *Archaeology*, May/June 1986. pp. 28—34.

Gedo, Mary Matthews. "The *Grand Jatte* as the Icon of a New Religion: A Psycho-Iconographic Interpretation," *Art Institute of Chicago Museum Studies*, vol. 14, nr. 2 (1989). pp. 223—37.

"Geographica," *National Geographic Magazine*, vol. 177, nr. 6 (June 1990), unpaged.

Gibson, Jon L. *Poverty Point: A Culture of the Lower Mississippi Valley*. Baton Rouge, Louisiana: Department of Culture, Recreation and Tourism, Louisiana Archaeological Survey and Antiquities Commission, Anthropological Study nr. 7, 1983.

Gilbert, Michelle V. "Art: The primitive View," *British Journal of Aesthetics*, vol. 22, nr. 2 (Spring 1982). pp. 167—71.

Gilbert-Rolfe, Jeremy. "Sculpture as Everything Else, Twenty Years or So of the Question of Landscape," *Arts Magazine*, January 1988. pp. 71—75.

Gill, Brendan. "A Sculptor's Obsession in Upstate New York," *Architectural Digest*, issue 46 (March 1989). pp. 46—54.

Gill, Sam D. *Mother Earth: An American Story*. Chicago: University of Chicago Press, 1987.

———. *Native American Religions: An Introduction*. Belmont, California: Wadsworth Publishing Company, 1982.

———. *Native American Religious Action: A Performance Approach to Religion*. Columbia, South Carolina; University of South Carolina Press, 1987.

Gillis, Kathy. Personal communication, Ottawa, August 9, 1993.

Gimbutas, Marija. *The Language of the Goddess*. San Franscisco: Harper & Row, 1989.

———. *The Prehistory of Eastern Europe: Part I: Mesolithic, Neolithic, and Copper Age Cultures in Russia and the Baltic Area*. Cambridge, Massachusetts: Peabody Museum, 1956.

Goldwater, Robert. *Primitivism in Modern Art* (1938). New York: Vintage Books. 1967.

Gopnick, Adam. "Basic Stuff: Robert Smithson, Science, and Primitivism," *Arts Magazine*, March 1983. pp. 74—88.

Gould, Stephen Jay. "The Creation Myths of Cooperstown," *Natural History*, November 1989. pp. 14—24.

Green, Johnathan, ed. *Says Who: A Guide to Quotations of the Century*. Essex, England: Longman Group, 1988.

Guédon, Marie-Françoise. Personal communication, Ottawa, 1989.

Guidoni, Enrico. *Primitive Architecture* (1978). New York: Rizzoli International Publications, 1987.

Haacke, Hans. *Earth*. Ithaca: Andrew Dickson White Museum, Cornell University, 1969.

Hall, Carol. "Environmental Artists: Sources and Directions." In *Art in the Land: A Critical Anthology of Environmental Art*, ed. Alan Sonfist. New York: E. P. Dutton, 1983. pp. 8—59.

Hall, James. "Landscape Art: Public Art or Public Convenience," *Apollo*, vol. 79, nr. 325 (March 1989) pp. 157–222.

Hapgood, Fred, "Roden's Eye," *Atlantic Monthly*, August 1987. pp. 46—52.

Harding, Ivy A. "South Africa's First A.R.A.," *Personality*, August 27, 1970. pp. 69—73.

Heizer, Michael, "Discussions with Heizer, Oppenheim, Smithson," *Avalanche*, issue 1 (Fall 1970). pp. 24ff.

———. *Michael Heizer*. Essen: Museum Folkwang, 1979.

Henes, Donna. Interview, in person, Brooklyn, New York, July 19, 1989.

Highwater, Jamake. "Art and the North American Indian," *Structurist*, issue 19/20 (1979/80). pp. 44—49.

———. *Arts of the Indian Americas: Leaves from the Sacred Tree*. New York: Harper & Row, 1983.

Higuchi, Tadahiko. *The Visual and Spatial Structure of Landscape*. Cambridge, Massachusetts: The MIT Press, 1983.

Hobbs, Robert. "Editor's Statement: Earthworks, Past and Present," *Art Journal*, Fall 1982. pp. 191—94.

Hoijer, Harry. "The Nature of Language." in *Exploring the Ways of Mankind*, ed. Walter Goldschmidt. New York: Holt, Rinehart, & Winston, 1960. pp. 77—89.

Holt, Elizabeth. *A Documentary History of Art*, 2nd edition. vol. 2., New York: Doubleday Anchor Books, 1958.

House, Dorothy. *Roden Crater*. Flagstaff, Arizona: Museum of Northern Arizona, 1988.

Hughes, Robert. *The Shock of the New: Art and the Century of Change*. London: British Broadcasting Corporation, 1980.

Hultkrantz, Åke. "Feelings for Nature among North American Indians," *Belief and Worship in Native North America*. Syracuse: Syracuse University Press, 1981. pp. 117—34.

———. *Native Religions of North America: The Power of Visions and Fertility*. San Francisco: Harper & Row, 1987.

———. *Prairie and Plains Indians*. Leiden: E. J. Brill, 1973.

Hunt, John Dixon and Peter Willis, eds. *The Genius of the Place: The English Landscape Garden 1620—1820*. London: Elek Books Ltd., 1975.

Hutchinson, Peter. "Earth in Upheaval: Earthworks and Landscapes," *Arts Magazine*, November 1978. pp. 19—21.

———. Interview, by telephone, Provincetown, Massachusetts, July 27, 1989.

Iseminger, William R. "Excavations at Cahokia Mounds," *Archaeology*, January/ February 1986. pp. 58—59.

Jett, Stephen C. "The Navajo Hogan." In *A Cultural Geography of North American Indians*, eds. Thomas E. Ross and Tyrel G. Moore. Boulder, Colorado: Westview Press, 1987. pp. 243—56.

Johanson, Patricia. *Art and Survival: Creative Solutions to Environmental Problems*. North Vancouver, B.C.: Galerie Publications, 1992.

Johnson, Dirk. "Life on the Great Plains: A Test of Survival Skills," *New York Times*, December 12, 1993, pp. 1, 28.

Johnson, Jory. "Presence of Stone," *Landscape Architecture*, July/August 1986. pp. 64—69.

Johnson, Yankee. "Earthworks: Combining Environmental and Land Issues," *The Arts*

(Earthworks): Newsletter of the King County Arts Commission, vol. 8, nr. 7 (July 1979). pp. 1—6.

Johnstone, Keith. "Touching the Earth: Primitive Artists and Western Theorists," *Structuralists*, issue 19/20 (1979/80). pp. 65—69.

Kastner, Joseph. "My Empty Lot: The Natural History of an Urban Patch." *The New York Times Magazine*, October 16, 1993, pp. 22—25, 41—44.

Kehoe, Alice B. *North American Indians: A Comprehensive Account*. Boulder, Colorado: Westview Press, 1987.

Kehoe, Thomas F. "Corralling Life," *Wisconsin Academy Review*, March 1987. pp. 45—48.

Kelley, Jeff. "Light-Years," *Art Forum*, November 1985. pp. 73—75.

Kiesler, Frederick. *Inside the Endless House, Art, People, and Architecture: A Journal*. New York: Simon & Schuster, 1966.

Kirkman, Terry and Judy Heviz. "Mortality Is the Message," *Montreal Star*, December 2, 1972. n.p.

Kluckhorn, Clyde. "The Personal Document in Anthropological Science." In *The Use of Personal Documents in History, Anthropology, and Sociology*. Louis Gottschalk, et al. New York: Social Science Research Council, nd. (C. 1945). pp. 79—173.

———. "Recurrent Themes in Myths and Mythmaking." In *Myth and Mythmaking*, ed. Henry A. Murray. Boston: George Braziller, 1960. pp. 46—60.

Kluesing, Cherie. "Site Artists: The Role of Outsiders in Landscape Design," *Landscape Architecture*, issue 78 (April/May 1988). pp. 120ff.

Kolodny, Annette. *The Lay of the Land: Metaphor as Experience and History in American Life and Letters*. Chapel Hill, North Carolina: University of North Carolina Press, 1975.

Korp, Maureen. *The Sacred Geography of the American Mound Builders*. Lewiston, New York: Edwin Mellen Press, 1990.

Kuspit, Donald B. "Caves and Temples," *Art in America*, April 1982. pp. 129—33.

———. "Charles Ross: Light's Measure." In *Art in the Land: A Critical Anthology of Environmental Art*, ed. Alan Sonfist. New York: E. P. Dutton, 1983. pp. 159—68.

———. "Concerning the Spiritual in Contemporary Art." In *The Spiritual in Art: Abstract Painting 1890-1985*, Maurice Tuchman, et al. New York: Abbeville Press, 1986. pp. 313—25.

———. "The Pascalian Spiral: Robert Smithson's Drunken Boat," *Arts Magazine*, October 1981. pp. 82—88.

Landes, Ruth. *Ojibwa Religion and the Midéwiwin*. Madison: University of Wisconsin Press, 1968.

Lane, Belden C. *Landscapes of the Sacred: Geography and Narrative in American Spirituality*. New York: Paulist Press, 1988.

Langager, Craig. "Getting a Symposium off the Ground: A Process in Itself," *The Arts (Earthworks): Newsletter of the King County Arts Commission*, vol. 8, nr. 7 (July 1979). pp. 1—6.

Langer, Susanne K. *Feeling and Form: A Theory of Art*. New York: Charles Scribner's Sons, 1953.

———. *Problems of Art*. New York: Charles Scribner's Sons, 1957.

Leavitt, Thomas W. "Foreword," *Earth Art*. Ithaca, New York: Andrew Dickson White Museum of Art, 1969. unpaged.

van der Leeuw, G. *Religion in Essence and Manifestation*, vol. 1 (1933). New York: Harper & Row, 1963.

Leroi-Gourhan, André. "The Beginnings of Art." In *Larousse Encyclopedia of Prehistoric and Ancient Art*, ed. Rene Hyghe. New York: Prometheus Press, 1962. pp. 26—29.

———. *Treasures of Prehistoric Art*. New York: Harry N. Abrams, 1967.

Lethaby, W. R. *Architecture, Mysticism, and Myth.* New York: George Braziller, 1975.

Lethbridge, T. C. *Gogmagog: The Buried Gods.* London: Routledge and Kegan Paul, 1957.

LeVeque, Terry Ryan. "Nancy Holt's 'Sky Mound': Adaptive Technology Creates Celestial Perspectives," *Landscape Architecture*, issue 78 (April/May 1988). pp. 82, 85—86.

Leveson, Paul. *A Sense of the Earth.* New York: Anchor Natural History Books, 1972.

Levin, Gail. "American Art." In *Primitivism in 20th Century Art: Affinity of the Tribal and the Modern*, ed. William Rubin. New York: Museum of Modern Art, 1984. pp. 453—74.

Levy, G. Rachel. *Religious Conceptions of the Stone Age* (published in 1948 as *The Gate of Horn*). New York: Harper & Row, 1963.

Lipke, William C. "Earth Systems," *Earth Art.* Ithaca, New York: Andrew Dickson White Museum of Art, 1969. unpaged.

Lippard, Lucy. *Overlay: Contemporary Art and the Art of Prehistory.* New York: Pantheon Books, 1983.

Littman, Sol. "Delights of a Female Voyeur," *Sunday Star* (Toronto), October 22, 1978. p. B-6.

Lockyer, Sir Joseph Norman. *The Dawn of Astronomy: A Study of the Temple Worship and Mythology of the Ancient Egyptians* (nd). Cambridge, Massachusetts: MIT Press, 1964.

Lonergan, Anne and Caroline Richards, eds. *Thomas Berry and the New Cosmology.* Mystic, Connecticut: Twenty-third Publications, 1987.

Long, Charles H. *Alpha: The Myths of Creation.* Chico, California: Scholars Press, 1963.

———. *Significations: Signs, Symbols, and Images in the Interpretation of Religion.* Philadelphia: Fortress Press, 1986.

Long, Rose-Carol Washton. "Occultism, Anarchism, and Abstracton: Kandinsky's Art of the Future," *Art Journal*, Spring 1987. pp. 38—45.

Lowenthal, David. "The Place of the Past in the American Landscape." In *Geographies of the Mind: Essays in Historical Geography in Honor of John Kirkland Wright.* eds. David Lowenthal and Martyn J. Bowden. New York: Oxford University Press, 1976. pp. 89—117.

MacDonald, George. "Cosmic Equations in Northwest Coast Art." In *The World Is as Sharp as a Knife: An Anthology in Honour of Wilson Duff*, ed. D. N. Abbott. Victoria: British Columbia Provincial Museum, 1981. pp. 225—38.

———. *Haida Monumental Art.* Vancouver: University of British Columbia Press, 1983.

Malone, Maggie. "The Great Outdoors: No More Giant Sculptures Plopped in Plazas," *Newsweek*, October 23, 1989. pp. 76—79.

Mansbach, S. A. "An Earthwork of Surprise: The 18th-Century Ha-Ha," *Art Journal.* Fall, 1982. pp. 217—21.

Margolis, Jon. "Them's Fightin' Words," *Chicago Tribune*, January 7, 1993, section 5, p. 1.

Marrett, R. R. *Faith, Hope and Charity in Primitive Religion.* New York: Benjamin Blom, Inc., 1972.

Massie, Sue. "Timeless Healing at Buffalo Rock," *Landscape Architecture*, May/June 1985. pp. 70—71.

Matteson, Esther, et al. *Comparative Studies in Amerindian Languages.* The Hague: Mouton, 1972.

Matthews, Anne. "The Poppers and the Plains," *New York Times Magazine*, June 24, 1990, pp. 24—26, 41, 48—49, 53.

———. "Slow Death at the 98th Meridian," *Outside*, May 1993. pp. 69—76, 179 ff.

May, Clifford D. "The Buffalo Returns: This Time as Dinner," *New York Times Magazine*, September 26, 1993, pp. 30—34.

McCrae, Rosalie Smith. "Art Photographs Use Myth to Test Belief," *The Ottawa Citizen*, December 6, 1980, p. 35.

McKibben, Bill. *The End of Nature.* New York: Random House, 1989.

McMann, Jean. *Riddles of the Stone Age: Rock Carvings of Ancient Europe.* London: Thames & Hudson, 1980.

McMillan, Alan D. *Native Peoples and Cultures of Canada: An Anthropological Overview.* Vancouver: Douglas & McIntyre, 1988.

Meadmore, Clement. "Thoughts on Earthworks, Random Distribution, Softness, Horizontality, and Gravity," *Arts Magazine,* February 1969. pp. 26—28.

Mellaart, James. *Çatal Hüyük.* London: Thames & Hudson, 1967.

———. *The Neolithic of the Near East.* New York: Scribner's, 1975.

Michell, John. *City of Revelation: On the Proportions and Symbolic Numbers of the Cosmic Temple.* London: Garnstone Press, 1972.

———. *The Earth Spirit.* London: Thames & Hudson, 1975.

———. *A Little History of Astro-Archaeology: Stages in the Transformation of a Heresy.* London: Thames & Hudson, 1977.

———. *The New View over Atlantis.* San Fransisco: Harper & Row, 1983.

Miller, Alan L. "Power," *Encyclopedia of Religion.* Edited by Mircea Eliade. New York: Macmillan, 1987. vol. 11, p. 468.

Miller, Naomi. *Heavenly Caves: Reflectons on the Garden Grotto.* New York: George Braziller, 1982.

Morgan, William N. *Prehistoric Architecture in the Eastern United States.* Cambridge, Massachusetts: The MIT Press, 1980.

Morris, Robert. "Statement by Robert Morris," *The Arts (Earthworks): Newsletter of the King County Arts Commmission,* vol. 8, nr. 7 (July 1979). pp. 1—6.

Morris, William, ed. *American Heritage Dictionary of the English Language.* Boston: Houghton Mifflin Company, 1978.

Muehlenbachs, Lelde. "Mixture of Print and Art Is Jarring and Distracting," *Edmonton Journal,* October 29, 1980, n.p.

Müller, Werner. "The Passivity of Language and the Experience of Nature: A Study in the Structure of the Primitive Mind." In *Myths and Symbols: Studies in Honor of Mircea Eliade,* eds. Joseph M. Kitagawa and Charles H. Long. Chicago: University of Chicago Press, 1969. pp. 227—40.

Munro, Eleanor. "Art in the Desert," *New York Times,* December 7, 1986. pp. 9, 38.

Murdock, George Peter. *Our Primitive Contemporaries.* New York: Macmillan, 1934.

Muschamp, Herbert. "When Art Becomes a Public Spectacle," *New York Times,* August 8, 1993. section 2, pp. 1, 30.

Nabokov, Peter. "Native American Architecture: Preserving Social and Religious Life," *Four Winds,* Winter/Spring 1981. pp. 43—47.

——— and Easton, Robert. *Native American Architecture.* New York: Oxford University Press, 1989.

Neihardt, John G. *Black Elk Speaks.* Lincoln, Nebraska: University of Nebraska Press, 1979.

Neuman, Robert W. and Nancy W. Hawkins. *Louisiana Prehistory: Anthropological Study nr. 6.* Baton Rouge: Louisiana Department of Culture, Recreation, and Tourism, 1982.

Nickel, Cheryl. "The Semiotics of Andean Terracing," *Art Journal,* Fall 1982. pp. 200—203.

Nikiforuk, Andrew. "Where the Buffalo Roam: Was the Settling of the Great Plains a Mistake That is Now Being Corrected?" *Harrowsmith Country Life,* July/August, 1993. p. 28.

———. "Wild about Buffalo: The New West Might Look as Untamed as the Old," *Harrowsmith.* December 1992, pp 46—52.

Nixon, Virginia. "Dickson's Creations Express Opposites," *Montreal Gazette*, May 24, 1980. p. 113.

Noel, Daniel. *Approaching Earth: A Search for the Mythic Significance of the Space Age.* New York: Amity House, 1986.

———. ed. *Paths to the Power of Myth: Joseph Campbell and the Study of Religion.* New York: Crossroad, 1990.

Norberg-Schulz, Christian. *The Concept of Dwelling: On the Way to Figurative Architecture.* New York: Rizzoli International, 1985.

———. *Genius Loci: Towards a Phenomenology of Architecture.* New York: Rizzoli International, 1979.

———. *Intentions in Architecture.* Cambridge, Massachusetts: The MIT Press, 1965.

———. *Meaning in Western Architecture.* New York: Rizzoli International, 1980.

O'Connor, Larry. "Where the World Changed," *New York Times*, December 9, 1990. Sec. xx, p. 41.

Orion, Ezra. "Sculpture in the Solar System: From Geologically Based Earthworks to Astro-Sculpture," *Leonardo*, vol. 18, nr. 3 (1985). pp. 157—60.

Oroschakoff, Haralampi G. and Wilfried W. Dickhoff. "A Reverberation in the Realm of the Sacred?" *Flash Art*, October 1987. pp. 86—89.

Page, Jake. "Hyeouma, *Native Peoples*, Summer 1990. pp. 30—36.

Paton, Bruce. "Paradise Expedition Comes to NFB," *Ottawa Revue*, January 8—14, 1981. n.p.

"Periscope," *Newsweek*, May 6, 1991, p. 21.

Pevsner, Nikolaus. *An Outline of European Architecture.* Harmondsworth, Middlesex: Penguin Books, 1968.

Pfeiffer, John E. *The Creative Explosion: An Inquiry into the Origins of Art and Religion.* New York: Harper & Row, 1982.

Phillips, Ruth B. *Patterns of Power: The Jasper Grant Collection and the Great Lakes Indian Art of the Early Nineteenth Century.* Kleinberg, Ontario: McMichael Collection, 1984.

Pinto, Jody. *Excavations and Constructions: Notes for the Body/Land.* Philadelphia: Marian Locks Gallery, 1979.

Pinxten, Rik; Ingrid van Dooren; Frank Harvey. *Anthropology of Space: Explorations into the Natural Philosophy and Semantics of the Navajo.* Philadelphia: University of Pennsylvania Press, 1983.

Pollan, Michael. "Autumn: It's No Garden Party," *New York Times Magazine*, September 16, 1990. pp. 54—57, 98, 100.

———. "Putting Down Roots," *New York Times Magazine*, May 6, 1990. pp. 38—40, 44, 82.

———. "Why Mow? The Case against Lawns," *New York Times Magazine*, May 28, 1989. pp. 23—26, 41—42, 44.

Popper, Frank J. Personal communication, July 22, 1993.

———. "The Strange Case of the Contemporary American Frontier," *Yale Review*, Fall 1986. pp. 101—21.

———. "Viewpoint," *Planning*, December 1990. p. 50.

———, and Deborah E. Popper. "The Future of the Great Plains," *Forum for Applied Research and Public Policy* (to be published, 1994), draft paper in typescript.

———. "The Reinvention of the American Frontier," *Amicus Journal*, Summer 1991. pp. 4—7.

Porter, Philip W. and Fred E. Lukermann. "Geographies of Utopia." In *Geographies of the Mind: Essays in Historical Geography in Honor of John Kirkland Wright*, eds. David Lowenthal and Martyn J. Bowden. New York: Oxford University Press, 1976. pp. 197—223.

Poser, Carol. "The Earthly Paradise," *Vanguard,* vol. 9, nr. 1, February 1980.

Potente, Eugene, Jr. "Man Is by His Constitution a Religious Animal," *National Sculpture Review,* vol. 28, nr. 4 (Winter 1979—80). pp. 14—15.

Prussin, Labelle. "West African Earthworks," *Art Journal,* Fall 1982. pp. 204—9.

"The Psychology of Lawn Ornament," *Ottawa Citizen,* June 10, 1989. p. D-1.

Ranney, Edward. "Excavating the present," *Aperture,* issue 98 (Spring 1985). pp. 42—47.

Reichel-Dolmatoff, G. "Cosmology as Ecological Analysis: A View from the Rain Forest," *Man,* vol. 11, nr. 3 (September 1976). pp. 307—18.

Richards, Caroline. "The New Cosmology: What It Really Means." In *Thomas Berry and the New Cosmology,* eds. Anne Lonergan and Caroline Richards. Mystic, Connecticut: Twenty-third Publications, 1987. pp. 91—101.

Riley, Thomas J. and Glen Freimuth. "Prehistoric Agriculture in the Upper Midwest," *Field Museum Bulletin,* June 1977. pp. 4—8.

Rödiger-Diruf, Erika. "Ausstellung: Zuruck zur Natur, aber wie?" *Du,* issue 6 (1988), pp. 78—86.

Rogers, E. S. "The Indian and the European: Two Views of the Land." In *Man in Nature: Historical Perspectives on Man in His Environment,* ed. Louis D. Levine. Toronto: Royal Ontario Museum, 1975. pp. 90—110.

Rooth, A. G. "The Creation Myths of the North American Indians," *Anthropos,* issue 52 (1957). pp. 497—508.

Rosenthal, Mark. "Some Attitudes of Earth Art: From Competition to Adoration." In *Art in the Land: A Critical Anthology of Environmental Art,* ed. Alan Sonfist, New York: E. P. Dutton, 1983, pp. 60—72.

Ross, Charles. Interview, by telephone, Las Vegas, New Mexico, September 12, 1989.

———. Personal communication, August 2, 1990.

———. "Star Axis: Where the Earth Meets the Sky." Unpublished prospectus, 1987, revised 1990.

———. *The Substance of Light: Sunlight Dispersion, the Solar Burns, Point Source/Star Space: Selected Work of Charles Ross, February 6—March 14, 1976.* LaJolla, California: La Jolla Museum of Contemporary Art, 1976.

———. "Sunlight Convergence/Solar Burns," *Co-Evolution Quarterly,* Winter 1977—78. pp. 104—7.

Ross, Thomas E. and Tyrel G. Moore, eds. *A Cultural Geography of North American Indians.* Boulder, Colorado: Westview Press, 1987.

———. "Indians in North America." In *A Cultural Geography of North American Indians,* eds. Thomas E. Ross and Tyrel G. Moore. Boulder, Colorado: Westview Press, 1987.

Ross-Bryant, Lynn. "The Land in American Religious Experience," *Journal of the American Academy of Religion,* Fall 1990, vo. 58, nr. 2, pp. 333—55.

Rubin, William. "Modernist Primitivism: An Introduction." In *Primitivism in 20th Century Art: Affinity of the Tribal and the Modern,* ed. William Rubin. New York: Museum of Modern Art, 1984. pp. 1—81.

Rushing, W. Jackson. "The Impact of Nietzsche and Northwest Coast Indian Art on Barnett Newman's Idea of Redemption in the Abstract Sublime," *Art Journal,* Fall 1988. pp. 187—205.

———. "Ritual and Myth: Native American Culture and Abstract Expressionism," *The Spiritual in Art: Abstract Painting 1890—1985,* Maurice Tuchman, et al. New York: Abbeville Press, 1986. pp. 273—95.

Russell, John. "Art Tells Us Where We Are (1981)," *Reading Russell: Essays 1941—1988 on Ideas, Literature, Art, Theatre, Music, Places, and Persons.* New York: Harry N. Abrams, 1989. pp. 184—89.

———. "James Turrell (1986)," *Reading Russell: Essays 1941—1988 on Ideas, Literature, Art, Theatre, Music, Places, and Persons.* New York: Harry N. Abrams, 1989. pp. 123—26.

Rybczynski, Witold. *The Most Beautiful House in the World.* New York: Penguin Books, 1989.

Saad-Cook, Janet. "Touching the Sky: Artworks Using Natural Phenomena, Earth, Sky, and Connections to Astronomy," *Leonardo,* vol. 21, nr. 2 (1988). pp. 123—34.

Sale, Kirkpatrick. *The Conquest of Paradise: Christopher Columbus and the Columbian Legacy.* New York: Alfred A. Knopf, 1990. pp. 74—91.

Saltz, Jerry. "Notes on a Sculpture: Alan Sonfist's 'Slice of Life,'" *Arts Magazine,* May 1989. pp. 13—44.

Sapir, Edward. *Time Perspective in Aboriginal American Culture: A Study in Method.* Ottawa: Canada Department of Mines, Geological Survey, 1916.

"Scorched Earth: An Elemental Work by Hideho Tanaka," *Crafts,* issue 76 (September—October 1985), pp. 28—31.

Scully, Vincent. *The Earth, the Temple, and the Gods: Greek Sacred Architecture.* New York: Frederick A. Praeger, 1969.

———. *Pueblo: Mountain, Village, Dance.* New York: Viking Press, 1975.

Seeman, Mark F. "Ohio Hopewell Trophy-Skull Artifacts as Evidence for Competition in Middle Woodlands Societies c. 50 BC—AD 350," *American Antiquity,* vol. 53, nr. 3 (1988). pp. 565—77.

Senior, Donald. "The Earth Story: Where Does the Bible Fit In?" In *Thomas Berry and the New Cosmology,* eds. Anne Lonergan and Caroline Richards. Mystic, Connecticut: Twenty-third Publications, 1987. pp. 41—50.

Shaffer, Diana. "Nancy Holt: Spaces for Reflections or Projections." In *Art in the Land: A Critical Anthology of Environmental Art,* ed. Alan Sonfist. New York: E. P. Dutton, 1983. pp. 169—77.

Shapiro, Gary. "Entropy and Dialectic: The Signatures of Robert Smithson," *Arts Magazine,* June 1988. pp. 99—104.

Sharp, Willoughby. "Notes toward an Understanding of Earth Art," *Earth Art.* Ithaca, New York: Andrew Dickson White Museum of Art, 1969. unpaged.

Sharpe, Eric J. *Comparative Religion: A History.* London: Duckworth, 1975.

Shearman, John. *Mannerism.* Harmondsworth, Middlesex: Penguin Books, 1967.

Sherrod, P. Clay and Martha Ann Rolingson. *Surveyors of the Ancient Mississippi Valley.* Arkansas Archaeological Survey Research Series, nr. 28, 1987.

Sherzer, Joel. "Areal Linguistics in North America." In *Current Trends in Linguistics,* ed. Thomas A. Sebeok. The Hague: Mouton, 1973, pp. 449—795.

Smart, Ninian. "Interpretation and Mystical Experience." In *Understanding Mysticism,* Richard Woods, ed. Garden City, New York: Image Books, 1980. pp. 78—91.

Smith, John. *Sucking-Stones.* Dunvegan, Ontario: Quadrant Editions, 1982.

Smith, Johnathan Z. *To Take Place: Toward Theory in Ritual.* Chicago: University of Chicago Press, 1987.

Sonfist, Alan. "Letters to the Editor," *New York Times Magazine,* December 10, 1989. p. 18.

———, ed. *Art in the Land: A Critical Anthology of Environmental Art.* New York: E. P. Dutton, 1983.

Spektorov, Bette. "The Impact of Megalithic Landscapes on Contemporary Art," *Studio International,* vol. 196, nr. 999 (April/May 1983). pp. 6—9.

Stevens, Mark. "Turrell's Celestial Vault," *Newsweek,* February 10, 1986, p. 71.

Stokes, Ann. *A Studio of One's Own.* Tallahassee, Florida: Naiad Press, 1985.

Streeter, Tal. Interviews, by telephone, Milbrook, New York, September 17, 24, 1989.

Swanson, Guy E. *The Birth of the Gods.* Ann Arbor, Michigan: University of Michigan Press, 1960.

Swimme. Brian. "Science: A Partner in Creating the Vision." In *Thomas Berry and the New Cosmology,* eds. Anne Lonergan and Caroline Richards. Mystic, Connecticut: Twenty-third Publications, 1987. pp. 81—90.

"This Art All Rock but Hard to Roll," *The Ottawa Citizen,* May 11, 1989, pp. D-10.

Tillich, Paul. *On Art and Architecture.* New York: Crossroad, 1987.

Tobey, George B., Jr. *A History of Landscape Architecture: The Relationship of People to Environment.* New York: American Elsevier Publishing Company, Inc., 1973.

Todd, John Emerson. *Frederick Law Olmsted.* Boston: Twayne Publishers, 1982.

Topitsch, Ernst. "World Interpretation and Self-Interpretation: Some Basic Patterns." In *Myth and Mythmaking,* edited by Henry A. Murray. Boston: George Braziller, Inc. 1960. pp. 157—73.

Treib, Marc. "Traces upon the Land: The Formalistic Landscape," *Architectural Association Quarterly* (London), vol. 11, nr. 4 (1979). pp. 28—39.

Trigger, Bruce. *Natives and Newcomers: Canada's 'Herioc Age' Reconsidered.* Kingston and Montreal: McGill-Queen's University Press, 1985.

Tuan, Yi-Fu. "Geopiety: A Theme in Man's Attachment to Nature and to Place." In *Geographies of the Mind: Essays in Historical Geography in Honor of John Kirkland Wright,* eds. David Lowenthal and Martyn J. Bowden. New York: Oxford University Press, 1976. pp. 11—39.

———. *Landscapes of Fear.* New York: Pantheon Books, 1979.

———. *Space and Place: The Perspective of Experience.* Minneapolis: University of Minnesota Press, 1977.

———. *Topophilia: A Study of Environmental Perception, Attitudes, and Values.* Englewood Cliffs, New Jersey: Prentice-Hall, 1974.

Tuchman, Maurice. "Hidden Meaning in Abstract Art," *The Spiritual in Art: Abstract Painting 1890—1985,* eds. Maurice Tuchman, et al. New York: Abbeville Press, 1986. pp. 17—61.

———. et al. *The Spiritual in Art: Abstract painting 1890—1985.* New York: Abbeville Press, 1986.

Turrell, James. Personal communication. Flagstaff, Arizona, March 24, 1989.

Tylor, Edward Burnett. *Religion in Primitive Culture* (1873). New York: Harper & Row, 1958.

Varnedoe, Kirk. "Abstract Expressionism." In *Primitivism in 20th Century Art: Affinity of the Tribal and the Modern,* ed. William Rubin. New York: Museum of Modern Art, 1984. pp. 615—60.

———. "Contemporary Explorations." In *Primitivism in 20th Century Art: Affinity of the Tribal and the Modern,* ed. William Rubin. New York: Museum of Modern Art, 1984. pp. 661—85.

———. "Preface." In *Primitivism in 20th Century Art: Affinity of the Tribal and the Modern,* ed. William Rubin. New York: Museum of Modern Art, 1984.

Vastokas, Joan M. "The Roots of Abstraction: An Introduction," *artscanada,* issue 226/227 (May-June 1979), pp. 2—23, 68.

———, and Romas K. Vastokas. *Sacred Art of the Algonkians: A Study of the Peterborough Petroglyphs.* Peterborough, Ontario: Mansard, 1973.

Vorren, Ørnulv. "Sacrificial Sites, Types, and Functions." In *Saami Religion,* ed. Tore Ahlbäck. Uppsala: Donner Institute for Research in Religions and Cultural History, 1987. pp. 94—109.

Walter, E. V. *Placeways: A Theory of the Human Environment*. Chapel Hill and London: University of North Carolina Press, 1989.

———. "A Shelter for Dreams," *New York Times Book Review*, May 21, 1989. pp. 1, 52.

Waters, Frank. *Book of the Hopi*. New York: Penguin Books, 1977.

Watson-Jones, Virginia. "Evidence of the Visionary Tradition in Contemporary Sculpture." Taped lecture, 60 minutes. Presented at the International Sculpture Center, Washington, D.C., June 6, 1990, for "International Sculpture '90."

Waugh, Earle H. and K. Paul Prithipaul, eds. *Native Religious Traditions*. Waterloo: Canadian Corporation for Studies in Religion, 1979.

Wedewer, Rolf. "Neuer Exotismus," *Kunstwerk Stuttgart*, vol. 33, nr. 5 (1980). pp. 3—34.

Wheeler, C. J. and A. P. Buchner. "Rock Art: A Metalinguistic Interpretation of the Algonkian Word for Stone." In *Papers of the Sixth Algonquian Conference, 1974*, ed. William Cowan. Ottawa: National Museums of Canada, 1975. pp. 362—71.

Whiteside, Carla. Interview, in person, Ottawa, July 12, 1989.

Whorf, Benjamin. "Language, Thought, and Reality." In *Exploring the Ways of Mankind*, ed. Walter Goldschmidt. New York: Holt, Rinehart, and Winston, 1960. pp. 103—7.

Wijsenbeek, L. J. F. "Mondrian und Kandinsky: Theosophische Einflüsse in den Jahren 1905 bis 1910," *Pantheon*, issue 43 (1985). pp. 141—43.

Wilford, John Noble. "What Unearth Is Going On? New Evidence Surfaces Man Migrated to the Americas 45,000 Years Ago," *The Ottawa Citizen*, June 18, 1989, p. E-7.

Wilkinson, Alan G. "Henry Moore." In *Primitivism in 20th Century Art: Affinity of the Tribal and the Modern*, ed. William Rubin. New York: Museum of Modern Art, 1984. pp. 595—614.

Williamson, Ray A. *Living the Sky: The Cosmos of the American Indian*. Norman, Oklahoma: University of Oklahoma Press, 1984.

Wilson, David J. "Desert Ground Drawings in the Lower Santa Valley, North Coast of Peru," *American Antiquity*, vol. 53, nr. 4 (1988). pp. 794—804.

Winkler, Daryold, Fr. Personal communication, Ottawa, January 1989.

Wittry, Warren L. "An American Woodhenge." In *Native North American Art History: Selected Readings*, eds. Zena Pearlstone Mathews and Aldona Jonaitis. Palo Alto: Peek Publications, 1982. pp. 453—58.

World Heritage Newsletter (World Heritage Centre, UNESCO, Paris), February 1993, nr. 1: electronic-mail transmission via ANTHRO-L UBVM.bitnet, May 19, 1993.

Wright, Ronald. "Beyond Words," *Saturday Night*, April 1988. pp. 38—48.

Young, T. Cuyler, Jr. "Pollution Begins in Prehistory: The Problem is People." In *Man in Nature; Historical Perspectives on Man in His Environment*, ed. Louis D. Levine. Toronto: Royal Ontario Museum, 1975. pp. 9—26.

Zelinsky, Wilbur. "Unearthly Delights: Cemetery Delights and the Map of the Changing American Afterworld." In *Geographies of the Mind: Essays in Historical Geography in Honor of John Kirkland Wright*, eds. David Lowenthal and Martyn J. Bowden. New York: Oxford University Press, 1976. pp. 171—95.

Zellweger, Harry. "Mythos und Ritual in der Kunst der 70er Jahre, Kunsthaus Zurich (5.6—23.8.81)," *Kunstwerk Stuttgart*, vol. 34, nr. 5 (1981). pp. 74—75.

Index